P9-CPZ-534

CRUCIAL ISSUES IN MISSIONS TOMORROW

Edited by
Donald A. McGavran

MOODY PRESS • CHICAGO

© 1972 by
THE MOODY BIBLE INSTITUTE
OF CHICAGO

Library of Congress Catalog Card Number: 72-77944
ISBN 0-8024-1675-6

Printed in the United States of America

CONTENTS

INTRODUCTION

by
DONALD McGAVRAN

THE CRUCIAL ISSUES in tomorrow's missions described in this book by the twelve authors must be seen in the light of today's terrain. Several features dominate the landscape. Consciously or unconsciously, those carrying out mission adjust to this terrain their convictions, programs and judgments of what is feasible and right. After all, it is here that God has placed them.

FIVE NOTABLE FEATURES OF TODAY'S TERRAIN

THE RETREAT OF WESTERN EMPIRES

The feature of the landscape which, perhaps, most affects missions is that, politically and militarily, *Eur*ope and Ame*rica,* which we shall conveniently call Eurica, have departed from *A*frica, Latin Am*erica* and *Asia,* which we shall call Africasia. Whereas in 1940 the nations of Eurica ruled most of Asia and Africa; today, with the exception of Angola and Mozambique, the nations of Africasia are entirely self-governing. While individually no Africasian nation except China has much military might, and except for Japan few have economic power, collectively they form a formidable block which some people call the Third World. In Africasia, the Western, erstwhile imperial, nations are notable by their absence. The fact is so well known that it needs no illustration. The West *has* retreated.

5

A COMPLEX PLURALISTIC SOCIETY

The second prominent feature of the terrain is that of many radically different religions living in friendship and equality. It is unpopular today to think in terms of one true religion and the others all false, for men tend to believe that each people has a right to its own ideas of God and its own religion. The common assumption is that all religions are what man thinks of God and, because each man has a right to his opinions, each religion is about equally true. If it is "true for you," that is all that matters. As anthropologists explore the complexities of various cultures, many conclude that all cultures are equally good and bad. Cultures are merely ways of acting which please certain men. It is, so some anthropologists teach, immoral to try to change the glorious culture of any ethnic unit. It is theirs. What right has anyone to alter it? Since the world view—or religion—is part of culture, a vast religious relativity billows out behind the science of anthropology. Such relativism is the anthropological form of scientism.

William Hocking in the early thirties taught that the era of church-planting was over and that the era of the reconception of religions, each standing in the presence of others, had begun. He held that actively aiding such reconception and zealously refraining from conversion evangelism was the form mission should take. While one may doubt whether this form is permitted to Christians, no one can doubt that a pluralistic world sees a great deal of reconception of religions going on. This feature of the landscape vitally affects missions in both theory and practice.

THE BATTLE FOR BROTHERHOOD

Christians have always believed in the brotherhood of man under the fatherhood of God. But today (when multitudinous have-not segments of world society have become politically powerful and marvelously vocal) the affluence of Eurican

Christians and their smug acceptance of it seem terribly sinful to the sensitive among them. Former imperial powers are seized with a guilty conscience at the depth of poverty and ignorance of their erstwhile subjects. Christians in North America—white and black—agree that the depressed and backward position of the blacks is a stench in the nostrils of God; He will not tolerate it. At all costs equal opportunity, schooling and recompense—in short, full integration—must go forward at full speed. Nothing, they hold, must interfere with the achievement of brotherhood now.

SECULARISM AND SCIENTISM

Secularism dominates the land we live in like snow-crowned Ranier dominates the great port of Tacoma. More and more people live as if there were no divine dimension to life; man is held to be all-sufficient. If secular man thinks of God at all, he considers Him as some vague First Cause, Totality, or the Ground of Being. Scientism reinforces the idea that the laws of nature rule supreme, and God neither does nor can interfere with them in any way. Hence, prayer is useless, except maybe as self-hypnotism. A thin deism, which at best considers God as the prisoner of His creation, becomes the dominant form of Christianity. Rationalism and existentialism are fashionable. New hermeneutics distorts the Bible to bring its teachings into line with the new look. Life becoming one-dimensional becomes also meaningless. Erosion of faith in the sovereign God makes some Christians believe that all that really counts is human action. The way of salvation taught by the apostles, compared with "salvation" offered by the "green revolution," seems vague and insubstantial. Jesus Christ as "Saviour," some say, seems scarcely credible to modern man. Faith in the immortal soul grows dim. The resurrection of the Lord Jesus becomes merely a mythic way of saying that when men believe on Him, it is *as if* He were present and aiding them. Some churchmen insist that mission is to "all of life," meaning that physical life must be improved. They precisely do not mean that mission should emphasize the immortal soul.

HITLERIAN FALLOUT

This feature of the landscape looms larger for German Christians than for others, but it affects millions all over the world. The deliberate killing of six million Jews, the snuffing out of freedom, and the fact that the orthodox churches did not furiously oppose Hitler have produced in many German Christian thinkers a tremendous guilt complex. They hold that the church—busy about its own life and wedded to its doctrines—failed to do God's will. From now on, they believe, the world will not listen to Christians when they say God is love. It will demand that they live a life of love. To those Christians in positions of leadership in the years 1930 to 1945, the twenty million or more who died in World War II, the several hundred thousand who died in Hiroshima and Nagasaki, and those who died in the following years of slaughter, all create a conviction that a different kind of Christianity must be developed to make this kind of happening impossible for evermore.

MINOR FEATURES

Minor features of the terrain, such as the following three, also influence missions: *Fear of manipulating men* has been created by the awesome power of calculated and callous persuasion using computers, chemicals, and mechanical means such as subliminal suggestion. Communist brainwashing and high-pressure sales campaigns make men do what others want done. As a result many men recoil from all persuasion. Permissiveness becomes the right style in life. *A sudden realization of the enormous extent of suffering* has flooded Eurica, brought close by television and seen against the confident assumption that no one ought to suffer. Earthquakes, starvation, the ravages of drugs, and the horror of refugee camps ought not to be. *Simultaneously nature is being controlled as never before.* Diseases are being wiped out. The power of the atom has been unlocked. During the 1971 exploration of the moon, Gulf Oil told several hundred million television viewers that atomic fusion is just around the corner. Inevitably multitudes ask, With abundant power at hand, what need of God? Why propagate speculations about ultimate questions when the really constructive thing to do is for men to manage global resources? Forget God. Stress development. Some such attitude as this is a well-known feature of the landscape.

BALEFUL EFFECT ON BIBLICAL MISSIONS

SOME DEFINITIONS

By biblical missions I mean those carried out primarily by messengers of the church sent specifically that men might repent of their sins and turn from idols to serve the true and living God. Biblical missions or missionary missions proclaim Jesus Christ as divine, and the only Saviour, and encourage men to become His disciples and responsible members of His church. Such mission is the God-given task of the church and is enjoined on all generations of Christians till Christ returns. The mandate does not change.

How mission is carried out, however, does change mightily from culture to culture and from year to year. It is effected by each phase in a denomination's history. When small and weak, the denomination carries out mission in one way; when large and powerful, in another.

To those who argue that the missionary mandate itself has in these fast-moving days been abrogated, or that it applied when Europe ruled the world, but does not in a family of free nations, I reply that I well understand what they are saying but believe they are mistaken.

At a seminary meeting some years ago, a group of enthusiastic ecumenicists were discussing the future. "As the nineteenth was the century of missionary expansion, so the twentieth and twenty-first are going to be centuries of a great uniting of the scattered fragments of the church. Missions are now over. Church union has begun." Believers in missionary missions hold such opinions to be either irresponsible or sub-Christian.

The duty of *the church* is, of course, much wider than missionary missions. It includes doing justice, loving kindness and walking humbly with God. In their spheres of influence, Christians should—and do—make every aspect of life sweeter. They are better mothers and fathers, wives and husbands, sons and daughters, neighbors and citizens. They teach better, manufacture better, and legislate better. They are redeemed souls in human bodies. They are the body of Christ in the world—salt and light, joy and peace. They are also sinners constantly confessing their sins, being forgiven, and making new starts. The church, but not the mission, touches all of life. The mission has its specific sphere of activity—the communication of the gospel. The missionary society is not the church, even as the surgeon is not the hospital. The mission plants church after church which, when established, touch every aspect of life, including both propagating the gospel and changing the culture so that it conforms more to God's will.

THE MAIN FEATURES OF THE TERRAIN ENDANGER MISSION

Dean Glasser maintains that Christians "are confronted anew with the significance with which He [Jesus] regards the task of preaching the Gospel of the Kingdom, discipling the nations, baptizing converts and teaching them what it means to bear His yoke." To biblical missions thus conceived, the main features of today's terrain present terrible dangers, which we briefly discuss one by one:

The retreat of Western empires is commonly interpreted as a retreat of Great-Commission missions. This danger has many faces. Some nationals, mistaking missions for Eurican governments, say the day of the missionary is over. He is an anacronism. Mistaking mission guidance (at no cost to Afericasian churches) for government control (entirely at the cost of the ruled colony), some nationals demand that the missionary society turn over its moneys and personnel. Missionary societies, also, mistakenly consider turning the whole country over to nationals and getting back to Eurica as the modern form of mission. They exclaim, "Let national Christians carry on whatever evangelization is proper in their countries. We are going home." The sending churches in Eurica feel that their nations are no longer empires but merely small countries among many other small countries. "It is not our task to win the world to Christ," they say. "In missions let us avoid all triumphalism. The servant church is the correct ideal." As this erroneous assessment of the situation gains ground, conversion missions appear to be a somewhat outmoded enterprise.

In pluralistic society, men easily conclude that all religions are about equally true. All are ways to God. All are "true" for their own believers. All are good adjustments to reality and are culturally right. Pluralistic societies incline to religious relativism as water runs downhill. The danger has many faces and threatens mission on many fronts.

The infallible Word of God becomes just one of many scriptures—the way in which Jews and early Christians perceived God. Jesus Christ becomes not "the only begotten Son of God" but one of many fine founders of religions—the eldest in a vast family of brothers. The inevitable result is that the basic reason for Christian missions disappears. If God is available to men in salvic power through many incarnations and religions, there is no need to reconcile men to God in Christ.

The battle for brotherhood displaces missions. Many sensitive Christians today argue—erroneously, I believe—that

till brotherhood among all colors and races becomes an accomplished fact, no one will listen to the proclamation of the
gospel. Since white Christians hold themselves aloof from
men of other colors, proclaiming Christ is rank hypocrisy.
Even the less sensitive tend to feel that justice has been so out-
raged, that the highest priority in Christian action must be
to establish brotherhood. "The most effective missions," said
a minister recently, "is vigorous action on the side of the oppressed masses of mankind. No more proclamation of Christ.
The day cries aloud for our being Christlike in our relationship to other men."

Thus the discipling of the nations is pushed off the stage,
while action to achieve justice and brotherhood leaps into the
spotlight. Many leaders of missionary societies feel the need
for brotherhood so keenly that they are prepared to use the
apparatus of missionary missions—the income, goodwill,
buildings, organization, salaried staff, and the missionaries
themselves—not to reconcile men to *God* in the church of
Jesus Christ, but to fight behind Che Guevara, battle for land
distribution, and rectify the wrongs of hundreds of years.
They have, in effect, hijacked the plane of missions which for
a hundred years has been dedicated to bringing the nations to
faith and obedience to Jesus Christ, and are taking it to Jordan to fight the battles of the refugees.

It is essential to see the distinction between the church
doing such things on budgets and with organizations created
for social action of this sort—which is good—and the missionary society doing them—which is bad. The missionary
society was created for the specific task of discipling the
nations.

Secularism quietly seduces missions. Concerning the good
goals toward which Christianity has been working, secularism
says in effect, "The goals are good. We seek them not because
God desires them, but simply because they are advantageous."
Every Christian goal—except enlisting men and women as

baptized followers of Christ—is adopted and promoted by secularists. The programs are the same—the same schools, hospitals, agricultural demonstration centers, leprosy homes, and social actions—but all are done as if convictions concerning the Bible and the Lord were matters of small import. Secularism is also called humanism.

Humanism has become the real religion of vast numbers of men—Buddhists, Hindus, Muslims and Christians. The welfare of the physical body and the visible society becomes the only welfare worth striving for. The power of man to create the good world is worshiped and adored, while all supernatural religion is suspect. The miracles recorded in the Bible are "of course, simply fables."

This thinking greatly afflicts the church as she carries out biblical missions. Many Christians think it more honorable to run a hospital than an evangelistic enterprise and strongly advocate hospitals which say nothing about the Saviour and refuse to "take advantage of helpless people to make theological profit of them." They hold it more constructive to dig wells and distribute heifers than to baptize believers and multiply congregations. The growth of the church earns their particular scorn. To them the only really valid mission is humanization.

This is the danger to which Peter Beyerhaus speaks in chapter 2 and from which he guards world mission in such an effective way. The famed Frankfurt Declaration plays a significant part here.

Hitlerian fallout emasculates Christians. Christians become paralyzed by guilt, forgetting that God forgives denominations (churches) as well as individuals. Curiously, as Beyerhaus says in passing, while guilt keeps them from multiplying Africasian congregations, it does not prevent them from multiplying fertilizer factories or hydroelectric plants there.

In his gracious chapter entitled "Salvation Now," Arthur Glasser recounts the way in which Christian leaders, reflect-

ing on the fact (?) that in "Germany those who were preoccupied with dogmatical purity lined up with Hitler, while
those who did not so believe withstood him," has led to widespread skepticism concerning dogmas and to a wholehearted
embracing of good works interpreted as God's real mission.
Since Dr. Glasser examines this danger and exposes this
fallacy, I do not comment on it at length. That it widely
threatens Christian leaders is evident. Within the last two
years a most eminent executive secretary of a large and famous missionary society wrote an article to the effect that
after the American aggression and savagery in Vietnam, it
would be a hundred years before anyone in Southeast Asia
would listen to the gospel! And this in spite of the fact that
during the very years of the American involvement in the defense of freedom in Vietnam, hundreds of thousands of Chinese, Indonesians, Taiwanese and Koreans have been not merely listening to the gospel, but accepting Christ and becoming
Christians. In those very years, for the first time in history,
over a hundred thousand Southeast Asian Muslims have become Christians.

The sins of countries in which Christians are in a majority
seem so heinous to some Christians that they embark on
furious crusades to atone for them. Each crusade becomes
"the mission of the church," and the propagation of the gospel
is assigned a very low priority. One can understand the emotional tumult which dictates such behavior while disagreeing
heartily with its theology and deploring its effect on the discipling of the multitudes perishing in a famine of the Word of
God (Amos 8:11).

The combination of features increases the danger. One time
Daniel Boone was exploring the wilderness which later became Kentucky. Suddenly he stumbled on a mother bear with
cubs, trod on the tail of a rattlesnake, and saw a hostile red-
skin slipping an arrow into his bow. An even more threatening combination of dangers now confronts missionary mis-

sions. The several forbidding features of the landscape *combine* to make travel difficult. Some missions are bogged down.

Each feature of the terrain exists not in isolation but in combination, with each supporting and reinforcing the other. Religious relativism is encouraged by secularism. Withdrawing missionaries under the mistaken assumption that Western nations should retreat from gospel proclamation in Africasia is hastened by the guilty conscience caused by Hitlerian fallout. This combination makes sincere and reasonably intelligent Christians devise hermaneutics which run directly contrary to the plain meaning of Scripture. Seeking a path congenial to the religious relativism and rationalistic secularism which dominate the scene, they interpret the Bible in a way which destroys its primary purposes. It is the combination which makes missionary societies and sending churches give the bread which perishes in place of that which men eat and live forever. The combination of dangerous features of the terrain creates the *Zeitgeist.* "Hemmed in by these swamps and precipices, this desert and that river," men say, "standing still and being Christians where you are—this new way of mission is the only possible way. It is right, whether men believe in Christ or not. We live in the age of the atom. Who knows whether belief in Jesus Christ is necessary or not." Some even maintain that "in this new world a non-evangelistic form of mission is the best way of obeying Christ."

WHAT SHALL CHRISTIANS SAY TO THESE DANGERS?

The crucial issues in tomorrow's missions discussed in this book, together with many not discussed, must be seen against the whole landscape—not merely against its unfavorable features.

Christ's mission of "making known the way of salvation to all men and incorporating in His body, the church, those who are being saved" will be here long after Christians have passed this terrain and left these features behind them. But in the next three decades the threats and dangers described will probably continue. What shall we say to them?

GREATLY OVERESTIMATED

Perhaps the first thing the missiologists in this volume say concerning the dangers of the terrain is that they have been exaggerated. Popular writers, vying for the attention of the public, have outdone each other in horrific descriptions. They have created an entirely false expectation of disaster. Our missiologists do not share the pessimistic outlook which charterizes prophets of doom. We well know the problems, but have there not always been problems? The religious relativism of today does not begin to be as dangerous to the kingdom of God as was that of the first three centuries. And the power of the church is so much greater than it has ever been. Is it not a little ridiculous for the largest, wealthiest church in history— the church in six continents—which has seen few martyred for their faith, to maintain tearfully that the dangers are really very great? The United States spends twenty-one billion dollars a year for alcoholic drinks, and a billion more for cat food! Can anyone suppose that the American church which spends a third of a billion a year for overseas missions is overdoing it? Is that sum not really only a beginning? A small part of what we shall one day spend? Should not the church in six continents increase missionary sendings? And press on, proclaiming to all men that Christ is the wisdom and the power of God?

MANY FAVORABLE FEATURES OF THE TERRAIN

It would be a first-class error to determine our Christian duty while looking at the dangerous features of the terrain, for there are also dozens of encouraging and favorable features. One of these is *the enormous number of earnest Christians in the world today*. If it were not for scores of millions of these and for hundreds of thousands of faithful churches, how truly hopeless and depraved the world would be! The advanced state of Christian nations is commonly attributed to the fact that they are mechanized, educated, and advanced in science and technology. But these things in themselves neither would have been born nor would bring about great good. That in their administration Christians are playing notable roles is a large part of what decreases their harmful effects and increases their benefits.

Another favorable feature of the terrain is the *increased understanding of the mind of Christ* among Christians and increased determination to reform society in a more Christian mold. Social customs and conditions, antithetical to the teachings of our Lord, which to our Christian forebears seemed an uneradicable part of life, now are recognized as sub-Christian. Slavery, poverty, ill health, and racial prejudices which once were accepted are now being attacked left and right. True, the curse of drink—to which may be attributed not only a hundred thousand needless deaths each year in the United States, but also untold shame and suffering—is temporarily triumphant, but it too is still challenged by courageous Christians and it too will be banished from Christian nations.

A third feature of the terrain most favorable to Christian missions is the *mounting conviction that God wills the growth and multiplication of churches of Jesus Christ.* After World War II this basic Christian conviction was eclipsed for nearly two decades, but now it is moving out of the shadow into the sunlight.

A fourth favorable feature is constituted by the *tremendous turnings to Jesus Christ.* True, these are not going on in every nation, and some segments of the population in every nation have set their faces like flint against the good news, but the tide toward Jesus is so great that without fear of contradiction one can affirm that never in the history of the world have there been more people hearing about Christ and accepting

Him. Never has there been more vigorous and widespread growth of His churches.

A fifth and most favorable feature is *the rising tide of revival and renewal.* The divine fire is graciously touching the church in many places and accomplishing more in half a day than ministers and missionaries can in half a lifetime. In answer to earnest prayer for infilling, the Holy Spirit is descending on His church and empowering it to be righteous, do justice, and rejoice in the Lord. A vast dedication of life at all levels is going on in the race-and-culture-transcending household of God, giving promise of new reservoirs of power for the many tasks which God, the righteous Judge, assigns to His servants.

EVEN UNFAVORABLE FEATURES HAVE FAVORABLE ASPECTS

It would be another first-class error to fail to observe that each difficult feature of the terrain has a balancing factor which aids missionary mission. The moon dust, which sensational writers feared might be fifteen feet deep and drown whoever landed in it, turned out to be so solid that the moon jeep made tracks only half an inch deep. The dust was there, but so well packed that it made for smooth riding! Just so, each of the dangers of our day is there, but in God's hands it turns out to advantage the propagation of the gospel.

Western empires *have* retreated. The British army is no longer quartered in cantonments all over India. The officers of the Royal Bengals no longer play polo on the maidan. The Dutch army remains in Holland, not Indonesia. Afericasian nations have seen China imprison British newsmen, *fedayeen* hijack and destroy planes—without Eurica firing a gun in protest. Truly an abject retreat. But, in God's mysterious providence, while the military might of Eurica has retreated, its culture and technology have never been so accepted. Country after country adopts the cultural trappings of the West—from high-rise apartments to fighter planes, from compulsory education to curled hair. Agricultural advances, sparked by fertilizers and improved seed, are so numerous that, despite the enormous growth of population, famine is years away.

A vast new receptivity toward innovations, a willingness to learn, and a readiness to experiment with new forms of government and to adopt new ideologies are apparent. Sometimes they favor Communism, sometimes Christianity, and sometimes new syncretistic religions. In India where, in British days, idolatrous popular Hinduism (the religion of 95 percent of the people) was seldom questioned and reformed Hindu sects made scant way, educated Indians are today rejecting it. The bawdy, irresponsible doings of the gods recounted in many Hindu scriptures now seem incredible to them. Fifty years ago, to become Christian was "to espouse the religion of our conquerers"; today the new generation, which has grown up in free India, has seldom seen a white man and thinks of Christianity as one of India's religions, which indeed it is. During the rule of Holland in Indonesia, it is doubtful whether a hundred thousand Muslims could have turned to the Christian faith; but twenty years after the Dutch left and becoming Christian was no longer unpatriotic, a hundred thousand Muslims were baptized. The fact of the matter is that political and military Eurica has retreated, but cultural and religious Eurica has advanced throughout the world.

Or consider pluralistic society—many religions living in friendship and equality, with its corollary that each people should practice its own religion and live in its own culture.

This does pose a very considerable danger. Careless Christians, ill-founded in their faith, can say as they skirt this swamp, "After all, why impose our faith on others? They have their religion which is good for them."

Pluralistic society, however, also presents a very great opportunity. Curiosity about Christianity pervades Africasia. Campus Crusade reports that university students welcome opportunities to talk about Jesus Christ and many profess the desire to receive Him. Bible correspondence courses flourish, and Christian radio is listened to with avidity. Those who become Christians are not boycotted. Semi-Christian sects are arising which regard the Bible as their sacred book, and meet to worship Jesus Christ. In India, a Hindu high school principal, Subba Rao, found out through a thrice-repeated dream that when he prayed in the name of Jesus for sick men to be cured, the Lord Jesus often cured them. Mr. Rao threw out his idols and urged people to believe in Jesus Christ. True, he warns them not to be baptized or to join existing churches, but his Bible study groups look very like unstructured Christian congregations.

Since the military and political retreat of Eurica, men can become Christians without appearing to be antinational. Since their countries so desperately need power, Christ's claim to give them power is heard gladly. True, millions are not battering down the gates of Zion to get into the church. In most places to become a Christian is still difficult. The individualistic pattern of becoming Christian which ages of stiff resistance to the Christian faith has made normal, still makes "becoming Christian" seem like action traitorous to the family and thus holds back multitudes. Nevertheless, it can be safely said that no era in the history of the world has ever been more widely favorable to the multiplication of Christian churches as this pluralistic world.

Third, consider the battle for brotherhood, its attendant guilty conscience, and its use of resources given for missionary mission, for advancing the cause of racial equality. Massive reallocation of mission resources is no doubt a danger. Most missions come to the edge of that precipice and some of them may slip over it.

Yet, the battle for brotherhood is being won and it is a good battle to win, for nothing could say more eloquently to the pagan world of both Eurica and Africasia that Christianity is highly relevant to the crying issues of each age. The battle is going well because of Christian churches. They are not doing as much as they ought, that is true, but they are doing very much more than would be done were they not there. The steady action in favor of equal treatment for all men—black and white, brown and yellow—is being fueled by the Christian consciences of ordinary church members in school administrations, supreme courts, legislative halls, publishing companies, television corporations, and neighborhoods—black and white.

As the battle is won, large numbers of missionaries from the brown and black and yellow segments of the church will launch out in gospel proclamation. The won battle is validating and will validate the good news.

Furthermore, the battle won in Eurica will encourage unnumbered millions of the depressed in Afericasia to fight for brotherhood. In Japan live four million Ettas, a very depressed segment of the population. In Africa live many "slave tribes" against whom ruler tribes discriminate. In India the seventy million members of the excluded castes are pressing up into education and fresh air—and the higher they get, the more they demand real equality. Increasingly all these see that only in Christianity does their *religion* assure them that they are equal before God and man. In Latin America the masses are turning toward Communism, believing that it will "give" them equality and justice. If this does come in, it probably will not give them land and good wages. But even if it should, the deepest levels of brotherly behavior are forever beyond Communism, for it does not believe in God the Father. The masses will turn to the Master.

In short, the battle for brotherhood, in the long run, advantages the spread of the gospel and the discipling of the nations. It is perhaps less a danger than a built-in advantage.

What shall we say about secularism? And the truly terrific danger of a weak, deistic Christianity, rampant rationalism, erosion of faith in the sovereign God, abandonment of faith in the soul and the resurrection, and consequent emphasis on mere humanism? No one can underestimate the forbidding nature of this part of the terrain. And yet, Christians must not imagine themselves the only ones afflicted. Secularism erodes Christianity, it is true, but it erodes other religions far more. It is secularism which makes the Hindu elite so scornful of the elephant-headed, ten-armed, monkey-faced and long-tailed gods of the traditional pantheon.

As secularism spreads, a huge vacuum of faith develops. When faith in the Divine diminishes, life becomes meaning-less and societies break down. Men turn to astrology and demon worship; spiritual hunger increases, and spiritual thirst rises. Men begin to listen to news about the bread of heaven and the water of life. The Jesus People on the West Coast of America are flourishing among the very youth who sought life in LSD, pot and speed. Vacuum of faith is camouflaged by increase in physical well-being, national affluence, and a rising gross national product, but it is there. If not filled by Christianity, it will be filled by new religions of all sorts. In-deed, it is being filled by these religions in areas where the fervor to multiply churches of Jesus Christ grows dim. Chris-tians are called, then, to proclaim Christ and lead men to be-come His responsible disciples in a world where secularism is making men increasingly hungry for just this good news.

As for the Hitlerian fallout, its heyday has already passed; it is a temporary phenomenon. Those who plan mission strat-egy on the basis that guilty Eurica has lost the privilege of preaching the gospel are running from a dust devil which comes whirling across a plowed field but will disappear be-fore getting to where we stand. The German pastors and ministers who filled responsible posts in the thirties and thus were, perhaps to some small degree, responsible for not oppos-ing Hitler, are now at least seventy years old. They have car-ried their guilt for twenty years and have been heard, but they are soon going to meet God the most merciful, who will, I am inclined to think, assure them that their guilt was not as great as they had imagined. As the new generation of Christian leaders in Eurica reads its Bible and receives its marching orders from the Lord, it is much more likely to hear "Go, disciple the nations" than "Sit, and blame yourselves and your fathers for their sins."

Horror of manipulating persons? Yes, they must not be manipulated; but as most ministers and missionaries can testify, there is much more chance of the people manipulating the minister than of his manipulating them. The church is *not* the totalitarian state; is is not likely soon to be powerful enough to persuade and manage men. Furthermore, persuasion and counterpersuasion are life. It would be a dull world in which no one ever persuaded anyone else.

The enormous extent of suffering? Yes, the world has always been a suffering world. We hear about it today. Much suffering is caused by an ingrained love of evil—what theologians call "original sin." The best men do has an unfortunate way of turning sour. Far from disproving the need for missionary mission, the suffering of the world cries aloud for heart transplants—excising these hearts of stone and substituting for them hearts of flesh.

"The control of nature and the miracles of technology are so great that God is no longer either necessary or credible. We can do everything for ourselves, thank you." We reply, "Indeed?" The temptation of pride besets man. Even while he fears the hydrogen bomb, he spends billions to develop limitless power for atomic fusion, believing with all his heart that if only he has enough electricity, and heat in the winter, and coolness in the summer, and dollars on payday, and cars in the garage, everything will be all right. Such convictions are the very stuff out of which conversions occur—the miry clay from which God lifts man. They are the ground on which men, seeing the bankruptcy of the natural life, turn to Jesus and take His yoke on them. To see multitudes voicing this pride is the best possible invitation to men indwelt by the Holy Spirit to tell them of the Saviour.

THESE CHAPTERS AND THIS TERRAIN

The following chapters are written by men intimately in touch with today's terrain. They have grown up in the midst of these swamps and have looked over the edge of these precipices, so they write as moderns. But they also write as Christians. They are picking their way among these bogs and mountains, but their eye is fixed on the unchanging mandate of the everlasting God. In their hand is the compass of an infallible Bible, *and they are finding a way through*. They believe that Christian mission, which for 1,940 years has been bringing the *ethne,* the families of mankind, to faith in Jesus Christ, is going to continue doing just that. God wills it.

However, since they are picking their way carefully between the mountains and forests, through which God has caused our path to lie, they talk a great deal about adjustments to present conditions. The road to world evangelization twists and turns to find solid ground and favorable grades, to avoid the canyons and to wind its way through the mountain passes. The twelve authors are in favor of good works, but oppose substituting them for belief in Christ. They are—perhaps a bit fanatically—in favor of the cultures of men, but they believe that cultures reach their optimum development as they are transformed according to the divine pattern revealed in the Bible.

The writers of these chapters may not refer to the features of the terrain to which I have called attention. Yet they are aware of them and are pointing out ways in which Christian mission can carry out its God-given task while adjusting to these temporary obstacles. Diversions in direction they hold are permissible, but only if the long-range goal is steadily pursued.

The long look characterizes the chapters of this book. We are describing aspects of Christian mission which will be here till our Lord returns. Till He comes, His church will be baptizing men in the triune name, teaching them all things He commanded, and multiplying churches of Jesus Christ. These —the most potent ingredients of a just social order—will, in turn, both multiply other churches and work that God's loving and just rule may extend more and more widely among the nations.

Drs. Beyerhaus, Glasser, Tippett and King address themselves to key theological issues which today confront Christian missions and threaten the propagation of the gospel. If anyone would understand basic, contemporary issues, he must read Arthur Glasser on "Salvation Now," Peter Beyerhaus on "The Kingdom, Humanization, and Mission," Alan Tippett on "The Holy Spirit and Responsive Populations," and Louis L. King, eminent Foreign Secretary of the Christian and Missionary Alliance, on "The New Shape." Nothing in this book is more contemporary and up-to-date than these brilliant essays.

Drs. Tippett, Mbiti and Kwast address themselves to certain anthropological opportunities and dangers which pluralistic society presents to Africasians and Euricans propagating the Christian faith across cultures. It is essential in such propagation to respect cultures, to affirm that they contain much that is good and must be preserved, and to deny that "the advance of Christianity is over the dead cultures it conquers." Equally truly, it is essential to remember that Christ is the only begotten Son of God, the Word who was in the beginning with the Father, through whom everything was made, and before whom all men and all cultures will be judged. The everlasting God has chosen to give His revelation to men in the Bible which passes from culture to culture, purging each of them repeatedly as new light breaks from it. It purges all cultures—Christian, partially Christian and non-

Christian alike. Since it purges twentieth-century Christianity in a way it did not purge seventeenth-century Christianity, it also purges twentieth-century Bantu religion and Marxist religion as their adherents come to believe on Jesus Christ.

How can Christianity purge and yet not destroy? How can a culture become Christian without being destroyed? To be specific, what parts of the Christianity practiced by those citizens of India, who have turned to Christ from an idolatrous culture, *must be transmitted* by Indian missionaries to Indonesian converts from Islam, and what parts *must be abandoned* as not of the essence of Christianity? This last question is usually asked in Eurican terms: What portions of the Christianity they knew in their homelands must Eurican missionaries transmit, and what portions must they abandon as accretions of Western culture? But to ask the question that way confuses matters because the guilt complex of Eurica so heavily colors the answers. The men writing to the anthropological issues are addressing themselves to various aspects of the puzzle just set forth.

"The Practical Issues"—Part III of this book—are also set in the forbidding terrain which is today. The mountains of the moon, which Scott and Irwin* traversed in their moon jeep, are no more dangerous to human beings than the features I have described are to Christian mission. In this particular combination of plains, mountains and bogs, if the mandate of Christ is to be carried out, specific actions have to be taken. They have theological and anthropological aspects, but primarily they are practical tasks. For example, in chapter 9, I argue that societies committed to the propagation of the gospel are essential. They must not turn from the task to which God called them; they must know they are *missionary* societies. Those who support them must be sure that the

---

* James B. Irwin is a devout Christian. He left on the moon photographs of a banner bearing the signatures of 700 people praying for him, of his church, and of its slogan, "Things Happen at Nassau Bay Baptist Church."

prayer and money they dedicate to the propagation of the gospel will go to the discipling of the nations.

The easy and fallacious argument that "quality" is a mysterious value which exists in a vacuum entirely apart from quantity is being employed these days to denigrate all evangelism. Evangelism is stigmatized as "numberolatry." Winning men to Christ is selfish; church growth is self-aggrandizement. In a scintillating essay, Ralph Winter discusses this curious but influential error, and argues for recognizing that quantities frequently measure qualities.

Presenting the gospel to great crowds, as Dr. George Peters so well points out, has been part of the Christian church's program since the beginning. Its modern form—great-campaign evangelism—is being greatly blessed of God during these decades. How to employ it more effectively is a crucial issue today. Dr. Peters helps us to see what must be done. His chapter—especially its concluding few pages—is "must reading" for all leaders of mission.

The rush to the city is transforming populations. Most men in the future are likely to constitute, not a peasantry but an urban proletariat. Therefore it is of highest importance that the church perfect forms of evangelism which will establish cells of Christians (units of God's peace and light, churches of God indwelt by the Holy Spirit) throughout the towns and cities of today and tomorrow. Dr. Roger Greenway, speaking out of years of experience as a missionary in Ceylon and Mexico City, contributes a luminous chapter on "Urban Evangelism." Not the least of its values is that it records an evangelistic campaign of several years' duration in which seminary professors and their students did multiply churches.

The Rev. Edward Murphy, Executive Secretary for Latin America of Overseas Crusades, out of twelve years' experience in city evangelism in Argentina and Colombia, writes the fine chapter entitled "Guidelines for Urban Evangelism." He argues that such evangelism must do much more than

reach the cities and proclaim the gospel. It must seed the
cities—inner cities and suburbs, barrios and wards, high-rise
apartments and shack towns, beautiful sections and ugly
sections—with congregations, assemblies of God, fellowships
of disciples, call them what one will. Each of them is what
Oscar Cullmann calls "an eschatological phenomenon . . .
constituted by the Holy Spirit." Each—no matter how humble
and how partial—is a sign that Christ has instituted the new
age. The redemption of the cities depends on urban evangelism.

CONCLUSION

As readers turn to the following chapters, I hope they will
share the excitement with which we view missions tomorrow.
We believe, with the late Cardinal Agaganian, head of the
Propaganda Fide in Rome, that the missions of the last two
centuries are but a prologue to the drama about to unfold.
The very fact that by and large only the primitive peoples
have been discipled, means that the tremendous populations
of secularists, materialists, Hindus, Muslims, Marxists, Buddhists and others have yet to turn to the Lord and be saved.
The great age of missions is about to begin. Africa south of
the Sahara is even now in the midst of a march to Christ so
huge that by the year 2000 there will be well over 200 million Christians there—David Barrett estimates there will be
357 million. Great turnings of Asian populations are going on
and will accelerate. As to Latin America, Stephen Neill says
in his *History of Christian Missions,*

> In South America the growth of the Churches numerically
> in the last fifty years has been startling; there is no sign that
> their evangelistic vigor and their eagerness to witness are de-
> clining . . . it seems certain that this type of Christianity
> will be one of the dominating influences in Latin America
> as it emerges out of political confusion and economic dis-
> tress into calmer and more settled existence. It is no exag-

geration to say that "Protestantism is the most powerful and transforming spiritual influence in Latin America today."[1]

Perhaps this is the feature of today's terrain which is most germane to missions tomorrow.

Note

1. Steven Neill, *History of Christian Missions* (Grand Rapids: Eerdmans, 1965), p. 567.

PART ONE
THEOLOGICAL ISSUES

1

SALVATION TODAY AND THE KINGDOM

by
ARTHUR GLASSER

INTRODUCTION

IN MANY WAYS the Fourth Assembly of the World Council of Churches, held in Uppsala in 1968, marked a watershed in relations between conservative Evangelicals and liberals. Never were they in such deep agreement over the importance of the Christian's "horizontal" obligation to love and serve his neighbor, that he might attain both individually and collectively that fuller humanity which is God's will for all. On the other hand, never were they in such sharp disagreement when man's "vertical" obligation to God was under discussion. The focus of their polarization was the essence of the gospel and its relation to the urgent task of human development. Conservative Evangelicals will not readily forget how they were politely and effectively contained in their efforts to modify Section II: *Renewal in Mission,* which appalled them with its secularized gospel and reduction of the mission of the church to social and political activism.

In the years since Uppsala, changes have taken place which have had a sobering influence on both parties. Liberals have been humbled by their impotence in humanizing society

33

and its structures. Their social panaceas have largely proved unrealistic and unworkable. Theological radicalism with its penchant for scolding biblically oriented church members has emptied pews and dried up congregational giving. A highly placed ecumenist laments the "worldwide malaise in the ecumenical movement, shared equally by Christians whether from the first, second or third worlds, whether they are church officials or radicals, administrators or innovators, traditionalists or progressives."[1] Fortunately, God has graciously begun to grant to some of the more disenchanted a new openness toward the transcendental dimension of reality. The essentiality of personal conversion in Christian experience has surfaced with new force. Not a few are seeking to recover the indispensables of prayer, Scripture meditation, the cultivation of the inner life, personal discipline and the *koinonia* of the people of God.

God has also been at work among Evangelicals. They too are a chastened people. A significant number of older leaders are becoming conscious of their singular lack of success in resisting the affluence and hedonism that mark the spiritual decline of the age. The religious stirrings within the youth culture have reminded them of their need for a more radical commitment to Christ, a clearer break with materialism, and a more positive response to the social, political, economic and ecological issues of the day. As a result, there is a new openness to Scripture and to the need for adopting a life-style that truly reflects the demands of biblical discipleship.

Nonetheless, no little tension still exists between conservatives and liberals. The editorialist who candidly admits to a worldwide malaise within the conciliar movement and chides its "left wingers" for "condemning themselves to sectarianism" through reducing their Christian witness to an "uncritical commitment" to nation building in the Third World, nonetheless feels he should downgrade the phenomenon of growing evangelical vigor throughout the world. "A wave of funda-

mentalism—in theology, in individual piety, in church poli-
tics—is sweeping all continents and almost all churches, a
flight to sacred texts, rituals, and orders."[2] Words such as
fascism and *regression* are darkly introduced to portray this
fundamentalism in unwholesome colors. Obviously, polarization will continue as long as Evangelicals are misunderstood
for their tenacious loyalty to historic, biblical Christianity and
to mission as traditionally understood. One cannot make
friends with a people while telling them that their response to
Jesus Christ is distorted by psychological weakness, anti-
intellectualism, and the fear of facing the harsh realities of
this generation.

Fortunately, a commonality is emerging that could con-
ceivably resolve the polarization. On all sides a question is
being increasingly asked: "What are the form and content of
the salvation which Christ offers men and women in the secular
world in our day?" What better question could be asked? If
liberals and conservatives were to leave their polemic trenches
and grapple with this question, much good might result.
Actually, this is the question that was raised but not answered
at the 1963 International Missionary Council meeting in
Mexico City. It may well become the great question for both
church and mission in the days ahead. Indeed, if the polarized
were to probe together the depths of Jesus' word to Zac-
chaeus, "Today salvation has come to this house," or Paul's
affirmation to the Corinthians, "Now is the day of salvation,"
new dynamism might be released for the ongoing of the Christian mission throughout the world.

Growing interest in the meaning of "salvation today" is
eclipsing the Uppsala assembly's hotly debated *Renewal in
Mission*. And few are sorry. This document has not proved
significant in renewing within churches the call to mission. It
is too ambiguous, too secular, too divorced from the harsh
spiritual realities of mankind. Its basic flaw is its failure to affirm that the spiritual hunger of man can only be satisfied

through the forgiving mercy and love of God displayed in the death and resurrection of Jesus Christ. More, it failed to include as "a chief and irreplaceable task of the church" the biblical mandate to proclaim this good news to all men with a view to persuading them to become His disciples and participants in the life and witness of His church.

The forthcoming meeting of the Commission on World Mission and Evangelism (scheduled to be held in Indonesia in December, 1972) will focus on "Salvation Today." Doubtless this is further evidence of the growing awareness within conciliar leadership of the disenchantment of many with the barrenness of a secularized gospel. The General Secretary of the WCC, Dr. Eugene Carson Blake, candidly admitted that the "first issue" to arise from Uppsala was "Does the Gospel, rightly understood eschatologically and historically, really support the present ecumenical preoccupation with social, economic and political questions such as the 'development' commitment of the Uppsala Assembly?" He defined the "second issue" by asking whether the WCC preoccupation with the study of man is "really more than a passing fashion . . . or worse, an indication that we along with the secularists have become agnostic about God."[3]

So then, the new conciliar focus is on "salvation today." Nonconciliar Evangelicals cannot but rejoice. What theme better summarizes Jesus' teaching and ministry? Why not listen to what men and women all over the world are claiming as the heart of their experience of salvation in Christ? The kernel must be recovered that it might be shared with this generation. But more, even the conveners of the Indonesian meeting of the CWME are saying that the time also has come to inquire of one another as to whether their claims are authentic expressions of "salvation in Christ." This is heartening. A standard is being introduced. Here is the possibility of personal claims being evaluated in the light of the normative witness of Scripture.

Possible Approaches to This Subject

How can we anticipate this dialogue and contribute to it? Several approaches suggest themselves. As has already been intimated, one could start with the worldwide Christian community and gather from a sampling of its members, representative claims to the experience of "salvation." But what would this prove? To confine an investigation to the empirical data of personal testimony would be to assume that all claims have equal validity. And Christian courtesy demands that all be listened to. But would this not open the door to the irrational and the fanatical? One recalls Wesley's memorable sermon "The Nature of Enthusiasm," in which he examined critically the subjective witness to salvation that revealed nothing more than "an awkward mixture of real heathenism and imaginary Christianity." He then went on to raise the very real possibility of a person walking in "a vain shadow, a shadow of religion, a shadow of happiness!" Finally, Wesley was pressed to reject the contention that any personal witness could ever be regarded as normative. "There is a real influence of the Spirit of God, there is also an imaginary one: and many there are who mistake the one for the other." In conclusion he had put one answer to those who sought some canon of judgment whereby personal experience might be evaluated: "To the law and to the testimony."[4] All subjective experience must be examined in the light of Scripture. So then, we would concur with a preliminary report of CWME that by itself this approach is invalid.

A second approach would be to underscore the thesis that whereas the meaning of salvation is to be confined to those who claim personal relationship to Jesus Christ, it must be recognized that in different historic periods and different cultures this has expressed itself in such a variety of forms that it is "not susceptible of conceptualization or logical analysis." Furthermore, since God's saving act in Christ is involved, one must allow for the dimension of "mystery." This approach implies that one cannot construct an integrated theology from the Scriptures that has universal validity for "test[ing] the spirits to see whether they are from God" (I Jn 4:1, NASB). In short, we are left with accepting a variety of statements as to the meaning of salvation: all temporal, culturally conditioned, and partial. Some might stress spiritual conversion— the personal, inward transformation of the heart by the Holy Spirit. Others might stress political liberation—the activity of finding one's identity through power encounter with those who previously dominated and dehumanized him. This would include the experience of demanding and attaining one's legitimate rights in society. Still others might stress self-development—the activity that enables the socially and economically depressed to help themselves and "their own kind." The above three groupings are to be regarded as signs of Christ's salvific force, pointing to His active presence and direction in the lives of men and women today throughout the world.

The Canterbury Consultation in 1969 on "Salvation Today" in cooperation with the CWME ranged rather widely over this tentative approach, and even suggested that light on the subject might be secured through dialogue with men of other faiths to ascertain the manner in which they understand "salvation." Although this suggestion would hardly evoke positive response among conservative Evangelicals, one of their observations was rather disturbing. It follows:

> The radical nature of salvation cannot be understood without a consideration of judgment, heaven and hell. Heaven and hell were cultural 'givens' in New Testament times (cf. e.g. The Apocalypse of Enoch). They were used by Jesus and the early church to express essential insights into the nature of God and the responsibility of man. What are the apocalyptic features of life today which will make this same message visible if seen in the light of Christ? How should our understanding of salvation today take seriously

these threats of hell and damnation, the power of the forces
of evil and our longings for heaven?[5]

This paragraph embodies an approach to Scripture foreign
to the Evangelical. Indeed, he cannot but take strong exception to a hermeneutic that fails to distinguish between cultural
"givens" and universal values. Such a hermeneutic opens the
door to a situational theology that confuses the changing
character of culture with the unchanging reality of God.
Whereas the Bible unfolds its message within several successful cultures, the God who speaks in its pages is consistent
with Himself. He doesn't change His mind from period to
period and from culture to culture. The unalterable "com-
mons" of His revelation are the lostness and condemnation of
man, the abiding divine desire to redeem, and the actions He
takes in history to effect this salvation. One cannot relegate
them to the category of the culturally conditional. Down
through the long history of the church, biblically oriented
Christians have been adamant in contending that they are
beyond debate.

A third approach to this subject would be to begin with the
gospel records. What do they tell us that Jesus Christ Himself
said about salvation? Does His definition provide a basis for
testing the authenticity of claims being currently made to
identify salvation with inward renewal, with social confrontation and liberation, or with self-achievement through economic betterment? Evangelicals contend that it does. Those
who participated in the Canterbury Consultation, referred to
above, found that when they listened to the witness of Scripture, it brought balance to their discussion:

> [Our] conversation [on "Salvation Today"] tended to ex-
> press the content of salvation in terms of freedom, although
> the Bible study reminded us of its connection with righteous-
> ness. To be saved is not, presumably, to be set free to ig-
> nore what God has shown us of His righteousness. Is then
> our understanding of salvation in Christ adequately expressed

only through the concept of freedom? What is the relation between Salvation and freedom?[6]

This observation is germane to our discussion for two reasons. First, it reminds us that in our day, salvation is popularly regarded as liberation. Second, it admits the distance between liberation and the biblical stress on divine righteousness. Jesus offers a cross and a yoke when He calls men to His lordship. "Seek ye first the kingdom of God, and his righteousness." The primary emphasis is on submission to authority and the pursuit of the "holiness, without which no one shall see the Lord," not on personal freedom and independence.[7]

One final matter remains. Sometimes Evangelicals are put off by the casual regard with which liberals treat their serious efforts to define theological issues. Here is where Evangelicals need a sense of historic perspective. Down through the years, in conciliar debates, there has long existed what has been euphemistically called "The Conflict." It exists between those who are primarily interested in formulating correct theological definitions of salvation and those who are primarily interested in the world and in the life-transforming effects of salvation. Apparently this conflict came to a vivid climax in the experience of men in the conciliar movement during the years 1934 through 1937. They have never forgotten to remind one another of its significance. At the Oxford Conference on "Life and Work" in 1937, on one side were the "correct definition" men with their preoccupation with "dogmatical purity." There were those in their number who kept defending what they felt was the moral renewal being brought to Germany by Hitler. On the other side were the "life and world transformers" who felt the German Church needed to be turned about (they used the word *converted*) that it might truly confess Christ and "think" salvation with reference to the conflicts and tasks of that day. Whereas no one now holds a brief for those Christians within the German Church who succumbed to Hitler's blandishments and denied Jesus Christ during the period of the Nazi madness, it is manifestly unfair to universalize their tragic failure and imply that only the liberal has "correct" political instincts.[8] Impartial accounts reveal that not all conservative Evangelicals in the Third Reich failed Jesus Christ. Many were active in the confessional church and sealed their witness with their blood. And yet, as late as 1970 this denigration is still being publicized.[9]

Let us turn from this polemic and reexamine together the heart of the ministry of Jesus—His proclamation of the good news of the kingdom of God. We believe this is foundational to our understanding of the present salvific activity of God in the world. We do not believe that our study will confront us with different types of salvation, all equally valid, or with separate gospels of personal, societal and economic salvation in conflict with one another. Rather, we will be confronted with one gospel of the kingdom with its announcement of the good news that God's salvific work in present fulfillment and eschatological consummation extends to all areas of human existence.

THE KINGDOM IN PRESENT FULFILLMENT

When one steps into the world of the gospels he is immediately confronted by the theme "Salvation Today." Indeed, how else are we to understand the import of the prophetic promise of John the Baptist, "The kingdom of God is at hand"? This meant nothing less than that God was about to intervene, act and liberate. This announcement of Messianic visitation meant the dawning of the day of salvation and the inauguration of the kingdom of God. The coming one would separate men, saving and baptizing the righteous with His Spirit, and judging the wicked with fire.

This dynamic picture was almost immediately enlarged by Jesus Himself. Whereas John proclaimed the imminence of the divine advent, Jesus spoke of its fulfillment: "The time is fulfilled, and the kingdom of God is at hand" (Mk 1:15). This ministry is announced by Luke as commencing with Jesus' public identification of Himself with Isaiah's "Servant of Jehovah" in the synagogue of Nazareth and His announcement of Messianic salvation. "Today this Scripture has been fulfilled in your hearing" (Lk 4:21, NASB). This is startling! The great promises of the Old Testament were being actually realized in His mighty acts: "The wretched hear the good news, the prison doors are open, the oppressed breathe the air of freedom, blind pilgrims see the light, the day of salvation is here" (Lk 4:18-19, Jeremias). Later when John's disciples complained that Jesus did not fast, He replied with the metaphor of the bridegroom and marriage feast. It would be inappropriate for these to fast who were already enjoying the essence of the new age, even though it had not yet come in eschatological consummation. To His disciples our Lord confidently affirmed, "I tell you that many prophets and kings desired to see what you see, and did not see it, and to hear what you hear, and did not hear it" (Lk 10:23, RSV).

We cannot emphasize too strongly the import of these words. What happened in the person and ministry of Jesus was nothing less than the beginning of an era marked by the fulfillment of the great Messianic promises of the Old Testament. This is crucial to our understanding of all missionary preaching. In the brief notes of all three of the missionary sermons of the apostle Paul recorded in the Acts—in the synagogue in Antioch in Pisidia (chap. 13), in Lystra (chap. 14), and in Athens (chap. 17)—one thing vividly stands out. Paul presented the coming of Jesus Christ as the decisive event of history. Apparently Paul had but one message for the human race. After the coming of Jesus of Nazareth, life cannot be the same again because God has entered the human situation by direct confrontation.[10] And all men must do something about this event; they cannot remain neutral.

Since this new age commenced with Jesus' call to men to

repent and follow Him, and since this summons likewise characterized apostolic preaching, we are face to face with the normative witness for the church for all time. Jesus was very explicit about this. He taught that God's reign (the new age) may be accepted inwardly by simple submission in "complete childlike obedience and trustful receptiveness." His parables of the treasure and the pearl (Mt 13:44-46) underscore the renunciation the repentant sinner makes of all else for this kingdom. When he opens his heart to Jesus' person and mission, the kingdom of God becomes dynamically active in his life.

So then, we must keep in mind the fact that the presence of the kingdom of God in this age should be seen as God's dynamic reign invading the here and now without transforming it into the age of consummation, which is yet future when God makes all things new (Rev 21:5). In this connection we find great significance in Jesus' exorcism of demons. If the ultimate coming of God's kingdom means the consummation of Jesus' universal triumph over evil, one would expect that at His first coming among men He would be challenged by the demonic powers. Indeed, He described this mission as an invasion of Satan's kingdom (Mt 12:26) to challenge, overthrow and despoil "that enemy" of his goods. It is striking to note how frequently He encountered demons and overcame them by an authority that amazed His contemporaries (Mk 1:27). In the end, at His cross He finally triumphed, once and for all, spoiling principalities and powers openly and overcoming all the counterassaults of the evil one (Col 2:15). The apostle John very pointedly states that "the reason the Son of God appeared was to destroy the works of the devil" (1 Jn 3:8, RSV).

All of which brings us back to the radical summons which Jesus issued to the men and women He confronted in His ministry. His gospel was not a new teaching, nor a new hope; it was a present event. When He spoke, demons fled, storms

ceased, the dead came to life, and sins were forgiven. "The
Kingdom of God acts powerfully and requires a powerful
reaction." This paraphrase of Matthew 11:12 gives the sum-
marizing picture.[11] And some of those who heard Jesus for-
sook all to follow Him.

Jesus' words cannot be separated from His person. The two
signs of the presence of His kingdom are His words and His
works (Mt 11:13; Lk 16:16). The authority He displayed,
both in preaching and healing, demonstrated the presence of
the kingdom of God among men. The kingdom He brought
was not the world-shattering, divine apocalypse of popular
imagination. Rather, it was present in His proclamation of
the good news. Jesus' parable of the sower is the key. The
present working of the kingdom among men is like the seed
that does not everywhere enjoy the same results. Only in
those who "hold it fast in an honest and good heart" does it
bear fruit (Lk 8:15, RSV). In others it may be completely
fruitless. Yet, Christ is adamant in affirming that *this is the
kingdom of God* in its present, dynamic activity and blessing
in the hearts and lives of men. Crucial, then, to the advance of
His kingdom is the widespread sowing of the good seed of the
gospel to the peoples of every tribe and tongue and people
and nation.

At this point we need to underscore the startlingly new
dimension in Jesus' revelation of His Father which is only
faintly perceived in the Old Testament. Whereas the God of
the Old Testament was active on behalf of His people, judging, delivering and blessing them, Jesus stressed an aspect of
His nature that greatly displeased the religious leaders of that
day. He portrayed Him as a seeking God, possessed by a love
that made Him take the initiative "to seek and to save the
lost." God must save. He must bestow on men His eschatological gift, delivering them from mortality through saving their
"true" life, that is, something contrasted with their mere physical life. But more, God must bring man into perfected fel-

lowship with Himself. He wants communion restored between Himself and men. He wants men gathered from all corners of the earth to sit with Him at a table in the midst of His Old Testament saints (Mt 8:11-12). He wants to bestow the free gift of forgiveness of sins. He wants to impart a righteousness that will make men fit for His presence and friendship. He wants to offer Himself as Father to those who come. And because He is a seeking, fatherly God, nothing is more central to kingdom work than this activity of inviting men to come to Him. Indeed, Jesus saw His mission largely in terms of "inviting sinners to the Great Banquet of the Kingdom."[12] He did not say, "Repent, or hell will swallow you up," but "Repent, for the Kingdom of Heaven is at hand."[13] And He has commissioned the church to continue this work of inviting sinners to His table. To do this is to extend to men nothing less than the gift of the kingdom of God.

But there is a note of urgency. His invitation may not be casually regarded. God is holy as well as loving, heavenly as well as fatherly. It is a serious matter to spurn seeking love. Intermingled with Jesus' winsome words of God's kingdom as present salvation are His stark words of impending judgment. Jesus wept over the realization of judgment coming upon those men and cities who were rejecting the "Salvation Today" which He offered them (Mt 23:37-39). His weeping was not meaningless; all know that within a few decades judgment fell on that generation.

So then, in summary, we would affirm that by the first advent of Jesus the redemptive rule of God, in salvation and judgment, entered history. True, it was in advance of the final event toward which all human history is moving. But this rule created an order of divinely initiated redemption in the hearts of men that, although hidden and ambiguous now, will in the final day be revealed as inherent in the eternal, glorious purpose of God.

The gospels do not come to a climax with the death, burial

and resurrection of Jesus, but with the giving of the Great
Commission. We are utterly unabashed when we make this
sweeping assertion, for it arises from the obvious implication
of John 20:21 (RSV), "As the Father has sent me, even so
I send you." Chronologically, this precedes all other statements of the Great Commission. And what is its import?
Nothing less than a deliberate identification of the mission of
the church with the central event in all salvation history. All
agree that the destiny of the human race turns on the incar-
nated coming of the Son of God into the world. But no one
would have the presumption to compare the sending forth of
the church into the world with the incarnation. And yet, the
Lord made this correspondence. So then, we are confronted
anew with the significance with which He regards the task of
preaching the gospel of the kingdom, discipling the nations,
baptizing converts and teaching them what it means to bear
His yoke.[14]

This missionary calling of the church is to be understood
as the continuation of the Messianic tradition of the Old
Testament. As Bright summarizes,

> His servants are indeed like the Servant (Isa. 42:1;
> 49:6), a light to the world (Matt. 5:14). If the Church
> remembered the last words of its earthly Lord as a com-
> mand to preach the Gospel in all the earth, it only under-
> stood His intention perfectly: to give them the Servant
> task. . . . In my opinion, that Jesus gave His disciples such
> a commission is absolutely certain, otherwise it is unlikely
> that they would ever have become so energetically mission-
> ary. Besides, if Jesus regarded Himself as the Servant, the
> missionary command follows necessarily—for it was part
> of the Servant's task.[15]

So then, conservative Evangelicals cannot but bow to these
massive affirmations of New Testament theology. They must
contend that the church regard itself as the people of the
kingdom. They must challenge the church to devote all its

energies in the period between the resurrection and the end
to proclaiming the good news of the kingdom throughout
the world. All men should be summoned to the rule of Christ.
The church is nothing less than "the missionary people of the
kingdom of God." It does not establish the kingdom but bears
witness to the fact that the kingdom has already been set up
by its King. In all the New Testament there is "no brave talk
of . . . ushering in his Kingdom—not so much as a syllable."[16]
Nor does the New Testament encourage Christians to identify
their ecclesiastical structures with the kingdom. They dare
not fall prey to the temptation to mark the advance of the
kingdom merely in terms of institutional growth. Actually,
only "the Church which is His Body" constitutes the people
of the kingdom, but local congregations and denominations,
still in this world, are not the kingdom. They are but mixtures
of the true and the false, always under the judgment of God,
always in need of spiritual renewal and the deepening of
commitment to the missionary priority. This is not the age for
ecclesiastical self-deification, but for the proclamation of the
gospel of the kingdom. And it is the age in which Christians
should never cease to pray: "Thy kingdom come!"

THE KINGDOM IN ESCHATOLOGICAL CONSUMMATION

We must now review Jesus' teaching of the relation between
the kingdom of God in its present dynamic invasion of present
history and its future eschatological consummation. Today,
through the missionary obedience of the church, God is
bringing the blessing of "salvation today" to men in all nations. Tomorrow, the Son of man will come in glorious manifestation, shattering the natural order, gathering together His
elect, bringing to pass His judgments in the earth, and revealing the kingdom in all its glory. Then the present age of sin
and death will finally end and usher in the era of righteousness and eternal life. The kingdom of God will have finally

overcome the kingdom of the god of this world. As T. W.
Manson summarizes,

> The essential thing for the understanding both of the
> ministry of Jesus and the theology of Paul is the doctrine of
> the two kingdoms: the Kingdom of God and the kingdom
> of Satan. All the evils under which men suffer, and all the
> evils which they commit, may be regarded as the manifesta-
> tion in history of the power of the evil kingdom; all men's
> hopes for the future—the future of the world or of the indi-
> vidual—are bound up with the triumph of the Kingdom of
> God over the kingdom of Satan. That, when it comes, is the
> coming of the Kingdom of God in power.[17]

This is the substance of the Olivet discourse, recorded in
Matthew 24 and 25 and parallels. Whereas we would admit
the complexity arising from Jesus' intermingling of the historical and eschatological in this discourse, we must underscore an obvious tension between His predictions of certain
historical events preceding the end and His warnings of its
imminence. Indeed, the very nature of this discourse makes
Jesus more of a prophet than an apocalyptist. There is no
mistaking His instruction that the eschatological consummation of the kingdom depends in some way upon what God is
now doing in history in and through the church. "Salvation
today" is related to "salvation tomorrow."[18]

When Jesus was asked for eschatological signs, He gave
none; rather, He pointed to the new thing that would charac-
terize the age from Pentecost onward—the church's preaching of the good news as a witness to all nations (Mt 24:14;
Mk 13:10). So then, God has not abandoned man to a meaningless prolongation of his existence on the earth. History
makes sense. By proclaiming the good news of the kingdom,
Jesus challenges the dominance of evil in the world and de-
livers men from its bondage. By announcing the end, He is
calling men to prepare for the climax of history, the time
when God's judgments will be poured out. Be ready for the

sudden event! This is His warning! The end will come! Let no one be pessimistic about history. God will win! Good will triumph over evil in the human heart, over evil in the structures of society, and over the demonic, superhuman source of all evil—that is, over Satan himself!

This brings us to affirm what the New Testament everywhere teaches: It is not in man himself either to effect his own salvation or to perfect human society. "History cannot save itself"—this is written large over the biblical view of man in this world. But in Jesus Christ, God has so decisively acted in history that "the consummation of the Kingdom, although breaking into history, will itself be beyond history, for it will introduce a redeemed order whose actual character transcends both historical experience and realistic imagination."[19] Inasmuch as this triumph tomorrow is related to the witness of the church to the nations today, biblically oriented Christians cannot but jealously guard the primary essentiality of this task. "Salvation today" means preaching the good news of the kingdom. Nothing can have higher priority for the "eschatological community" caught between the tension of proclaiming that the kingdom of God has come and even now is in the world and looking for the kingdom that is yet to come. This community regards itself caught in the midst of a cosmic struggle. Whenever it contends for the truth committed to its keeping, whenever it performs Christlike deeds among men, whenever it witnesses to the gospel, it is participating in the ongoing of the kingdom of God among men. This is its mission. As Bright has well summarized,

> The Church is not to conduct missions as one of her many activities . . . she is a missionary people—if she is not that, she is not the Church. Her gospel declares that the salavtion of man lies only in the Kingdom of God, and that salvation she announces to the world . . . and summons men to it. . . . She campaigns for the spirits of men; she captures men for the redemptive fellowship of the Kingdom of

Christ. . . . Mankind has no hope save in a redeemed race of men; this is the soberest realism. We ought to know by now that well-planned short cuts which promise a just world order through external programs are uniformly a delusion. The redemption of man awaits precisely the birth of a new and redeemed race of men. And the Kingdom of God is that new race of men, God's living Church. In her is that ever-coming Kingdom.[20]

"SALVATION TODAY" AND ETHICS

We have already intimated that bearing the yoke of the kingdom today involves submission to Jesus' ethical instruction. Indeed, His ethics only makes sense when it is related to the dynamic nature of God's kingdom rule in the hearts of His people. This obligation is societal as well as personal. God not only brings men under His rule, but by effecting their moral transformation He makes possible a new quality of life characterized by righteousness. True, non-Christians contend that Jesus' standard is so absolute as to be unattainable; even He failed to transform history and purify society. And yet, a careful examination of His ethical teaching reveals a stress on inward character that is both realistic and practical. Furthermore, one wonders what this world would be like if He had not come!

But Jesus did not merely stress the essentiality of right attitudes. He called the "children of the kingdom" to be the faithful representatives of its divine rule within a world dominated by the enemy.

This brings us to the crux of the ethical teaching of the New Testament. One looks in vain for any approach to the ethical life or to social activism that does not presuppose a prior inward spiritual renewal. Only by the new birth can men enter the kingdom and receive the dynamic for the kingdom ethic (Jn 3:3, 7). True, the gospels contain little explicit teaching on social ethics, but Jesus never gave the least encouragement to those who would ground social ethics in something other than personal ethics.

It is at this point that we also need to remind ourselves that whenever Christians pray "Thy kingdom come," they are re-affirming the biblical perspective that this world with all its social patterns and relationships will end. This Christian hope and expectation means "the end of all social and political Utopias which expect to achieve a perfect pattern of peaceful society by human means and human strength."[21]

This does not mean an "eschatological negation" of the world but a frame of reference by which Christians can re-spond positively to society as it is. That the kingdom of God is at hand provides impulse, capacity and urgency to the task of subjecting the whole of human society to radical criticism in love and in hope.

"Only a social ethic based on eschatology can really recog-nize both the need for and the weakness of social systems, be-cause it sees those systems involved in the struggle between the demonic and divine realms for control of God's creation, of man and of human relationships."[22] So then, Jesus expects His people as "salt" and "light" to make an impact on society that can be felt and measured. This impact is not to be confined solely to the spiritual realm, for Jesus' redemptive concern ex-tends to the whole man in the totality of his existence: physi-cal, psychological and social. His kingdom cannot but be con-cerned with the evils, personal and societal, which bring suf-fering to man. In this sense we must believe that the New Testament implicitly teaches that there is a "social gospel."

Once again, we turn to Bright for a summarization:

> Jesus did not present his ethical teachings as a program which he expected the secular order either of his day or ours to carry out. . . . He did not set out to reform society, but to do far more: he summoned men to the Kingdom of God and its righteousness. . . . This new order even now bursts in upon the present one and summons men to be its peo-

ple. . . . We cannot as "liberals" have done, preach the ethics of Jesus and leave aside his person and work as if it were a cumberous and superfluous theological baggage. Nor can we, as "conservatives" have tended to do, urge men to salvation through faith and feel no need even to confront ourselves and our people with the demands of the righteousness of the Kingdom. This, too, is not to preach the Christ of the New Testament.[23]

CONCLUSION

What is the biblical meaning of "salvation today"? It is personal relationship to Christ by the new birth, embracing nothing less than the blessing and obligation of bearing the yoke of His kingdom. No pietistical, passive acquiescence to the evils of society! Rather, the refusal to be neutral toward the moral issues of the day. But more, those who enter this kingdom and receive God's salvation are called to a life of missionary obedience. They are a missionary people whose chief task is to summon men to the lordship of Jesus Christ.

Notes

1. Ernst Lange, "The Malaise in the Ecumenical Movement," *The Ecumenical Review* 23, no. 1 (Jan. 1971): 1.
2. Ibid., p. 6.
3. Eugene Carson Blake, Report of the General Secretary, *The Ecumenical Review* 21, no. 4 (Oct. 1969): 333-34.
4. John Wesley, "Sermon 33," *Forty-Four Sermons* (London: Epworth, 1951), pp. 416-28.
5. "Salvation Today: Issues for Further Study," *Study Encounter* 5, no. 4 (New York: Division of Studies, World Council of Churches, 1969), p. 210.
6. Ibid., p. 210.
7. Mt 6:33; Heb 12:14.
8. Indeed, one has but to examine critically and in the light of subsequent events the pronouncements of liberals on political and social issues from 1914 onward, to be confronted by a shocking instability of viewpoint and a very low level of discernment. With the fall of France, *The Christian Century* looked to Hitler to "give the rest of the world a system of inter-relationships better than the trade-strangling and man-exploiting system of [British] empire capitalism" (June 26, 1940, p. 815). When its editors learned that the Allied postwar occupation of Germany was under consideration, their considered advice was: "Let Stalin gain our postwar aims for us! Let Stalin take charge of Germany's future" (Sept. 29, 1943, pp. 1095 ff.). For details of this sort, consult the heavily documented articles by Frank Farrell, "Instability of Liberal Social Ethics," *Christianity Today*

6. no. 7 (Jan. 5, 1962), pp. 308 f.; no.·8 (Jan. 19, 1962), pp. 365 f.; no. 9 (Feb. 2, 1962), pp. 515 f.; "Liberal Social Ethics: Confronting the Four Horsemen" *Christianity Today* 7, no. 3 (Nov. 9, 1962), pp. 107 f.; no. 4 (Nov. 23, 1962), pp. 174 f.

9. For some startling and sobering details, consult *Study Encounter* 6, no. 1 (1970), pp. 17-18.

10. For an illuminating contemporary analysis of these sermons, see the essay by William Barclay, "A Comparison of Paul's Missionary Preaching and Preaching to the Church" in the *Festscrift* honoring F. F. Bruce, *Apostolic History and the Gospel,* ed. W. Ward Gasque and Ralph P. Martin (Grand Rapids: Eerdmans, 1970), pp. 167 f.

11. G. E. Ladd, *Jesus and the Kingdom* (New York: Harper & Row, 1964), pp. 154-60. Dr. Ladd's treatment of this key text is very helpful.

12. Ladd.

13. Helmut Thielicke, *The Waiting Father* (New York: Harper, 1959), p. 26.

14. In the gospel of Matthew, the formal teaching of Jesus ranges over such themes as ethics, discipleship, mission, corporate life and stewardship. To bear His yoke involves submission to His will in these five categories (chaps. 5-7, 10, 13, 18, 24-25).

15. John Bright, *The Kingdom of God* (Nashville: Abingdon, 1953), p. 211.

16. Ibid., p. 234.

17. Quoted by Ladd, p. 116.

18. For a comprehensive treatment of the manner in which the apostle Paul related the missionary motive to the eschatological coming of "salvation tomorrow," consult Oscar Cullmann's essay, "Eschatology and Missions in the New Testament" in *The Theology of the Christian Mission,* ed. Gerald Anderson (New York: McGraw-Hill, 1961), pp. 42-54.

19. Ladd, p. 333.

20. Bright, pp. 217-18.

21. Heinz-Dietrich Wendland, "The Relevance of Eschatology for Social Ethics," *The Ecumenical Review* 5, no. 4 (July 1953), p. 365.

22. Ibid., p. 368.

23. Bright, pp. 221-24.

2

MISSION, HUMANIZATION, AND THE KINGDOM

by
PETER BEYERHAUS

WORLD MISSION, world history, and social change are inseparably interrelated in a dialectical tension. For the motive and goal of world mission is the kingdom of God, which in spite of all resistance is also the goal of world history and which already permeates human society. This destination, the kingdom of God, has always been in the consciousness of Christian missions.

THE KINGDOM OF GOD

The nature of the kingdom has not always been conceived in the same way. In his penetrating essay "The Meaning of World Mission," Walter Freytag developed the thesis that none of the four successive waves in the missionary movement has been able to express the whole biblical concept of the kingdom. Rather, in each we observe a narrowing down, a contraction, of the total significance of God's kingdom:

> In Pietist missions the Kingdom of God was narrowed to a purely individualist-ethical outlook. They concentrated on the salvation of individuals. . . .
> Second, came those who held that the goal was not so

54

much individual converts but self-supporting, self-governing and self-propagating churches. These missiologists did not teach that the churches *must* be identical with the Kingdom of God, but acted as though they were. . . .

Third, philanthropic missions, mainly with Anglo-American background, conceived of the Kingdom in terms of bettered social conditions in the world. This view, which today is celebrating an unexpected comeback, Freytag called the idealistic and socio-ethical contraction. . . .

Finally, the fourth wave, in sharp contrast to the former three, which held that the Kingdom was already present in this world, believed that the Kingdom is yet to come. The apocalyptic evangelists, men like Frederik Franson and Grattan Guiness, believed the Kingdom to be an eschatological phenomenon and located it in the totally transcendent realm. The only object of mission, they said, is to speed up the second coming of the Lord and the consequent establishment of His apocalyptical Kingdom.[1]

Freytag does not try to answer the question, Why has no mission movement succeeded in combining these four emphases? Each gives one true part of the total picture—but only one. In my judgment, the reason for this shortcoming lies in the *mystery* of the kingdom, a mystery which Jesus Himself underlined. Jesus took up and also rejected the Messianic expectations of His time. He referred to the "Agenda of the World," but did not second its motions. He made it clear that the forces of the kingdom were at work in His person and ministry, but refused to present Himself as the earthly Messiah or to be elected to this office. In His parables He indicated that the kingdom would not come at once with visible power, nor would the apocalyptical transformation take place soon. The kingdom He described was rather a progressive, dynamic process. The decisive and constitutive act in this process was to be—as Jesus gradually disclosed to His disciples—His atoning death as the "ransom for many" (Mk 10:45).

We can conclude that the kingdom is founded in God's saving act of redemption on the cross of Calvary. Membership in it can be acquired only by men who *believe in the gospel* and are thus rescued from the wrath of the holy God. This is the abiding tenet which Evangelicals and, indeed, all who take the Bible seriously, can never give up.

The kingdom finds its first societary expression in the *Ekklesia,* which is the gathering of the Messianic community—of those, who through the means of grace communicate with their risen Lord and receive His gift of salvation. Here Christians must defend their conviction against all attempts to reduce the role of the church to that of a mere instrument. Only the wording of the formula "extra ecclesiam nulla salus" was coined by Cyprian; its truth lies in the epistles of the New Testament.

But the kingdom, which rules over the minds and bodies of Christians not only when they are assembled for worship, exercises its transforming effects in their *society* as well. People, truly indwelt by the Spirit of the gospel of liberty, work for the elimination of inhuman structures and principles and for a reconstruction of society which does justice to the dignity of man for whom Christ sacrificed His life. The humanists are right when they insist that the kingdom is reflected already in this world in the appearance of visible signs of the coming *shalom* (reign of peace).

But the *full shalom* is not to be expected within the present age of history, while the forces of the new aeon are rigorously opposed by those of the old. The kingdom will find its unrestricted establishment only through the visible *return of the uplifted Lord*. Then He will openly triumph over all His enemies. He will bind Satan, so that the nations will be willingly ruled by the Messianic justice which will go forth from Zion. Here the apocalyptic evangelists play an important role in correcting this worldly optimism of the old theological evolutionists or the new theological revolutionaries. As these men (the humanistic wing of philanthropic missions) demythologize the futuristic elements of biblical eschatology, they are constantly developing a naïve enthusiastic concept of world history, in which the millennium is swallowed up by the utopias of ideological action programs. But God has not yet given the precondition of His millenary *shalom* when the Lord will bind the forces of the evil one. Therefore the position of the humanists must necessarily lead to substitution of the law for the gospel. Violence takes the place of following in the steps of the suffering Servant. Missions become more active in liberation movements than in church growth.

Even the kindom of Christ in power, however, will not be the absolute end of history. The real end, described in Revelation 22, will consist in the creation of a *new heaven* and a *new earth* by the Father. The Fourth Assembly of the World Council of Churches should never have yielded to the exegetical blunder by which the prophetic words "Behold I make all things new" were misinterpreted as announcing a series of ecumenical projects in the seventies!

If our perspective of the history of the kingdom is correct, then we were right to state that the history of the world and the history of the church in mission stand in a growingly more obvious inner relation to each other. God the Father directs history. In the resurrection of His Son He has installed Him as Lord of all powers. Thus, in spite of all antagonism between the two, the final goal of the world and of the church can only be one. Christ as the Head of the church wills to be acknowledged also as the Ruler of the world. Thus He lets humanity as a whole share in the salvation which He has wrought at His cross.

This assigns to mission its historic destination. The church in mission is to make known the gospel to ever more people, ever more nations and spheres of life. Ever more people shall be redeemed, ever more churches shall be established, ever more nations or societies shall be given the opportunity to reshape their structures and principles according to the commandments of the kingdom and draw spiritual support from its forces. Thus the course of the proclamation of the gospel is manifesting itself by a process of *humanization*.

But in the light of its ultimate vision, the kingdom of Christ in power, mission will see only a partial success of its labors during the present aeon. The proclamation of the gospel, the offer of salvation, and the claim of sovereignty of Jesus Christ lead not to the unification of humanity, but rather to a new and most antagonistic separation. The double answer of belief or unbelief, called for by the gospel, means a *division of the spirits*. Thus the birth and growth of each new church are to the surrounding world both a sign of hope and a sign of judgment. The world is told that the offer of grace under the lordship of Christ is the answer to its legitimate hope, but it is also told that its negative response to Christ is directing and accelerating its course toward the final cataclysm.

The Role of the Church

This truth has molded the church's understanding of her role both in New Testament and in postapostolic times. It expressed itself in the name given to the early Christians as the "Third Generation," the new people which came forth from the two peoples, Jews and Greeks, and was destined to take their places in the coming kingdom. This conviction, as Harnack remarks, gave to the confessors of the new faith at once a political and historical self-consciousness which could not be surpassed in its comprehensiveness, perfection and impressiveness. Harnack sums up the relevant utterances from early Christian literature as follows:

> Our people is older than the world. The world has been created for our sake. It is also preserved for our sake—it is we who hold up the extreme judgement. Everything in the world is subjected to us and has to serve us. Everything in

the world—in the beginning, middle and end of history—is revealed and transparent to us. We shall participate in the judgement of the world and shall enjoy eternal beatitude.

Such statements were the real cause for the hatred and the persecutions in those times. In the ears of the non-Christians they sounded as absurd and arrogant as they sound in the ears of those theologians who have resolutely reversed the pattern God-church-world and now read it God-world-church.

It is highly significant to observe the dialectic social behavior of the Christians. The consciousness of being the Third Generation led them to dissociate themselves in many internal and external ways from the world. It also gave them a powerful sense of civic responsibility.

As God preserved the world for the sake of His people (the community already gathered and still to be gathered), early Christians felt themselves responsible for this preservation of the world. Dr. U. Wickert, an expert of patristics, calls their attitude to the state a "mixture of critical reservation and solidarity." We read in an anonymous tract of the second century that

the Christians obey the laws, but in their specific way of life they surpass the laws. . . . What the soul is in the body, this the Christians are in the world. . . . The soul lives in the body, but it is not of the body. Christians live in the world, but they are not of the world. . . . The soul is enclosed in the body, but it is the soul that keeps the body together; likewise the Christians are arrested in the world, but it is they who keep the world together.

According to their conviction, two things enabled the Christians to preserve the world: their superior civil obedience, which was inspired by their new ethics of love, and their unique ability to exorcize the demons. Thus, paradoxically, the Christians of the early church conceived themselves as the healing dimension in a world doomed to eventual cataclysm.

In the midst of the worst persecution, Origen confidently wrote that Christ, who had already conquered the world, would finally establish His visible lordship over it.

Thus the church—in spite of being aware of her separation from the old world—manifested a strong social concern for it. She believed both that world history in virtue of God's rule had to serve her, and that she had to serve Christ within the framework of His world's history.

To describe how this concept was manifested in the succeeding epochs of history would take a whole volume treating of the two medieval syntheses of church and empire, in other words, Constantine's theocratic form in the East, where the emperor ruled the church, and Augustine's ecclesiocratic form in the West, where the pope ruled the empire.

A further volume would treat of the colonial imperialism of the last four and one-half centuries, whose aftereffects still handicap Western relations to the Third World. Eurican missionaries for the most part accepted the economic and political openings or even annexations on three continents. Rightly or wrongly, they interpreted them as vehicles which God, the Ruler of history, had prepared for the messengers of His gospel.

It would be incorrect, however, to allege that missions in the colonial age were governed by this-worldly aims. Their determining aim was the eternal salvation of those who apart from Christ were lost. They also labored zealously for the well-being of the ethnic groups they were serving. Missionaries constantly tried to rescue people from sickness, poverty, illiteracy and fratricide. Thus they too maintained the dialectic social behavior which marked the church in patristic days.

In passing, one notes that in spite of many deplorable effects, the often defamed cooperation between colonial rulers and missionaries has born many abiding positive fruits. The emergence of new independent nations in Africa and Asia could hardly have occurred apart from this cooperation. And we should not forget that it was men of mission like William Wilberforce, John Philip, David Livingstone and Charles Lavigerie who place a decisive role in destroying the scourge of slavery in Africa.

Today we are often told that Western churches have forfeited the "privilege" of doing mission work in the Third World, because their name has been scandalized by their association with Western imperialism. An absurd statement! Observe, first, mission work is no privilege, but an irrevocable mandate given by a sovereign Authority. Second, it is sub-Christian to maintain that there is a guilt which cannot be removed by contrition and forgiveness. Third, such unremovable guilt would invalidate all other Western concern for and aid to the Third World. Finally, the wholesale condemnation of the work of our predecessors is an act of phariseeism. These critics of missions should distinguish between contrition which leads to a constructive new beginning, and a paranoid guilt complex, which causes spiritual paralysis and inefficiency. Such a guilt complex cannot be the fruit of the Holy Spirit!

Let us not be immobilized by judgments concerning the work of our predecessors. They will give account for their obedience or disobedience to the Great Commission in their own historic situation. Our main concern should be to respond in a constructive missionary way to the challenges of our historic situation. We too in our day, like our predecessors in theirs, must obey the Great Commission.

Today's Task for the Church in Mission

The task of the church in mission in each historic moment is to ask *what opportunities God gives us to testify to the non-Christian world about His whole purpose of love.* We shall keep firmly in mind that this purpose aims toward the salvation of all those who believe in His Son and become His responsible disciples.

Today there are two contesting answers to this question, each represented by a respectable missionary force throughout the world. The pity is that they seem to be unable to work out a constructive synthesis of both answers.

THE FIRST IS THE EVANGELICAL ANSWER

Consistent with the tradition of Protestant world missions as a whole, Evangelicals—I am speaking of those with a statesmanlike vision—regard as today's new opportunities those responsive populations which the gospel finds. In them they would concentrate as strong missionary forces as possible both from the small indigenous churches nearby and from the larger churches in Eurica in order to secure a maximum of new disciples. In the past, Evangelicals used to call such openings "awakenings" and ascribed them solely to the work of the Holy Spirit. Today, while not diminishing the stress on prevenient grace, which is at work in group movements, many Evangelicals believe that sociological factors also play an important part. This is, at least, the conviction underlying the worldwide studies of the Institute of Church Growth at Fuller Theological Seminary in Pasadena, California. Anthropological and historical questions are treated in a scholarly fashion, as are theological and biblical questions.

The whole purpose is to find out where at present within non-Christian populations conditions appear which could make them responsive to the missionary challenge. These situations become the main points of concentration of a wise strategy of mission.

This concept has been officially adopted by American evangelical missions at the Wheaton Congress on World-Wide Missions in 1966. Regretting their former "complacency with small results long after a larger response could have been the norm" and their "failure to take full advantage of the response of receptive peoples," the Wheaton Declaration urged

that research be carried out by nationals and missionaries in

all parts of the world to learn why churches are not growing . . . to evaluate church growth opportunities now overlooked, and to review the role, methods and expenditures
of our agencies in the light of their significance to evangelism and church growth.

This strategy combines the theologically valid conviction of
the absolute priority of eternal salvation with a new understanding of history as a dynamic process which conditions the
kairoi toon ethnoon, that is, the opportunities when people
become responsive to the proclamation of the gospel.

This evangelical view not only shares the soteriological
concern of the first apostles, but is also verified today by
major ethnic movements which contribute greatly to the increase of church membership in several parts of the world.
Contrary to the popular impression that the advance of the
world missionary movement has been brought to a standstill
by nationalism and renascent religions, the church today faces
greater missionary opportunities than ever before in its entire
history.

In Africa south of the Sahara during the years 1950 to
1970 the number of Christians has risen from twenty to fifty
million. In Indonesia in the years 1965 to 1968 four hundred
thousand people applied for church membership, and the
movement is still going on. One might object that the Indonesia movement has more political than spiritual causes,
but this is exactly our point: In mission history we cannot
neatly divide the motives and factors which influence the
process of Christianization. The decisive question for the
church is whether she is responsive to the occasions in which
God as the Ruler of history demands her special attention
and obedience. The gospel has the inherent power to transform even such inquirers who at first embraced it from very
mixed motives. Otherwise Europe would always have remained a heathen continent!

Evangelical mission leaders are worried today that within

many churches and mission societies the awareness of such evangelistic opportunities has considerably declined. As a matter of fact, as far as Western churches are concerned, the old eagerness to preach the gospel to those who never have heard it, "that they may turn from darkness to light and from the power of Satan to God, that they may receive forgiveness of sins and a place among those who are sanctified by faith" (Ac 26:18, RSV), has greatly diminished. Today, only in evangelical mission societies does this biblical motive seem to spur men on to become missionaries. Only among Evangelicals do we find organizations like the World-Wide Evangelization Crusade or the Sudan Interior Mission which still are moved by the concern for the unevangelized in areas which have recently opened up for mission work.

THE SECOND IS THE ECUMENICAL ANSWER

Within the other churches, and not the least within those missions which are affiliated to the Commission of World Mission and Evangelism, the evangelistic drive seems to have been more or less replaced by a social-ethical interest. Since the preparation for Uppsala, 1968, not *Christianization* and church-planting but *humanization* and attempts to change the structures of society seem to be the new ecumenical missionary strategy. In the Draft for Section II, "Renewal in Mission," the place formerly given to the mission fields was dedicated to the "fields of tension within society," that is, to racial strife, social upheaval and student revolts. The chief emphasis has been on achieving more satisfactory horizontal relations rather than on Paul's interpretation of his apostolic ministry: "We beseech you on behalf of Christ, be reconciled *to God*" (2 Co 5:20, RSV). The concern caused by such apparent "displacement of their primary tasks" in ecumenical missions, as the Frankfurt Declaration later called it, caused Dr. McGavran in the *Church Growth Bulletin* to put the searching question to all assembly delegates: "Will Uppsala Betray the Two Billion?"

Goaded by this provocative question, some delegates thought that converting non-Christians and rendering social service were being offered as exclusive alternatives. This erroneous thought no doubt contributed much to the strong polarization between "evangelicals" and "ecumenicals," "traditionalists" and "progressives," which marked the heated deliberations in Section II.

The two tasks of proclamation and service need not form exclusive alternatives. It was a committed British Evangelical, the Rev. J. R. W. Stott, who after Uppsala in the same *Church Growth Bulletin* proposed the new formula: "Evangelicals should proclaim the equation 'mission=witness+service,' "—a view in which Dr. McGavran heartily concurs.

Christian mission is complex, however, and we do the cause no favor by oversimplifying it. There are many different forms of society and of human need. Mission meets them all. No narrow view of mission is sufficient—either one which emphasizes evangelism or one which emphasizes social action. Mission should meet many forms of society in many ways.

For example, newly opened geographical areas and ethnic units are one form in which even today missions meet the challenge of history. Mission societies, like World-Wide Evangelization Crusade, are right and deserve our wholehearted support. Even today there are wholly untouched tribes in the valleys of central New Guinea, on the heights of the Himalayas, and in the deep forests of Amazonia, where the first cultural contact calls for pioneer missions. Here the task is making disciples of these tribes.

Much more important, in well-missionized countries like India, Ethiopia, Thailand, urban Japan, or Brazil, enormous populations exist which are being evangelized by neither the present missions nor the small younger churches of a few thousand or a few hundred thousand members. In such countries, the task is not pioneer missions but continued vigorous proclamation of the gospel and service of mankind through *and beyond* existing churches. The great bulk of mission labors will no doubt be spent in these great countries for here is where most men live.

In addition to these two main forms of mission, we also have to consider where mission is called on to open up new areas of life by witness and service. I mention three examples to illustrate this point:

1. In Asia and Africa one of the main problems is that which in India is called "communalism," and in Africa "tribalism." As N. Sithole has shown, European and American missions helped create the spiritual foundation of modern nationalism in Africa. But since nationalism in its initial stage has been a reaction against Western colonialism, the unifying force of that colonialism has been lost in the newly independent states. Old unresolved frictions of tribes and castes mount. They frustrate the unifying efforts of national governments and can cause horrible fraternal wars. Who is able to point out a spiritual force which could reconcile such dissensions? Here the national and regional Christian councils have demonstrated a significance which has been taken seriously by some national governments.

2. All young nations introduce industrialization to solve their economic problems, but industrialization produces estrangement from the familiar patterns of life and brings forth new social antagonisms. Who will help the factory laborer find meaning in his job at the conveyor belt? Who will help various groups see each other not as opponents but as partners? Who will exhort managements not to sacrifice men to productivity and efficiency? All these questions explain the growing significance of industrial missions (Christian attempts to help bring in a more just and humane social order) in many parts of the world.

3. Industrialization necessarily means *urbanization*. Migration to the towns exceeds the creation of new jobs in speed. In Calcutta, Bangkok, Lagos and Rio de Janeiro the cultured hearts are surrounded by septic belts of an uprooted proletariat afflicted by many hygienic, social and moral evils. Who helps heal these raw wounds and integrate these displaced persons into the new society? The answer of the National Christian Council of Kenya was the creation of a number of exemplary communities in Nairobi, which were built in partnership with the cooperating missions.

These three examples show how the social and political problems of the nations form a genuine field of Christian mission. Giving aid to people out of the love of Christ, in emergency or in developmental crises, overcoming old or new enmities through the power of reconciliation, witnessing courageously for the dignity of discriminated persons because Jesus died for them—all these are occasions where the oral proclamation of the gospel and multiplication of churches in these cities can be verified by the serving fellowship of love and thus demonstrate its winning power.

I myself saw in a Nairobi community center how the help given toward the social integration of stranded migrants from the tribal areas made them very receptive to the Christian message. Each Sunday, three services in different vernaculars were held at this center. Loudspeakers had to be used for the people who could not find room in the church. We must serve the *whole* man—his spirit as well as his body. We must multiply churches as well as distribute powdered milk.

In the countries of the Third World, Christian missions still meet many who are prepared to listen to a religious interpretation of their social need. These people are aware that today's new culture needs an integrating religious center. The social challenges are at the same time chances for church-planting evangelism.

Thus we find that the two ways of developing a missionary

strategy which relates the saving message to an opening situation need not be exclusive alternatives. If mission means to
cross new frontiers, there is no reason to define these frontiers
in geographical and ethnic ways only. To cross sociological
and functional frontiers can also be legitimate mission.

THE DECISIVE THEOLOGICAL DEVIATION?

What then is the decisive reason why men holding the two
concepts of finding a missionary strategy relevant to the present historic situation have failed to meet each other and work
out a complementary synthesis?

I think the main reason lies not in differences of opinion
about policies, but in the Evangelicals' belief that ecumenical
attempts to redefine the goal of mission in terms of humanizing the social structure reveal a decisive theological deviation
at the very heart of the Christian faith. The shock of the deliberations in Uppsala Section II, where Evangelicals had to
struggle with their utmost strength to have included in the report such elementary Christian convictions as the need for a
new birth and a biblical nurture of the congregation in mission, will not easily be forgotten. Neither will it be forgotten
that Canon Douglas Webster had to make three abortive attempts to get in a reference to "the two billions who have not
yet fully heard the Christian message," before it was reluctant-
ly included in the form of a somewhat reduced number. According to Douglas Webster, the weakness of the report "is
less in what it said, then in what it refused to say."[2] Why,
Evangelicals ask, was there such a resistance to statements
which affirmed the central concern of Christian missions
ever since the days of the apostles? Could it be that social
compassion has swallowed up soteriological compassion? Or
that, with some of the most vociferous protagonists of humanization, the doctrinal convictions underlying soteriological compassion have faded away?

Opening up to historical situations exposes Christian mis-

sion to the danger of seduction. For, in world history, we encounter not the *Deus revelatus* but the *Deus absconditus*. Far
too easily we forget that in world history the rule of Christ is
still contested by the prince of this world.

In past epochs, missions were tempted to pervert the sign
of the cross into a symbol of imperialistic aggression. Today
our temptation is to yield to the voice of syncretistic tolerance
and perform our service silently "with no ulterior motive."
But by so doing, we are subjected to sub-Christian ideological
motives which our non-Christian partners keep tenaciously in
mind.

The malady, which most major missions have never dared
to look at, is the insidious paralysis in the biblical convictions
of many theologians and ministers in our churches. Critical
methods of exegetical research have undermined the authority
of the Scripture. Demythologization and existential interpretation have dissolved the concept of Christ's expiatory sacrifice as well as the reality of His future kingdom still to be
established in power by His second coming. Situationalist
views of the Bible deprive its texts of their normative significance for faith and ethics and reduce them to answers of men
to the sociopolitical problems of their times. What remains
are a few vague principles like responsibility, solidarity, and
openness to the future, which can be completely abstracted
from the specific history of revelation and salvation in which
they occur.

Even Jesus becomes merely the prototype of an ideal social
attitude, the "man for others" whose resurrection and lordship
mean hardly more than that the community of His followers
is still inspired by His example. Christological affirmations
thus are abstracted from the living person of Christ. They
arise, in fact, from reflections of the church about her own
mission. The conclusion drawn by the members of a missiological seminar under the guidance of a well-known ecumenical
theologian sounds like this:

> Traditional statements about the Return of Christ, "that God
> be all in all" and the like, aim functionally at man's be-
> coming man, a goal to which Christian mission is calling and
> paving the way, but which to reach is not at his disposal.

By such theological methods, biblical prophecies are deprived
of their essential content. They are not disputed in form and
their original content is not directly negated, but by a process
of philosophical or sociological abstraction they are transformed into anthropocentric statements which in spirit and
wording merely reflect current humanistic ideology.

It is obvious that in such a general theological situation
the primacy of oral witness in Christian mission is viewed
more and more skeptically. We encounter today the strange
concept that socially desirable consequences allow us to call
our activities "mission" even if we deliberately abstain from
calling on people to believe in Christ and to be baptized in
His name. To quote the revealing minutes of the missiological
seminar again,

> . . . it cannot be regarded as the goal of Christian mission to
> "make" non-Christians Christian, to "convert" them, to
> "win" them, etc. To practice the function of the Christian
> faith—in a theoretically responsible way—is the only method
> of spreading it. Thus to communicate Christian ideas (e.g.
> of "God and sin") and practices (e.g. prayer, worship, bap-
> tism, eucharist) without being asked, to non-Christians and
> children, is an obstacle to mission. (The Christian educa-
> tion of children is always authoritarian. To abandon it
> would be a sign of *shalom*.)[3]

The argument defending such mission—mission without
encouraging men to accept Christ as Saviour from the guilt
and power of sin—is that any form of humanization, such as
the breaking down of caste in India, can occur only by the
power of Christ, who is understood to be the anonymous
directing power of world history. Thus it does not matter
who brings about desirable change—Christians, Marxists,

humanists or Hindus. World history is the result of God's mission, and in all good transformation of the social structures, we recognize the features of the coming kingdom of God. From here the conclusion is easily reached that any good action is mission—that is, participation in the *Missio Dei.*

The above argument is a most dangerous and erroneous shortcut in theological reasoning. The whole construct has abandoned two indispensable biblical foundations—the crucifixion and the second coming of Christ. The dialectical tension between world history and salvation history, which is expressed by these two events and which is not removed within this present aeon, is overlooked. Church and mission are leveled down to the one dimension of this world's self-understanding. In such a concept the eschatological kingdom of Christ is swallowed up by the achievements of current progress. Even if such progress is ascribed to the work of the anonymous Christ, we are nearer to the monistic philosophy of history of Georg Hegel and Karl Marx than to the prophecies of the Bible.

The argument defending this form of mission runs on like this: "When you agree to this program you sacrifice nothing indispensable. When social structures are humanized according to the will of God, the coming kingdom becomes visible. We should be happy that present political ideologies and syncretistic movements have received their dynamic direction from the unquenchable hope of Christianity. Are not such liberation movements more genuine fruits of Christian mission than many quarreling younger churches? We should, therefore, support revolutionary movements as our partners or agents in the struggle for justice. Freytag and Newbigin observed long ago that many revolutionary movements have produced their own political and/or religious messiahs and have been shaped according to the pattern of Jesus of Nazareth in His struggle, suffering, death and resurrection. Here Christian missions have achieved an exciting effect which they never anticipated! Why not accept this modern secular form of mission?"

THE EVANGELICAL ANSWER

Let us speak directly to this argument. What *does* hinder us from recognizing such unexpected and indirect results as legitimate fruits of mission? Why is it really impossible for us to rejoice at revolutionary transformations of society which may exceed by far the social results of classical missions? Our reason is simply that for those advocating humanization as sufficient mission, the ultimate aim is a perfect society in which there is neither demand nor room for salvation. Humanization—to these advocates—has become separated from the evangelization of the world. Man is putting himself into the center, declaring himself to be the measuring stick of all things and creating for himself a paradise *without God*. He needs no God because he himself replaces God.

Man's constant temptation is to declare that he needs no god. Ernst Bloch (quite mistakenly) holds that the secret atheistic theme of the Bible is the emancipation of man from the erroneous concept of a sovereign God. Bloch calls this a "theology of the snake" and bases it on the serpent's statement, "Ye shall be like God." In this odd view, Bloch merely echoes Karl Marx who in 1841 wrote in the introduction of his doctoral thesis:

> The Confession of Prometheus—"With one single word, I hate all gods"—is the confession of philosophy itself, its verdict against all celestial or terrestrial gods who do not acknowledge the human self-consciousness as the highest deity. There shall be nobody besides him.

Being aware of this inherent atheistic trend within the whole history of humanism, we are shocked to see how naïvely current ecumenical missiology can take up the concept of humanization and put it into the center of its moti-

vation and goal. True, the New Testament does describe
Jesus as the new man and the beginner of a new humanity.
But this is a complementary exposition to the other, more central, declaration that in Jesus Christ we are meeting the pre-
existent Son of God who wrought our salvation and is risen
to receive our adoration and obedience. Separating these two
concepts and putting His human nature into the foreground
risks perverting the Christian faith into a humanistic syncretism and removes the ontological interval between biblical
faith and non-Christian religions and ideologies. Ecumenical
missiology tells us to discover the manhood of man together
with the adherent of other "living faiths."

One text in recent ecumenical documents goes to an un-
surpassable extreme in separating the concept of humanization
from the doxological and soteriological context of biblical
faith. It occurred first in the American contribution to the
Church for Others and was quoted in the "Commentary on
Section II" in *Drafts for Sections, Uppsala 1968:*

> We have lifted up humanization as the goal of mission be-
> cause we believe that more than others it communicates in
> our period of history the meaning of the messianic goal. In
> another time the goal of God's redemptive work might best
> have been described in terms of man turning towards God
> rather than in terms of God turning towards man. . . . The
> fundamental question was that of the true God, and the
> church responded to that question by pointing to him. It
> was assuming that the purpose of mission was Christianiza-
> tion, bringing man to God through Christ and his church.
> Today the fundamental question is much more that of true
> man, and the dominant concern of the missionary congrega-
> tion must therefore be to point to the humanity in Christ
> as the goal of mission.[4]

That is, in former ages men were religious and asked for the
true God, and Christian missions directed them to Him. Today people do not care for God anymore, but for better hu-

man relations. Thus mission today should not speak of God, but should direct men to "the humanity in Christ."

True, this is advocated in the interests of missionary accommodation. By confining ourselves to humanization we hope to find common ground with Hindus, Muslims, Marxists and humanists. Yea, according to the concept of the anonymous Christ working outside the walls of the church, we are sharing in Christ if we, with them, work for the humanization of mankind. Perhaps by means of dialogue, if non-Christians ask us for the motive of our actions, they might even accept Christ and build Him into their present faiths!

Here we are encountering nothing less than the bankruptcy of responsible missionary theology. Ecumenical missiologists who reason thus forget that being missionaries means being the heralds of a sovereign Lord who has entrusted to them an unchangeable message, the true knowledge and acceptance of which decides the eternal life or death of those who hear the message. By contrast, according to the new view, the hearers themselves, as well as what they think needs to be said, determine the scope and content of the message, even if this strips from that message its essential meanings.

Anyone who argues like the quoted section of the "Commentary on Section II" in *Drafts for Sections, Uppsala 1968* also forgets that missionary proclamation calls for a wholehearted decision to follow Christ. The Christian cannot offer the gift and withhold the Giver. The non-Christian, however, can and often does grasp the gift and reject the Giver. This is what all post-Christian religions and ideologies have done. They have readily accepted principles and visions from the Christian message, greatly enriching and transforming their previous systems. When engaging in dialogue with representatives of such syncretistic movements, we therefore are likely to discover a certain common ground in regard to situational analyses, general principles and visions of hope. But all these conversations, including the Christian-Marxist dialogue, come to a sudden stop when we speak of Christ and Him crucified. What does a Marxist do with the cross? At best, he, like Ernst Bloch, places Christ's cross with the thousand crosses of the followers of Spartacus at the Via Appia. But he does not accept the cross as the altar at which our guilt was expiated and our peace with God was restored. There is no bridge which leads us over from a social concept of humanization to the everlasting truth that by Christ's sacrifice we were not only invested with true humanity according to His image, but made children of God and thus partakers of His divine life.

Because of this syncretistic rejection of the unique offer and claim of Christ, all post-Christian movements betray either a mild but intransigent, or an aggressive anti-Christian character. In God's plan, their function is to prepare for the final dramatic conflict with the community of Christ, where the dominating figure will be the Antichrist. He will fulfill the program of a Christless humanization by claiming to be Christ Himself. He will unite humanity under his rule, which will appear to be a paradise of social justice, but end in terror, blood and tears.

There is one basic and fatal error in any theology of mission which locates God's mission one-dimensionally in world history: It overlooks or belittles the demonological crack which runs right through history from the fall to the end of the world. Therefore, it is unable to put the cross of Christ with all that it stands for in the center.

No road leads from the present state of injustice through the transformation of all social structures toward a united humanity which is equal with the Messianic goal. The Bible clearly teaches that the world finds its way toward salvation only where its encounter with Christ's messengers results in the obedience of faith in Christ. Where, however, the world rejects His offer of grace and His royal authority, it falls under the wrath of God and proceeds to meet its final judgment. Missions, according to Lesslie Newbigin, constitute the cutting edge which God introduces into the stream of history.[5] By this edge, people are forced to make their decision about Christ. Thus the saved new humanity and the doomed old aeon are separated. It is the specific mandate of mission to erect the cross of Christ in all human spheres of life. This cross is a power of salvation for those who believe, but "a fragrance from death to death" among those who are perishing (2 Co 2:15 f., RSV).

Fully aware that world history ends on these two roads, Christian mission still rejoices at all truly humanizing changes in society. It evaluates them as direct or indirect effects of the ministry of reconciliation and as anticipatory reflections on the coming kingdom, which God will inaugurate on Christ's return. But it believes that abiding salvation is to be found only where people who were alienated from God are rescued and incorporated into the body of Christ. This truth determines the priorities of our missionary functions and keeps alive our hope in the coming Christ. For He Himself will resolve the tension between world history and mission history. He will remove their tragic dichotomy by His final victory in the anti-Christian cataclysm of world history. Then the common goal of world history and mission history, that is, the kingdom in power, will definitely be established.

Notes

1. Walter Freytag, "The Meaning of World Mission," *International Review of Missions* 39 (1950): 153-61.
2. Douglas Webster, *Bible and Mission* (London: British & Foreign Bible Society, 1970), p. 3.
3. This quotation is taken from the mimeographed minutes, p. 4, of a University Seminar on Mission led by Prof. H. J. Margull in the summer of 1970.
4. "Commentary on Section II," *Drafts for Sections, Uppsala 1968*, p. 34.
5. Lesslie Newbigin, *The Relevance of Trinitarian Doctrine for Today's Mission* (Edinburgh: Edinburgh House, 1963), p. 37.

3

THE HOLY SPIRIT AND RESPONSIVE POPULATIONS

by
ALAN R. TIPPETT

"The Holy Spirit and Responsive Populations" looked harmless enough when the title was given to me. What subject would be more natural in a symposium of this kind? The business of Christian mission is to seek conversion responses, and certainly in the final analysis this is the work of the Holy Spirit.[1] However, on deeper reflection, the title brings together two much-debated issues in current missionary theory and theology, both with serious consequences in the existential missionary situation. I shall discuss first the *fact* of responsive populations so that we may understand the conversion phenomena to which the theology of the Holy Spirit is to be applied.

Responsive Populations

Why *populations,* one may ask, why populations and not *persons*? In this context the word *populations* directs one to the non-Western world of extended families, clans, tribes, castes and age-grades, where whole villages may represent precise ethnic entities, and where such groups may elect to turn from animism to Christianity as total units at one precise point of time. This kind of religious movement may be positive *toward* Christianity or negative *away from* it. For purposes of differentiation we may describe the former as a *people movement* and the latter as a *nativistic movement*. Spiritually they are direct opposites, but psychologically they comprise almost identical dynamics. When we speak of "responsive populations" we are thinking of large homogeneous units of people who, once they have made their decision, act in unison. Many peoples have become Christian in this manner; indeed, most parts of the world where Christianity is solidly entrenched were originally won from paganism in the first place by people movements. A decade ago the debate on the validity of this kind of conversion complex was quite heated. Today the people-movement idea is more widely accepted by evangelical missionaries and strategists because it is better understood. Many of its critics still speak of it wrongly as *mass movement*. Church-growth writers, however, have been working on people movements for years and have resolved the basic problem by means of the term *multi-individual* to describe the phenomenon. This came into use about 1962 and has been written up at length in statements which demonstrate its anthropological and theological validity.[2]

CHURCH-GROWTH AND PEOPLE MOVEMENTS

Church-growth writers have also engaged in considerable research with respect to the use of group structures in "the transition from animistic to Christian forms" in the process of church-planting.[3] Generally this has been well received by both anthropologists and nationals. Side by side with this, some new dimensions, and warnings, have been developed about the *indigenous church concept* to make it more theological and more realistic on the practical level.[4] Likewise Bavinck's idea of *possessio*[5] has been appropriated and given a little more depth[6] by tying it in with the notion of the *functional substitute*. The concept relates to the *permanence of culture change* when the social group accepts it, and speaks especially to *directed* change and therefore is significant both in anthropology and mission. The cultural ramifications of functional substitution in church-planting has been discussed by this writer on the theoretical level,[7] on the existential level with respect to data from Fiji[8] and the Solomon Islands[9] and as a principle to be allowed for in planning church-planting.[10] These ideas bear on the handling of people movements and have been well received by Christian nationals who have known this type of experience. The development of this concept permits the preservation of many cultural features in the church being planted—thus a more indigenous church emerges from the beginning because it allows for the congregation acting as a multi-individual group. At the same time it is a safeguard against syncretism—a long-standing criticism against some group movements. The people-movement idea is thus culturally acceptable and Christian mission can be undertaken with a minimum of cultural disruption and a maximum of indigenity.

The character of missionary role has changed, but there must be a *continuing* missionary role. Now that the era of the old mission-station approach[11] has virtually given way to a new era of partnership with, or fraternal-worker service in, indigenous churches, there is no other feasible option before the Christian mission in communal and tribal societies, but that which is commonly called "the church-growth approach." The church-growth viewpoint is anthropologically based, indigenously focused and biblically orientated. It is certainly not, as some superficial critics have maintained, mere statistical "denominational extension," although the church-planting may be denominationally serviced.

THE THEOLOGY OF PESSIMISM AND PEOPLE MOVEMENT

The missionary strategists who nonchalantly reject church growth as an adequate approach to mission are usually con-

ditioned by a *theology of pessimism*. This may be universalist
or liberal or even conservative and still be pessimistic. This
pessimism may spring from any one of three causes:

1. The wartime experiences of Christianity driven under-
ground in Europe and the philosophical adjustments demanded by existence in the oppressive situation.

2. The current frustration and despair because of the en-
croaching secularity, the scientific agnosticism, the selfish individualism and permissiveness, the multi-individual rejection
of the establishment, including institutional religion, and the
frequently articulated idea that the church is fighting for its
survival.

3. The experience of nongrowth in the resistant mission
fields, where after a century or more of our foreign missioning, there has been created only a small, foreign church, worshiping in English, French or German instead of the vernacular, with our own foreign denominational structure, content to remain dependent on foreign funds and leadership, and
who (if they have produced any leaders of their own) will
be so foreignized as to be seen as foreigners by their fellow
countrymen.

Many of the vocal theologians of today, and likewise many
makers of mission policy, are victims of one or more of these
factors, so that we do not wonder at the cloud of gloom and
pessimism over everything*; and the futile attempts at re-
evaluating missionary philosophy to meet these conditions.
The error here lies in the assumption that the *whole* world

---

* The manner in which missionary policy can be influenced by the background of home officials came home to me some years ago when I was
researching an African situation where a rapid conversion intake was suddenly stopped. Eventually I discovered that a missionary from India, who
had been in a location where he had seen extremely small and slow
growth, upon retirement was given a portfolio with authority over this
African tribal situation. He had demanded that, as missionary staff did not
permit further intake, the men on the field *consolidate* the existing gains,
and let the accessions not begin again until the personnel was adequate
to handle the movement. It never did get started again. Thus, a responsive
movement had been sealed off, and a community which might have been
won whole was left half Christian and half pagan.

is resistant: that there are no ripe fields waiting for harvest anywhere. This error is tragic.

It is tragic because it accepts a wrong criterion. The idea of mission (i.e., bringing peoples to discipleship in terms of accepting the name of Father, Son and Holy Spirit) is not determined by the physical and social conditions that cast the gloom about us, but by the word of the Lord. He said that all power was now given Him, that His followers were to make disciples of all nations, and that He would be with them to the end of the world. If you accept that word, the implication is that mission in these terms goes on to the end. The idea that "the world sets the agenda" is true only in one sense. There is another sense in which it is false. That the needs of the world should or should not claim our attention is not argued; what is argued is that the Great Commission has not been withdrawn.

It is tragic because it is a wrong evaluation of the world situation. This view presupposes there are no responsive populations and no doors wide open. It overlooks hundreds of communities in Africa, in Latin America, in Indonesia and New Guinea, and bypasses what has really been happening in these postwar years. Dr. Winter, a provocative church-growth historian, realist and yet an optimist, pointed out in *The Twenty-Five Unbelievable Years: 1945-1969*:

> The church in Korea grew more in the years 1953-60 than it had in the previous sixty years. The church in Sub-Sahara Africa more than tripled from thirty to ninety-seven million. In Indonesia at least fifty thousand Moslems became Christians. . . . The South India Conference of the Methodist Church in the face of persecution grew from 95,000 to 190,000 members. The Presbyterian Church in Taiwan between 1955 and 1965 engaged in a "Double the Church Campaign" concluded it successfully. In Latin America, largely due to ceaseless and effective personal evangelism on the part of the Pentecostal family of Churches, Protes-

tants grew from about 1,900,000 in 1945 to at least 19,-
000,000 in 1970. In Brazil alone, by 1970, new congregations of the evangelical variety were being founded at the
rate of three thousand per year.[12]

The battle is by no means lost. If the church has her back to
the wall in some places it is certainly not so in others—even
if it means that the responsibility of the church is being taken
away from the West.

*It is tragic because a theology of pessimism can never
handle these responsive population opportunities.* The great
majority of these people movements have beeen husbanded
by Christians with a simple, biblical faith of a conservative
type and spirit of optimism. Another factor which frequently
comes to notice in church-growth case studies is the way missionaries explain nongrowth as due to their "being in resistant
fields" and being quite convinced that this is so; while comparative analysis reveals that the Pentecostals or some neo-
pagan religious movement is going ahead by leaps and
bounds. We find the growth may be Baptist here, Methodist
there, Presbyterian over yonder, but I have never found
growth in a church or society clouded with a theology of
pessimism. There have always been a vibrant missionary
drive, a clear goal and a simple clear-cut faith.

Those pagan movements which are bounding forward in
our day are frequently using the techniques of evangelical
Christianity, and they indicate that people are open for religious change and probably looking for it. For a century or
more Christians have been striving to win the American Indians. Some are Christian, usually where they got caught up
in revivals or people movements. Now, before our eyes, 45
percent of the Navahos are reported to be involved in the Peyote Cult. It may be that missionaries have used the wrong
methods. It may be that few have learned the Navaho language. It may that they have offered a foreign church. It
may be that the white man's poor relations with the Indians

through history was too great an obstacle. But we can never say Indians are now resistant to religious change. No one who has investigated the spread of peyote among them can say that. We are surrounded by winnable peoples in locations we call resistant.

It is tragic because it is satisfied with something less than the best. As long as we are in the world as Christians, being there and finding God's presence there, merely "witnessing" by our presence, or "being faithful" and engaging in dialogue with men of other faiths—the theology of pessimism leaves it there. To strive to bring the pagan to a decision for Christ, what church-growth theory calls *verdict theology,* is to create a *dialogical crisis,* and this is frowned on. This attitude of "if you cannot bring men to decision, then come to terms with them and co-exist" is certainly not scriptural. It eliminates the existential cross of the disciple of Christ from his ministry in the world. We turn to a missionary theologian who came from people-movement experiences in New Guinea, whose opinion was that:

> Today we have a Christianity that shies away from suf-
> fering, which still goes on dreaming of a Christianized world,
> appeals to the rights of man and the freedom of conscience
> and wants to put them into operation; all this in order to
> escape suffering and to make that suffering impossible in-
> stead of recognizing her call to suffer. Suffering does not fit
> into the Church's need for security nor into the modern
> philosophy of men.[13]

Vicedom's book throughout is one which realistically faces up to the confrontations of the Christian with the world, and sees the mission of the church in the world and "the congre- gation as the point of breakthrough for the Holy Ghost in the world" with a responsibility to lead men in the world to com- mitment.[14] In a smaller book he described down-to-earth events which showed converts being formed into congrega- tions by people-movement patterns.[15] Here is the Holy Spirit at work on a responsive population, and here is a book which fits in with the church-growth case studies. His *Mission of God* reacts against the theology of pessimism because the defeatism of the latter has no way of dealing with people-movement responses and therefore ignores them.

To recapitulate to this point, I have claimed that the fields open for mission are not as resistant as often imagined, that the people who await the gospel should be seen as large groups—tribes, peoples, populations—that they may be expected to turn Christian as social groups, that from these multi-individual people movements we may expect indigenous churches—formally cultural, rather than denominational extension. I have also pointed out the current theology of pessimism that controls much missionary policy-making, and I find it a wrong criterion, a wrong evaluation of the world situation, unable to handle the responsive situations, and less than scripturally prescribed in that it avoids responsibility to which we have been called. Against all this the Bible calls us to a theology of encounter and does not promise any escape from a way of the cross. Nevertheless, we are encouraged to go forward with expectation and optimism, knowing that ultimately victory will be with the Lord. It is important that we *recognize the existence of responsive populations.* Anthropology has taught us much about how to handle them, but this is not enough, we have to bring ourselves into tune with the Spirit of God and put ourselves under His direction.

THE HOLY SPIRIT

The other dimension of our title is the Holy Spirit. Some Evangelicals still relate cross-cultural missions to their own Western conversion requirements. They cannot see a people movement as "under God." I have known some Western missionaries to refuse to harvest a field "ripe unto harvest," and even in one case to hold off people at gunpoint when they came as a tribe to burn their fetishes and thus demonstrate their change of heart. These missionaries wanted them to come one by one, against their tribal cohesion. Church-growth literature has not bypassed this problem; it is one of the most recurring themes. The multi-individual conversion pattern has been examined on a basis of its New Testament precedents and prototypes, and usually Evangelicals who take the trouble to follow through the relevant passages are soon convinced that multi-individual people movements are quite biblical.

In my earlier writing I have been mostly concerned with simply demonstrating that many types of people movement are found in Scripture, and that these may therefore be presumed to have been "under God." But one can go further. These movements, which followed social structure, were under the specific direction of the Holy Spirit and the biblical writers have said so. It was only when I began following them as a theme through the book of Acts that this recurring feature struck me. I had studied the Holy Spirit as a doctrine. I had been instructed in His role in conversion, in the life of faith, in the church and its ministry and so on. When I thought of the Holy Spirit I tended to recall certain specific passages of Scripture, but the Spirit as a recurring feature of the episodes of church expansion was a belated realization. I had read about this in Roland Allen but it had not registered until I discovered it for myself:

> Missionary work as an expression of the Holy Spirit has received such slight and casual attention that it might almost escape the notice of a hasty reader . . . it is in the revelation of the Holy Spirit as a missionary Spirit that the Acts stands alone in the New Testament. The nature of the Spirit as missionary can indeed be observed in the teaching of the gospels and the epistles; but there it is hinted rather than asserted. In Acts it is the one prominent feature. . . . Directly and indirectly it is made all-important. To treat it as secondary destroys the whole character and purpose of the book.[16].

In this essay I am concentrating on a single aspect of the work of the Holy Spirit, namely *His relationship with responsive populations, with the winning of human communities to Christ.*

The mission to the world to which our Lord called His followers was built on *the prototype of His own mission to the world.*[17] This is clearly stated in John 17. His coming to this world, as the nativity stories in Luke show, was charged with the power of the Spirit (Lk 1:35; Mt 1:18, 20). Even those persons associated with the nativity complex received the Spirit—Elizabeth, Zacharias, Simeon (Lk 1:41, 67; 2:25-26). The Spirit was at the Lord's baptism (Mt 3:16; Jn 1:33), His temptation (Lk 4:1) and with Him throughout His ministry (Ac 10:38). Jesus Himself lived in the power of the Spirit and accomplished His mission to the world in that power. It was in the same power that He commissioned the apostles both before (Mt 10:20; Jn 17:18) and after the resurrection (Mt 28:19), promising them the resources of the Spirit, a promise He had made on other occasions for other purposes also (Jn 15:26; 16:13). Not only are we sent *as He was sent* into the world, but we are to teach what He taught (Mt 28:20) and love as He loved (Jn 15:12, 13:15). The Spirit was clearly with Jesus during His lifetime (Mt 3:16; Mk 1:10; Lk 3:22; 4:1; 10:21; Jn 1:32; 3:34; Ac 1:2), and in this power He achieved His mission on earth (Mt 12:28; Lk 4:14-15, 18 ff.; Jn 3:34, etc.). Furthermore, He took His stand on a basis of prophecy related to the Gentile world mission (Mt 12:18 ff. and Lk 4:18; cf. Is 42:1-4; 61:1-2).

So Jesus taught His followers to interpret His own mission to the world as a prototype for, and a prelude to, their own. Quoting the Scriptures, He claimed the Spirit (Lk 4:18), and the gospel writers who reported what they remembered of Him certainly declared that the Spirit was with Him. *Thus for their mission to be built on the prototype He had pro-*

vided, there had to be an event something like Pentecost. The mission of the apostles presupposes the *availability* of the Spirit as a source of power. An intellectual or social Christian "mission" without the power of the Holy Spirit is invalid because an essential ingredient is missing. When Jesus gave His own model for mission it implied the power and activity of the Spirit.

There is one other thing to be noted about this prototype of our Lord—one other implication besides the availability of the Spirit: He also implied the *importance of the social group.* If we are to relate the Holy Spirit to responsive groups, as distinct from individuals, we must pause here for a moment. We have emphasized Jesus' dealings with individuals and, of course, He was deeply concerned with individuals. But our Western individualism has closed our eyes to the fact that individuals belong in groups. Jesus was moved by the individual without *a group,* the individual *isolated from his group,* and the joy and salvation of the healing of a leper or a demoniac was not merely a matter of physical restoration but that *now he belongs.*[18] He could go back to the group from which he had been alienated and tell them what the Lord had done to him (Mk 5:19). This is the point of the three parables in Luke 15: the isolated one now belongs again; the lost sheep is no longer lost; the lost son is home again. Jesus' concepts are *collectives*—folds and flocks (Jn 10:16). Even when He deals with individuals He has the total group in mind. The episode with the woman of Samaria is a good example of this: Beyond the woman, Jesus saw the group to which she belonged. He sent her back into the village (Jn 4:16), knowing she would talk (vv. 27-30). He saw Sychar as a field ripe unto harvest—a responsive population (v. 35)—and He was quite right, for many of the Samaritans of that city believed on Him (vv. 34-43). When He preached the gospel to the poor and deliverance to the captives, though this may have been directed to an individual at times, I believe He was

speaking here of collective man—the communities that He
desires to restore. Jesus concentrated His ministry on groups
like the publicans and sinners, village groups, occupational
groups (Lk 15:2; Mk 2:16; Jn 1:24, etc.), He sent His disciples to households and villages (Lk 8:1; 10:5, 8-9, etc.)
and the Great Commission is in terms of ethnic units within
ecumenicity.

Therefore, from among the features of Jesus' model for
mission I have selected two only for this article: (1) the
presupposition of the availability and the activity of the Holy
Spirit as the source of power, and (2) the implication that
the human group is a thing to be preserved, that the isolated
individual needs to be restored to the place where he belongs,
and that groups are winnable. Thus the two elements of the
subject assigned to me for this article are both found to have
been clearly articulated in the mission of our Lord Himself.
As He Himself determined what the apostle's model for mission was to be, this surely ought to be valid for us today.
Pessimistic theology has to be rated against this model.

NEW TESTAMENT CHURCH-PLANTING

Our Lord gave us to understand that the Holy Spirit would
be operative within the Christian mission (Mk 13:10-11).
We also have the word that He operates to the end, together
with both the witnessing church and convert (Rev 22:17).
The whole sweep of church history lies between these points.

Pentecost itself, the historic happening when the Spirit was
manifestly given to the waiting apostles, was followed by their
first missionary proclamation (Ac 2). The proclamation was
in terms of trinitarian action. The audience was reminded of
the promise of the Spirit (v. 33) which was not, in reality,
offered to a wider audience than the apostolic band (v. 38).
This is verdict theology—repentance and response. Three
thousand souls is a people-movement figure (v. 41). These
converts were baptized together and immediately consolidated

into a physical fellowship, as Jesus bound together the disciples. Thereafter in their travels they left behind little social groups as Jesus Himself had left in Sychar. Thus the churches or fellowships, with doctrine, fellowship, breaking of bread and prayers, began to grow organically from the very start (v. 42). They went from house to house and praised God (vv. 46-47), and their numbers grew day by day. Although this was a strong people movement that went on day after day, it was not a mass movement, for the biblical recorder speaks of *"every soul"* (v. 43).

In the following chapter the lame individual was cured, but the incident was used by Peter as a subject for a sermon to the total group. This sermon to the people (men of Israel) involved an encounter with a select group (4:1), and imprisonment. Asked by their judges to give an account of themselves, they spoke of the Holy Spirit (v. 8). Peter spoke at length and they were released with warning. Subsequent preaching and healing and fellowship led to another outpouring of the Holy Spirit (4:31). The movement had grown so much that by Acts 6 it was out of hand and murmurings arose. The church was already bicultural. Under the leadership of the twelve, the community was called together and the multi-individual group operated as decision-maker. The ideas put forward by the leaders were ratified by the populace (vv. 3-5), new roles were created, and men were appointed—further organic growth. The three criteria for this position were "honest report, full of the Holy Ghost and wisdom." One of the appointees was a proselyte. They were ordained by the laying on of hands. As a result of this organic growth under the Spirit of God, a number of priests joined the community. This phase of the people movement was terminated, as far as the written record shows, with the death of Stephen, whose message was rejected in spite of the fact that he was full of the Holy Spirit (7:55). He had point-

ed out plainly to his audience that they were resisting the
Holy Spirit (v. 51).

This episode is a bridge to the story of Paul after a series
of rural incidents. Word came to Jerusalem of interest in Samaria. We might call it a *mood of inquiry,* or a readiness to
listen to the gospel (8:14), and so John and Peter were sent
there. As yet there was no spiritual movement, no outpouring
of the Spirit (v. 16); but after prayer directed to this end
(v. 15), they of Samaria also shared the experience (v. 17).
This gift of the Spirit was so manifest that a local magician
wanted to buy it, as animist magicians trade their secrets to
this day. Thus the early church was alerted to a danger
and given a useful piece of instruction. The preaching extended through the villages (v. 25).

We are now introduced to Philip who was directed to
Gaza to meet the Ethiopian and lead him to Christ, under
the guidance of the Spirit (vv. 29-38). Subsequently the
Spirit led him away to Azotus and the cities of Caesarea (v.
40), leaving the convert to take the gospel to the nation
where he had great authority (v. 27). Also from the Petrine
narrative we have the people movements at Lydda and Saron
where whole villages ("all that dwelt at") turned collectively
to the Lord. Peter was itinerating. There were already Christians at Lydda and he visited them for pastoral encouragement. These movements were sparked off by a healing mir-
acle (9:32-35), as also happened at Joppa (vv. 36-43). In
the following chapter Peter was with Cornelius at Caesarea,
whither he had been called. Cornelius had "called together
his kinsmen and near friends" (10:24) and they were many
(v. 27). Peter witnessed (vv. 39-41), that is, he shared his
experience, and the Holy Spirit fell on those who heard
(v. 44). This extended-family conversion in the Gentile
community surprised those "of the circumcision," but the
converts were baptized because they had received the Holy
Spirit (vv. 44-48).

All this demonstrates that Jesus led the apostles to expect expansion from Jerusalem, to Judea, to Samaria, to the uttermost parts of the earth when they had received the Holy Spirit (1:8). One of the reasons for this diffusion is found in chapter 11. Persecuted converts scattered to Phoenicia, Cyprus and Antioch and preached to the Jews of the dispersion. However, at Antioch some of those who had come from Cyprus and Cyrene preached to Grecians, and "a great number" believed (11:19-21). Barnabas, who was sent from Jerusalem to investigate it, rejoiced at the expansion of the Christian community, exhorted them to faithfulness, and went to Tarsus for Saul, whom he brought along in order to help him with instruction for a whole year (vv. 22-26). He knew of Saul's conversion and of his powerful testimony among the Jews at Damascus (9:22).

The Pauline missionary experiences are similar to those already summarized. The Holy Spirit was always active, some movements were quite extensive, and groups of converts were formed into congregations. From this point as the gospel spread in the Graeco-Roman world we meet house-churches (Ro 16:11; Phile 1). Lydia was baptized together with her household (Ac 16:15), as was the Roman centurion in the same city (v. 33). Paul preached to the household and obtained a group response (vv. 30-34). The word *all* appears three times in these verses, with respect to his preaching to all, and all believing and all being baptized. It is a good picture of the total multi-individual group. In chapter 18 there is the house of Crispus, the chief ruler of the synagogue, all of whom believed and were baptized (v. 8). The household was the social unit, the small group which made its own decisions at the level of personal religion as distinct from national loyalty.

In Acts 19 is recorded the disturbance which Demetrius the silversmith caused. The previous episode reveals why the craftsmen were so alarmed. Verses 17-20 record a strong

movement away from the magical arts to Christianity in
Ephesus. It must have been a large and significant movement
(because of the implications of the passage). The magical
books and paraphernalia were worth 50,000 pieces of silver,
and they were destroyed by burning, as animists burn their
fetishes upon conversion as an ocular demonstration of their
change of faith: belief, confession, demonstration—the regular pattern.[19] A people movement among the magicians
brought a counterdemonstration among the craftsmen whose
trade was in jeopardy; it was a movement on the basis of occupation. People movements in occupational classes or castes
may reach a great size, as for example, Xavier's movement
among the fishermen in India.

To Paul's experiences at Antioch, Philippi and Ephesus
we could add those at other places. Each place had its own
uniqueness. In Asia Minor he began in the synagogues and
presented a study arising out of the history of Israel as a
stepping-stone to Christ (Ac 13:14 ff.). Sometimes he had
Jews, proselytes and Gentiles who responded (vv. 42-43),
but organized opposition from the more envious Jews made
these would-be converts less stable. In Iconium also, Jews
and Greeks both believed (14:1). Paul now identified the
troublemakers as "unbelieving Jews" (v. 2), but before de-
parting from the district he ordained elders in the churches he
had planted, so the organic church grew (vv. 22-23).

At Rome it was quite different. This Christian community
emerged by migration growth. Merchants, soldiers, craftsmen and others moved into the capital along the network of
Roman roads. Many of them met in Rome in private homes
and secret places; they were even found in the household of
Caesar. From Romans 16 it is apparent that Paul knew
many of them before they had gone to Rome. Their names
are often Greek or Roman—craftsmen, kinsmen, fellow
prisoners. Eventually he reached the capital himself and, although a prisoner, he lived for two whole years in his own

house, receiving all who came, preaching the kingdom, teaching of the Lord Jesus (Ac 28:30-31). A similar ending is used in his letter to Rome, in which the preaching of Jesus Christ was made manifest to all nations (16:25-27). Where better than at Rome! From the Scriptures he wrote to Rome, "I will confess to thee among the Gentiles, and sing unto thy name . . . the God of hope fill you with all joy and peace in believing, that ye may abound in hope, through the power of the Holy Ghost" (15:9, 13).

To sum up this biblical unit, two things stand out clearly: (1) the activity of the Holy Spirit in the New Testament church-planting, and (2) the operation and approval of the Spirit in the conversion of social groups. The control of the Christian mission by the Spirit may be seen in His initiation of mission (Ac 1:2; 13:2, 4) and His deployment of it (16:6-7). As the blessing and power of the Spirit were promised the mother of our Lord when the incarnation was announced for His earthly mission (Lk 1:35), so the same blessing and power of the Spirit were manifested in the mission of the apostles (Heb 2:3-4). The New Testament church was planted by the apostles, through group-movement patterns, by the power and under the direction of the Holy Spirit. The church grew from a recurring spiritual experience that brought conversion responses to multi-individual communities upon their receiving of the Spirit. Where they did not respond, this was said to be "resisting the Spirit."

THE SPIRIT IN THE GROWTH PROCESS

Essential to the possibility of the idea of Christian mission is the existential reality of a discrete fellowship group. We call this the church, though it has other biblical names—the flock, the body, the fellowship, the household, the temple, the priesthood, all of them corporate groups into which converts are to be incorporated (1 Jn 1:3).[20] The Bible does not bind us to any single structural form for the church (either cultural or denominational), but it does commit us to a group of some kind. Our Lord formed the apostles into a group in His lifetime with the precise intention of leaving it behind in the world after His departure: a fellowship of those sharing the kingdom experience, says Bowman, the remnant called out by the Messiah.[21] He promised them the Holy Spirit, using another term, the Paraclete, who would dwell within them, and whom the world could not know (Jn 14:16-18). He would remain with them after the bodily departure of our Lord (16:7). He would be their Teacher as Christ had been (14:26), and both the Paraclete and the disciples would bear witness to Christ in the world thereafter (15:26-27). This small body of material in John's gospel, where this word is used, is addressed to the disciples collectively. Jesus sees them as a group whom He sends back into the world to represent Him there. The burden of this gospel is *witness to Christ* (20:31): witness for a verdict of acceptance. Yet, it recognized the possibility of rejection (1:11). Acceptance (i.e., believing) means power to become sons of God (1:12) and gives one a place in the fellowship group and assurance of the presence of the Comforter, which means a peace that the world cannot give (chap. 14).

John 14 takes us far beyond the other religions, for it shows Christ as the only way to the Father (v. 6). It is thoroughly trinitarian and therefore will allow no dialogue which eliminates the uniqueness of the Son and seeks a compromise on the basis of God and Spirit. It shows the Christian's spiritual separation from the world no matter how much his ministry may be in it. The world cannot receive the Paraclete (v. 17) or mediate His peace (v. 27).

Jesus brought the disciples together and made them a fellowship that they might stand together and support each other. In a good deal of the New Testament teaching that calls for Christian maturity and growth in grace, the collective form, as the idea of "perfecting the saints," is used.

Ephesians 4:11-12 shows both the perfecting and organic growth expected of the church. If we look forward we find the church as a body fitly joined together, with every part working effectually so that the body edifies itself in love (v. 16). If we look back we find we are instructed to keep the unity of the Spirit in the bond of peace, for there is one body and one Spirit (vv. 3-4). Here is diversity in unity. Here is the multi-individual group. This is possible only in the presence and power of the Spirit.

The moral living and virtues that are expected of converted Christians, either of individuals or groups, are also possible only in the presence and power of the Spirit. This is the Spirit who witnesses with our spirit that we are sons of God by adoption and heirs of Christ (Gal 4:5-7; Ro 8:8-17). Through the Spirit the Christian man has his spiritual gifts (1 Co 12:13; Ro 5:1-5). His Christian graces are sometimes described as the fruit of the Spirit (Gal 5:22-23; Eph 5:9). Thus it is the Holy Spirit which enables the church to be the church ministering the life and love of Christ to the world, in New Testament times and today.

One of the features of the New Testament church which may be traced to the work of the Spirit, quite apart from the service ministry and the mutual edification within the fellowship, was the vital experience of *power, joy* and *faith,* which Hunter calls *the concomitants of the Spirit's presence.*[22] You will find men described as "full of faith and of the Holy Spirit" (Ac 6:5, NASB; 11:24, etc.), and these terms, with *joy* and *power,* cluster together in the record. These concomitants of the Spirit give a zest and thrust to the group. When the Holy Spirit falls on a group, that group becomes transformed. It is this new dynamic that gives the group outreach and makes it witness, and leads to what Roland Allen called "spontaneous expansion." In my case studies of the planting and growth of the church in the south-central Pa-

cific, and in the archival documents on which I have worked
for years, I have invariably found this to be true of the great
people movements to Christianity.[23] The narrative vibrates
with power, joy and faith, in spite of the persecution and
military pressure from enemy groups.

Another concomitant of the Spirit's presence which I have
found in the island records is the assurance of the ultimate
triumph in glory with God. This was a radiant and exciting
experience and was certainly associated with the work of
the Spirit. The apostle Paul spoke of the earnest of the Spirit,
the Spirit being, as it were, a pledge and a promise of more
to come, a foretaste of glory for Christians to enjoy here on
earth (2 Co 1:22; 5:5; Eph 1:13-14). This also for the
island converts was a matter "to be told abroad" and shared.
They communicated it with power by dialogue, by dancing,
by chanting and proclamation. It was part of the excitement
of the people movements. As Green points out, the power of
the Holy Spirit was for the New Testament church a "guaran-
tee of the coming Kingdom," and "eschatology and mission
were irrevocably united in the person of the Spirit."[24]

The church in the New Testament was not supported and
controlled from some overseas board or other foreign-sending
body. True, a missionary program went out from Antioch,
but the churches stood on their own feet from the beginning,
and were indeed themselves missionary churches. Without
organized training programs and seminaries, how did the
early preacher get his message? Without our printed resources, Bible and commentaries, how did he know what to proclaim? The message was certainly preached with power. Jesus
had led them to expect that the special role of the Spirit
would be to teach them all truth (Jn 14:26) and to testify
of Christ (15:26), and they were to bear witness of what they
had learned from being with Him (v. 27). Paul (1 Co 2:13;
1 Th 1:5), Peter (1 Pe 1:12; 2 Pe 1:18-21) and John (1

Jn 5:6) all speak of the role of the Holy Spirit in revealing the message of truth and life.

To sum up the role of the Holy Spirit in the growing process of the church, we have seen first that there must be a physical entity we call the church, a discrete group. This has been preserved and nourished by the Spirit since the departure of Jesus to the Father. From the Spirit the fellowship group has a peace the world cannot give and an experience the world cannot share. The operational pattern of the group is to have members mutually supporting each other, building each other up in virtue and service. United and diverse, they are a multi-individual group. All this is possible only in the power of the Spirit, from whom we have also the gifts of the Spirit and the fruit of the Spirit, which enable us to operate as the body of Christ in the world. Other concomitants of the Spirit are power, joy and faith, which frequently occur together and are features of the church in times of spontaneous expansion, a fact borne out also in history. These are often accompanied by a strong eschatology with assurance. Eschatology and mission unite in the person of the Spirit. The message which is preached with power is that revealed and verified by the Spirit. These are the features of a church growing at the qualitative level of what McGavran calls *perfecting* in church-growth theory.[25]

RESPONSIVE POPULATIONS TODAY

Not all populations are responsive. Fields *come* ripe unto harvest. The harvest time has to be recognized, and harvesters have to be sent in at the correct season. A discussion of how fields ripen is another subject, but what happens to a crop which is not harvested when it is ripe goes without saying. In this essay I have argued that many ripe fields exist, some of which are large and promise an abundant harvest. Responsive populations should mean many people movements and great numerical church growth. Identifiable groups are waiting to be won for Christ. When the group responds, a congregation has to be created, preferably with the same structure as the group itself. Those responsible, as the stewards of the ingathering, need common sense, humility, anthropological understanding, and a strong personal faith to be good stewards; but, above all, they need obedient submission to the Holy Spirit, without whose power and blessing there could be no mission at all.

Also related to our subject, but worthy of separate treatment of its own, is the subject of the thousands of new churches (denominations) emerging all over Africa. A large body of literature is growing, and this discloses the wide range of religious ferment in Africa.[26] Some of these movements seem to be quite heretical, others quite conservative as far as their Christianity goes, others are boldly experimental. All are intensely enthusiastic. Neither is this religious ferment limited to movements that are Christian or syncretistically Christian. Some relate to the other faiths and some are quite new-pagan. Neither is this confined to Africa. In Japan there are Soka Gakkai and many other movements, the statistical rise of which may be set off against an inverse fall in Christian baptismal intake figures of the traditional churches, dating from about 1957. The greatest Christian growth is among groups little known in the West, such as the Spirit of Jesus Church. What I am saying as I draw this chapter to a close is that great multitudes which no man can number are currently either modifying their religious position or changing their religious affiliation. Viewing the matter on a world scale, there probably never has been such a period in history when such a large percentage of the world's peoples have been so open for religious change. Far from being a secular age, it is intensely religious, even in our Western cities. This dynamic situation calls for reevaluation of missionary techniques, and a deployment of men and resources so that missionary thrust is directed where the populations are most likely to be responsive. But having said that, the thrust must carry religious conviction, it must meet both the physical and spiritual needs of man in society, it must have power, joy, peace and vitality, it must not make individual converts into religious and social isolates, but bind them together into a fellowship community. All this can only be done under the direction of the Holy Spirit. As Starkey has said, "The most striking purpose of the Spirit's advent . . . is to be found in his gift of community."[27] I see no hope for the way of individualism in our modern world. The individual must feel he belongs. The interacting, multi-individual aspect of the community must be brought to maturity. Nearly all the basic problems of human society spring from carrying the interests of the individual too far so that they deny the rights of the neighboring individual. Individuals belong in context and the context requires balance— loving one's neighbor as oneself. All this has a superb backing from the anthropology of communal society, but this is theory. The theory has to come to root in real-life situations. The world needs not merely a world understanding, but understanding in all the cohesive subunits that make up the various levels of human society. For us in mission this means the local churches at grass-roots level, the fellowship groups which are the body of Christ, ministering His mind, and service, and love and mission in their neighborhood. In the last analysis, it is here that the church grows or does not grow. You can take a Christian fellowship group and study it anthropologically as an institution, and see "how it ticks," but if you carry your research to the ultimate conclusion you will have to admit that there is still one element which registers in your data but cannot be explained in human or processual terms. I call this the *noncultural factor*. It is, of course, the Holy Spirit. He is at work. Anthropologically I know how the church ticks, but another factor has to be introduced before the ticking is regulated as it should be. Given the current mood for religious change, and considering the missionary program in such a responsive population, I see no better way of handling the situation than by planting Christian fellowship groups that fit the local social structure and encouraging the people to pray for the gift of the Holy Spirit. If such a group is both indigenous in character and filled with the Spirit, and the religious mood of the location is innovative, we may expect a spontaneous expansion of the church. This is the regular pattern of people movements, and God has most certainly blessed it.

Notes

1. For the place of the Holy Spirit in church-growth theory and theology, see Donald McGavran, "Authentic Spiritual Fire," *How Churches Grow* (London: World Dominion, 1959), pp. 55 ff.; and Alan R. Tippett, "The Non-cultural Factor," *Church Growth and the Word of God* (Grand Rapids: Eerdmans, 1970), pp. 42 ff.
2. See Tippett, *People Movements in Southern Polynesia* (Chicago: Moody, 1971), pp. 251-61, 338; and "Religious Group Conversion in Non-Western Society" (Research in Progress Paper No. 11, School of World Mission, Pasadena, 1967); McGavran, *Understanding Church Growth* (Grand Rapids: Eerdmans, 1969), pp. 296-315.
3. For example, see Tippett, *Solomon Islands Christianity* (London: Lutterworth, 1967), pp. 269-85.
4. Tippett, *Verdict Theology in Missionary Theory* (Lincoln: Lincoln Christian College, 1969), pp. 126-41; and McGavran, *Understanding Church Growth,* pp. 335-53.
5. Johan H. Bavinck, *An Introduction to the Science of Mission* (Philadelphia: Presbyterian & Reformed, 1964), pp. 179-90.
6. Tippett, *Verdict Theology . . .,* pp. 105-6.
7. Tippett, "Initiation Rites and Functional Substitutes," *Practical Anthropology* 10, no. 2 (March 1963).
8. Tippett, "The Integrating Gospel" (Bound ms. School of World Mission, Pasadena, 1958).
9. Tippett, *Solomon Islands Christianity.*
10. Tippett, *Peoples of Southwest Ethiopia* (South Pasadena, Calif.: William Carey Library, 1970).
11. McGavran, *Bridges of God* (New York: Friendship, 1955), chap. 5; Malcom R. Bradshaw, *Church Growth Through Evangelism-in-Depth* (South Pasadena, Calif.: William Carey Library, 1969), p. 27.
12. R. D. Winter, *The Twenty-Five Unbelievable Years: 1945-1969* (South Pasadena, Calif.: William Carey Library, 1970), p. 67.
13. G. F. Vicedom, *The Mission of God* (St. Louis: Concordia, 1965), p. 139.
14. Ibid., p. 93.
15. Vicedom, *Church and People in New Guinea* (London: Lutterworth, 1962).
16. Roland Allen, "Pentecost and the World" in *The Ministry of the Spirit,* ed. David M. Paton (Grand Rapids: Eerdmans, 1962), p. 21.
17. This theme is the subject of Tippett's "His Mission and Ours," a bound manuscript at the School of World Mission in Pasadena, Calif., 1960.

47260

18. For the church-growth theology of belonging, see Tippett, "The Convert and His Context" and "Belonging and the Process of Incorporating" in *Church Growth and the Word of God.*

19. Tippett, "Religious Group Conversion. . . ."

20. Tippett, *Church Growth and the Word of God,* pp. 58-61.

21. John W. Bowman, *The Intention of Jesus* (Philadelphia: Westminster, 1943).

22. Archibald M. Hunter, *Paul and His Predecessors* (Philadelphia: Westminster, 1961), pp. 92-93.

23. Tippett, *The Christian: Fiji—1835-67* (Auckland, N.Z.: Inst. Printing & Pub. Soc., 1954).

24. Michael Green, *Evangelism in the Early Church* (Grand Rapids: Eerdmans, 1970), p. 273.

25. McGavran, *Bridges of God,* pp. 13-15.

26. See Bengt Sundkler, *Bantu Prophets in South Africa* (New York: Oxford U., 1961); Harold W. Turner, *African Independent Church* (London: Oxford, 1967); G. C. Oosthuizen, *Post-Christianity in Africa* (Grand Rapids: Eerdmans, 1968); and D. B. Barrett, *Schism and Renewal in Africa* (New York: Oxford U., 1968).

27. L. M. Starkey, Jr., *The Holy Spirit at Work in the Church* (Nashville: Abingdon, 1965), p. 23.

4

THE NEW SHAPE

by
LOUIS L. KING

In 1959 Martin E. Marty in *The New Shape of American Religion* exposed "the erosion of particularity, the smoothing of the edges of witness, the loss of religious content" in American Protestantism.

Using Dr. Marty's phrase, I view the missionary situation under three heads and then propose a fourth as the ideal.

1. The New Shape of Protestantism
2. The New Shape of Catholicism
3. The New Shape of Missions
4. The New Testament Shape as the Ideal

It is my intention to be descriptive, not polemical. As Evangelicals look out on the world scene, read largely of what is being written, face the opportunities and dangers of this fast-moving age, and evaluate the whole, something like the following is their considered opinion.

The New Shape of Protestantism

Without detailing the process whereby mainstream Protestantism has come to be so radically altered, I shall simply state that it is dominated by ecumenical concerns. The overarching aim is church union—union that can readily give up biblical and theological certainties—union that absolutizes the principle of a "relative hold on relative truth" so that ultimately we know nothing, love nothing, and believe nothing to be true except the principle that one must be relative.

Last year Dr. Linwood Barney arranged, and the Rev. Jack Shepherd moderated, a unique and exciting "Dialogue on Ecumenism" at Jaffray School of Missions. It began with Dr. David Stowe, Associate Director of the Division of Overseas Ministries of the National Council of Churches, presenting "My Personal Views or Convictions About the Ecumenical Movement." I immediately followed with a presentation of my personal views. In the exciting interchange and sometimes free-for-all discussion that ensued, Dr. Stowe admitted my presentation mirrored a fair "image" of Protestant ecumenism as represented in the World Council of Churches. What then is that "image"?

We see in the World Council of Churches certain downgrade tendencies gravitating in the direction of New Testament apostasy. When the plain, scriptural accounts of the possibility, the nature, and the onset of apostasy and its eschatological implications are placed alongside certain elements in the World Council, we see a degree of likeness.

The liberal theological thrust of some of its permanent, full-time personnel, the writings of some of its leading proponents, and the admittance of the Orthodox Churches have produced within the World Council of Churches theological uncertainty and ambitious ecclesiastical intentions, as well as vague hints and ambiguous silences. There is dangerous uncertainty on matters on which there is every biblical reason for forthrightness and clarity. The writers of its official and semiofficial documents do not treat the Bible with exegetical fairness, nor submit to its authority. They destroy the Bible in the form of exegesis. They destroy it in the way they deal with it. They destroy it by not reading it as written in normal literary form, by ignoring historical-grammatical exegesis, by changing the

Bible's own perspective of itself as propositional revelation in
time and space and in history. They are not speaking for God,
but are merely taking the social consensus of the day and
speaking as though that were the Word of God. They say the
same things the unbelieving philosophers and sociologists are
saying; the only difference is that theological language is
used. This is especially true when we consider their treatment
of the following:

CONCEPT OF THE CHURCH

The ecumenical idea of the church is that it is a genial, all-
inclusive, united church where it matters little what a man
believes. The notion is that all religion is the same and (not
the New Testament but) membership in the movement is the
all-important arbiter of religious truth. In a word, ecumenism
does not endeavor to settle upon any critical appraisal of New
Testament standards for the church. Further, this cooperation
and unity have not led to purity of life and purity of doctrine.
Indeed, the late D. T. Niles admitted before his untimely
death, "Much disagreement exists in the WCC as to who
Jesus Christ is, where He is found, and how He is to be
identified."

BELIEF OF UNIVERSALISM

The writings of many men within the World Council of
Churches and one of its approved books, namely, *Fire upon
the Earth* by D. T. Niles, reveal an abandonment of belief in
the final judgment and in an eternal hell. To this end, the
grand New Testament words *gospel* and *salvation* are invested with meaning that is different from that which the New
Testament warrants. For instance, "The gospel is the approach that blends together the social, political, and religious
issues of our day."

Salvation comes to mean "both the end of the enemy and
the oppressor, both internal and external, and the establish-

ment of *Shalom*—viz., a society of peace and joy, without oppression and exploitation, with plenty of food and drink for all—nourishment for the body as well as for the mind and spirit."

Evangelism is not to convert men to Christ; it is "to renew and revitalize the fabric of human society by becoming involved in economic, social, and political affairs." Another says that "evangelism is the involvement of Christians in social and political tasks for the good of all men." In a word, the aim is to remake and run this world. It has led to a massive movement to the *left*. To finance this new, vast, and secular salvation of society, conciliar leaders want to utilize the church's missionary and educational funds. Even though they use traditional Christian terminology, a great chasm exists here. They are giving wrong definitions and secondary solutions to secondary problems and calling it all evangelism.

TOLERATION OF SYNCRETISM

As a result of universalism, syncretism is glowingly commended, for it is said that God's hand can be seen in, and values found in, all the religions of the world—that no particular religion possesses anything final or absolute. The position is one of relativism and synthesis.

DISCOUNTENANCING PROSELYTISM

The WCC at New Delhi passed a resolution condemning proselytism and suggesting that member churches abstain from this activity, for it was said to be incompatible with brotherly relations. The action was due largely to a strong plea by Archbishop Theophilus of Ethiopia who objected to what he considered misplaced evangelistic zeal which was drawing people away from the Orthodox Church. The ecumenical movement thus expressed itself as not favorable to evangelical missionary work in Orthodox Church areas.

Since then, evangelistic activity leading to conversion has

been treated as a kind of "imperialism," as pressure tactics to get men to change their religious allegiance. It is considered improper in any area or context—a natural corollary for those who believe that all men will be ultimately saved.

FAVORING COMMUNISM

There is an inordinate hostility toward the United States' involvement in Vietnam and Laos, with little criticism of North Vietnam, China, or the Soviet Union. The published documents of the 1966 Conference on Church and Society and the Uppsala General Assembly show a strong preference for open-ended Marxism.

PREACHING REVOLUTION

Despite the New Testament teaching that governments are ordained of God and that the duty of Christians is to obey civil law and to abide by the "absolutes" of the Bible, the World Council of Churches proclaims that the redemption of society is the church's responsibility. This should be brought about by open opposition to government and by the use of violence when necessary. Someone has stated that "if the World Council heard, 'Come over into Macedonia and help us,' they would send over some specialists to enter into dialogue with the priests of Jove and Venus, and others to assist in a revolt against Roman oppression and slave holding." Bloodshed is advocated if it will capture the attention of the populace. They have abandoned the spiritual salvation of individuals and societies through the cross in order to proclaim the redemption of society through demonstrations, riots, strikes, and a radical restructuring of all society.

DOWNGRADING MISSIONS

For the size of their membership and financial resources, the missionary outreach of the WCC is simply pitiful. Their main effort appears to be to get churches to unite rather than to get men outside of Christ united to Him.

American missionaries related to the World Council through various mission boards are fewer in number today than twenty years ago when the council had 64 percent of the total missionary force. Between 1956 and 1960, the percentage of missionaries from ecumenical churches in the United States declined from 43.5 percent to 38 percent. In the past ten years it dropped another 12 percent to 26 percent. This means that 74 percent of American missionaries are not with council-related boards. Canada had 3,700 Protestant missionaries in 1960, but only 700 came from the council-related churches. Today only 523 Canadian missionaries are sent out by council-related Churches. Organic union has not increased missionary passion or resulted in a missionary upsurge; rather, it has resulted in the opposite. In 1968, Dr. David M. Stowe, then Associate General Secretary for Overseas Ministries of the National Council, stated that "the center of gravity of Protestant missionary sending agencies is shifting constantly away from the 'ecumenical' agencies toward conservative and fundamentalist ones." In ecumenical churches there is such a doubt about the uniqueness of Christ, the full authority and integrity of the Bible, and the lostness of the lost, that missions and evangelism no longer receive the goodwill or commitment of a few years ago.

DRIFT TOWARD ROME

Since the 1961 New Delhi Assembly, the drift toward Rome has been accelerated. In 1962, sixty Protestant pastors and six Roman Catholic bishops and two archbishops met and, after attending two masses, signed an agreement that they would mutually renounce proselytizing in each other's sector. Approximately forty Protestant church leaders have gone to Rome to confer with the pope, and the pope has gone to Geneva. The various councils of churches have now incorporated Roman Catholics into their memberships. Roman Catholics serve on various commissions of the National Council and the World Council. This Rome-ward movement goes on even though Rome has not shifted her view of the mass, the authority of the pope, the validity of traditional and papal declarations, and the mediation of Mary, saints, and angels.

UNETHICAL METHODS

Through inter-church aid, money is used to gain the allegiance of churches not connected with World Council. This proselytism with the use of money is actively practiced on Africasian churches.

THE NEW SHAPE OF CATHOLICISM

Prior to the Pontificate of John XXIII, the Roman Catholic Church was a solid wall. Her creeds, dogmas and rituals were held with particular strictness. The picture was that of a rigid ecclesiastical colossus with crushing metallic qualities. Relations between Protestants and Roman Catholics were clear-cut but almost totally negative. Where Romanists were a majority people, Protestants' civil rights and religious liberties were restricted. At times evangelical Protestants were sorely persecuted.

Today, however, a remarkable, all-embracing attitude and a new philosophy have entered Catholicism. The "new shape" of Catholicism, which began to develop after World War II in France, Germany and Holland, came to fruition in Vatican II (1962-1965)*. It created a new spirit in the Roman Church—a change in thinking, in attitude, in atmosphere. Catholicism has taken on some supple, adaptable and movable qualities, and this "new shape," especially observable in our overseas areas, needs to be seen and under-

---

* Vatican II began October, 1962, and ended December, 1965. During this period, 168 sessions were held. The delegates took 544 votes and approved sixteen decrees.

stood correctly. The following are some of the very important
changes in Roman Catholicism:

1. *Change in Self-Definition.* Prior to Vatican II, the
Catholic Church was the hierarchy under the pope, and the
laity *belonged* to the church but *was not* the church. Now the
emphasis is on the church as "the people of God."

2. *Change in Attitude Toward the Outside World.* A new
ecumenical spirit is being wafted east and west from the papal
apartments. Ecumenism has been accepted, and dialogue
structures established with other Christians and nonbelievers
such as Jews and Muslims.

3. *Change in Attitude Toward Human Freedom.* The
Catholic Church has acknowledged certain principles of religious and civil liberty that to a large extent are already the
common heritage of mankind. This change contrasts greatly
with the extreme reluctance prior to five years ago to grant
human freedoms to Christians outside the Catholic Church.

4. *Change Regarding Episcopacy.* Efforts are being made,
with some success, to recognize the Catholic bishops as the
leaders of the church under their head, the pope. The pope
is being called upon to share leadership with the bishops.

5. *Change in Liturgical Worship.* A substantial shift has
taken place from the use of Latin to the vernacular in public
worship. The laity now actively participates in the mass, and
the priest has turned and faces the congregation. Wherever
possible, he stands closer to the people. Some of the "magical" aspects of the mass have been removed. Liturgy is permitted to be adapted to the local cultural conditions, so that
if kneeling is not a meaningful act of homage, it is eliminated.
Protestant hymns such as Luther's "A Mighty Fortress Is Our
God" are a part of public worship.

6. *Change in Attitude Toward the Bible.* All Catholics are
now allowed to read the Bible, and there is a deep and widespread interest in it. Many Catholic biblical scholars, how-

ever, have come out openly for "higher criticism" and "form criticism," which are quite incompatible with biblical inerrancy.

7. *Change in Methods and Tactics.* Previously the tendency was to use the slow-moving boa-constrictor "squeeze and crush" approach toward minority opposition to Catholic aims and claims. Today we are confronted with a changed, "pleasantly sweet, Pied-Piper, theological musical score" which has become an ecumenical "hit."

8. *Change on Hold on Priests.* The Vatican reported in July, 1969, that 7,137 priests had left the priesthood during the five-year period of 1963 to 1968. And Rome is making it easier for priests to make their exodus.

But in spite of these changes—most of them commendable —there is no official evidence that Rome is giving up a single dogmatic iota regarding the mass as a real and true sacrifice, papal infallibility, tradition as a source of faith, the sacraments as the means of grace, and the mediation of Mary, saints and angels. There are, however, subtle changes called "developments" taking place. Present-day Catholic scholars do this by making a distinction between "intention" and "formulation"—that *what* Rome affirms is invariable, but *how* she affirms is variable in form. This approach is bringing about a certain relativity in dogma and doctrine. One thing is obvious: modern situational ethics appear to be infiltrating Catholic dogmatics, and avant-garde theologians are having a heyday.

"New shape" Catholicism, then, is an improved, updated, remodeled, more compatible-with-the-times church. Vatican II has smashed many separating barriers and opened up avenues of communication, and some of Catholicism's most irritating aspects have been amended. However, the same alarming avant-garde theological concepts that have corrupted Protestantism are gaining ground in Catholicism, while the offensive nonbiblical, non-Protestant dogmas remain.†

THE NEW SHAPE OF MISSIONS

Today is a time of great testing in connection with the whole matter of the mission of the church. No one can gainsay that. It is evidenced by the multiplicity of conferences held by mission boards or mission fellowships to assess mission-church relationships, social concerns, dwindling personnel, and mission finances.

The retired leader of a respected evangelical mission recently wrote:

> We have entered the twilight of foreign missions. Along with gas lamps, the Stanley Steamer, and the buggy whip, this once glorious instrument of the Church is now consigned to a niche in the museum of antiquity. Any vestigial remnant would serve only as an embarrassing nuisance, a reminder of another era when indeed it served some useful purpose.

He continued:

> Missionaries are, as never before, on the move—back to the homeland. Here in —————, one major denomination will have withdrawn all foreign missionary personnel by the end of 1971. A second major denomination (having the largest number of churches in —————) has re-

† In light of this, ours ought not to be the deadening outlook of conformity or the weakening approach of compromise. Evangelical Christians ought not to be guilty of die-hard segregation or of blindness that is oblivious to changing reality. The Catholics are reading their Bibles. How wonderful! Let our attitude be based on dynamic witness—a readiness to grasp the golden opportunity. Let us distribute the Scriptures to them. Let us accept invitations to preach to Roman Catholic groups as long as no limitations are imposed on our message and as long as the church with which we are working understands and does not object to our doing so. By all means establish personal relationships with Catholic leaders, and with lay people too. We ought, however, to avoid formal and public meetings with Roman Catholic leaders that involve minutes, reports, photographs, or newspaper articles. This dims the distinctiveness of the gospel as contrasted with the Roman Catholic system. Beware, too, of joint debates and prayer meetings, for they may be a waste of time.

moved 50 percent of its foreign missionary personnel within the last four years. The logic upon which the homeward move is based sounds plausible indeed: "The National Church is now largely indigenous. Tasks once performed by missionaries are now done better by nationals. Moreover, now that the offspring of missionary enterprise can walk, 'the crutch' can be thrown away. The missionary's task is all but complete. It is time to leave."

Quoted in the 1970 edition of *North American Protestant Ministries Overseas,* R. Pierce Beaver, discerning writer and professor of missions at the Divinity School of the University of Chicago, has struck this sobering note:

"The 70's will be the most critical decade in the history of . . . Protestant Missions." To back this up he presents a trenchant analysis of mission organizations to date:

What is now called "mission" is a gigantic system of inter-church aid (personnel and funds) which is the consequence of some poor principles and methods in the earlier stages of mission, leaving the young churches dependent. The personnel are "ecumenical deacons," not real missionaries.[1]

Very few are sent to encounter unbelief directly. They are lent, not sent.

REVENUE

The new shape is observable in financial support to missions: the ecumenical mission boards, and now a few evangelical missions, have entered into serious financial decline. The following excerpt from *Christianity Today* epitomizes the stark situation:

Ten Anglican missionary societies—including some of England's biggest and oldest—are in dire financial straits and their work in overseas fields is threatened, according to a joint statement by their general secretaries.

The message, published in London last month, asserts that the societies' income is static or declining in the midst of constantly increasing costs. Churches overseas continue to ask for mission help and personnel, but "we are having to delay or refuse many of these requests," the statement said. "We are facing the prospect in 1971 of withdrawing workers already on the field. There are men and women ready to train for service overseas. What is lacking is the money to support them."[2]

Also under the heading of revenue, the NAPMO directory includes the following quotations:

Harold J. Ockenga, president of Gordon-Conwell Theological Seminary and former pastor of Boston's Park Street Church with its famed missions program, states that "if present trends continue, the support for the missionary enterprise will be more difficult to attain in the decade ahead":

The situation is parallel to that in the 1930's when the book *Rethinking Missions,* by Ernest Hocking, pointed out that the decrease in missionary giving of that decade was due, not to a lack of resources, but to the cutting of the nerve of missionary motivation by means of a neglected theology, except for that within the churches.

The trend is now toward a secular theology which in turn, will again quench the vigor of missionary passion on the part of the average layman.

From contacts I have had in the churches, I sense an impression that missions are no longer needed in certain areas because of the rapidity of technical and social developments. This mistaken impression must be counteracted by better information. . . .

Deterioration of spirituality in our churches and depletion of membership will reflect itself in missionary giving. While a remnant of God's people will be as committed, if not more committed, than ever to getting the Gospel to every nation, tongue and people, the general run of church members will have less interest in missionary activity.[3]

. . . And David M. Stowe points to yet another threat to missions: . . .

The average pew-holder might enjoy being convinced that charity begins and ends at home in a black ghetto or a lobbyist's office, hence no need to give or go.[4]

PHILOSOPHY

Notable changes in the atmosphere and attitude toward missions are observable within the ecumenical churches and, strangely enough, among Evangelicals also.

There is widespread belief in the principle of religious toleration and of a pluralistic society. It expresses itself thus: In religious matters everyone has the right to live together in harmony and amity; everyone must be free to observe the tenets of his religion or of no religion, as his conscience directs him. To attain to, and to continue in, this happy state of affairs, the principle of noninterference with the religion of others must be straitly observed. No conversion should be attempted. In all secular universities, this teaching is promulgated by cultural anthropologists and sociologists.

Bishop Stephen Neill of missionary fame informs us that there is a pervasive belief within the church that each religion is integral to the culture of which it forms a part. A society needs cement to hold it together, and this cement is provided by their religious ideas and ideals. The people are dependent upon their myths, their sacred dramas and liturgical rituals. Anthropologists say when you change or undermine its religion, the society as a whole will fall to pieces; its existence as a society has been destroyed, and they are deprived of their reason for existence. When this happens the people will begin to die out; therefore, it is wrong to attempt to change any man's religion.

There is also the widespread belief that we have made a tragic mess of things in our Western civilization. We have failed to solve our problems. Twice in this century we have plunged the whole world into war and carried on localized conflicts in Korea and Vietnam. By our ineptness we have drawn Asians and Africans into our difficulties, ecological blunders, and crime. Therefore, we have no right to treat our culture as an article of export. We should not attempt to impose our ways and our religion on people when our ways and our religion have not helped us with our massive problems.

SOCIAL CONCERN

Social concern is being pushed in evangelical circles as the new shape and thrust of missions. There is scarcely an Evangelical Foreign Missions Association or Interdenominational Foreign Missions Association meeting where social concern does not receive attention and commendation. It is talked of as the lost dimension in mission work and therefore needing special attention. Without seeming to know it or to care if they do know it, social-concern advocates sound suspiciously like the social gospelizers of the early 1900s.

Dr. Donald McGavran of the School of World Mission at Fuller Theological Seminary says that this push among Evangelicals is not at all a new dimension. He observes that for 150 years missions "have integrated social concern and evangelism—often to the tune of 80 percent social action and 20 percent evangelism." The danger now is that the percentage will be 110 percent social action and minus 10 percent evangelism.

MISSION-CHURCH RELATIONSHIPS

Beginning after World War II, the ecumenical missions changed the pattern of their relationship to the younger churches. Saying that the missionary era had ended because an "ecumenical age" had come, they stopped sending missionaries for apostolic witness to the world and began lending missionary servants to Afericasian churches. They stopped sending missionaries for proclaiming the gospel, and they began sending men and money for inter-church aid. They gave mission-owned property, the mission's annual budget, and missionary personnel to the churches. In a word, on the field the mission ceased to exist by being fused into the churches. But even after they had done all of this, the problem of mission-church relationships still exists.

Dr. Herbert C. Jackson, Professor of Missions at Union Theological Seminary in New York City, has listed four unresolved problems in the ecumenical mission-church relationships:

1. The younger churches have an overanxiety to control the missions.

2. Neither the ecumenical mission nor the ecumenical church has sought to find or to follow the biblical requirements for a church.

3. Ecumenical mission and church leaders have allowed anti-Western criticism to dominate them.

4. The younger churches exercise an unintentional tyranny over the mission. This has stifled the further spread of the gospel.

Evangelical missions also are having problems in their relationship with the younger churches. As with the ecumenical missions, changing the organizational pattern has not diminished the problem.

The New Testament Shape Is the Ideal

The secret of the Holy Spirit's blessing and power is wrapped up in those churches that see and carry out Christ's worldwide mission. This is the obvious truth of the book of Acts. Nothing will more truly stimulate and enrich the spiritual life of any church than its unselfish, sacrificial effort for this poor world, this world so full of weakness, emptiness, unworthiness, corruptions, and great unbelief—this world that is like a crushed moth, a bruised reed or a smoking flax.

Actually, an enormous task is before us with the population explosion. When Christ was born, the world's population was one-tenth of what it is now. In 1830 the world's population reached its first billion. One hundred years later, in 1930, it attained the second billion. In 1962 the third billion mark was reached. In 1969 it was three and a half billion. By the year 2000, it is expected to be between *six and seven billion.* We have, therefore, a gigantic task to complete, with one billion more people today than thirty years ago. Every year there is an increase of 73 million people. And, of the almost three thousand languages, more than one thousand await the translators.

The missionary task, however, must never be thought of in terms of millions, for figures mean little to us. We must think instead of individuals—men and women who are like ourselves. If our gospel is hid, it is hid not just from a percentage of the population, but it is hid from definite individuals that the apostle Paul described as "perishing" (1 Co 1:18). They must be rescued. To this day and to the end of the age, no province or area or country should be exempt from devout preaching by the missionary—a preaching which intends to convert. The Head of the church emphatically orders us to seek converts from among the perishing sons of earth.

This we know and accept: the key to missionary endeavor is not opportunity but obedience. The church has advanced in spite of opposition and persecution and peril. It has never been dependent upon the friendship of rulers and favorable political conditions. It is true that the welcome given the foreign missionary in former years may not always be accorded us, and possibly the church and mission here and there may be entering a period of testing and even persecution. Such a prospect should not appall the servant of the Lord who remembers Paul's exhortation that we must through much tribulation enter the kingdom of God. Since Jesus calls us to constancy in spite of lack of security, we should not hesitate to serve in lands where changing conditions may make missionary work impossible in a few years' time. We should not ask, "Is it right to risk wasting several years learning a difficult language and then being forced to come home?" or "If I do have to come home, will I fit into work back in the homeland?" Trustful obedience is prepared to leave the responsibility for the future in God's hands rather than have it supplanted by the spirit of fear or conditioned by opportunity. "He who observes the wind will not sow; and he who regards the clouds will not reap" (Ec 11:4, RSV). If the work is undertaken at God's command, there will undoubtedly be eternal results both in the life of the missionary and in the lives of the people to whom he is sent.

The endeavor of all true Christians and every real missionary society must ever be the redemption of lost men through Jesus. Ours is not a program of political or even social action. No ecumenical organization should be promoted by missionary societies in order to further the solidarity of Christians. It is not for us to campaign for new and promising secular methods or for a changed political, social, economic and educational structure which will assure the church a more important voice in affairs, a stronger position in power. All these ideas are directly opposed to, and foreign to, the Lord's purpose for the church's existence.

Christ created the church, in part, as a missionary organization. Missions was and is its primary purpose. If we do not remain true to our missionary task, we will become fatally corrupted. If we watch our neighbors, we shall forget our mission and fall into a trap. Success will come from strength, not weakness—by stressing what we can do best, rather than spending time comparing ourselves to others or competing with others. A successful organization, like a successful person, must have an outstandingly clear and definite personality and stick to its beliefs. It must not violate its personality. It must be careful of its "shape." Integrity of purpose is all-important, for when we forget our purpose or deviate sharply from it and fail and flounder, we have outlived our need for existence.

The church was meant to be a missionary movement. Into its soul was breathed the Master's word, "Go." The true church is not geared for standing still, for its very equilibrium depends upon forward motion. It will wobble only when speed is slackened; it will topple over into the ecclesiastical scrap pile if it stops.

More than anything else, we should be concerned to align our purposes with those of God as revealed in the Bible. We must go forward to aggressive evangelism, to simplicity and fervor of soul and spiritual power. We should be less concerned about being up-to-date in regard to organization, equipment, and novel devices. Our concern should be to be up-to-date in regard to the New Testament—its truth, its missionary principles and practices.

The church of Jesus Christ has been set in this world for the purpose of carrying the gospel to the ends of the earth. This should be the all-pervading center of thinking. We need to leave our safe harbors and put out to sea—to be "sacred fools"—reckless gamblers with life—mobile and spontaneous. We need to do this

> not because the church is endangered
> not to recapture the past glories
> not because our powerful rivals will outrun us
> not for any kind of self-aggrandizement.

We must do it because

> We are the living outreach of God to the world (Jn 20:21). Jesus sends us into the world just as He was sent into the world.

Our work is to continue His work.

Jesus said: "I came down from heaven, not to do mine own will, but the will of Him that sent me" (Jn 6:38).

This comprehends all the details.

We are sent to do God's will, not our own.

We are not upon our own errand, but God's.

We are God's servants, God's representatives, God's light in a dark world. Faithfulness to this mission of God is costly, for world evangelization is a difficult and dangerous task. It is ever a blood-marked, sacrificial, and sometimes heart-rending task. We must not turn from it by psychological and theological rationalizing.

The new shape of missions has a striking resemblance to the shape lived out in Galilee and Judea nineteen hundred years ago. It is the only true shape.

Jesus calls us to total surrender:

> to a discipleship that breaks us away from our own ideal of life
>
> to place ourselves completely at His disposal
>
> to listen henceforth to no other voice
>
> to cause all earthly ties to fade into insignificance
>
> to dissolve any delay-causing affiliation
>
> to allow nothing to draw us away from Him or place us in opposition to Him
>
> to lay our lives completely in His masterful hands
>
> to make no provision for retreat or sidestepping
>
> to say "whether by life or by death, Christ shall be glorified in my body"
>
> to concede to Jesus the responsibility and accountability for our lives and ministry, and not to assume them ourselves
>
> to consider decisive the will of God—and the course of the kingdom of God
>
> to know that God cannot carry out His mission if we are ruled by consideration of our well-being, the security of our lives and our financial incomes.

The missionary shape remains constant—unchanged—the same. "If any man will come after me, let him deny himself, and take up his cross daily and follow me" (Lk 9:23). "As my Father hath sent me, even so send I you" (Jn 20:21).

Notes

1. *North American Protestant Ministries Overseas Directory,* 9th ed., p. 9.
2. *Christianity Today,* Apr. 9, 1971, p. 46.
3. *North American . . . Directory,* pp. 11-12.
4. Ibid., p. 12.

PART TWO
ANTHROPOLOGICAL ISSUES

5

POSSESSING THE PHILOSOPHY OF ANIMISM FOR CHRIST

by
ALAN R. TIPPETT

SINCE THE FUNDAMENTAL TASK of missions is to reconcile men to God in the church of Jesus Christ through the preaching of the gospel, and since several hundred million animists are in the valley of decision in these last decades of the twentieth century, one of the most crucial issues in missions today is the conversion of the animists. Essential to any incorporation of animists into the church is the possession of their philosophy for Christ.

PRESUPPOSITIONS

Recently it fell to my lot to react to an address of a certain psychologist who had pressed the point that the only hope for man's salvation and realization of human brotherhood was in the area of the *potential commonality of mystical experience*. I do not deny the potential commonality but I do deny its power to save. And, as for its universality, I believe this is only possible at the *level of awe* or the *numinous*. Granted, this is an experience which men of all faiths may share: a sense of a presence, or, shall we say, the supernatural. However, the fact that a savage and a Christian can

125

both feel that presence, does not indicate that they both attribute the same *meaning* to it, or that they are even capable of this, their concepts of God being so different. So I fear my psychological friend was pinning his hopes for ecumenical harmony on a chimera.

I must confess that I see no hope for either salvation or harmony, *except in Jesus Christ.* I see no hope for this unless Christ be *universally presented.* I see no relevant presentation in terms other than those of a *power encounter.* Please note those three facts: salvation in Christ alone, a universal mission, and a manifestation of power. In bringing sinful man to God, or in bringing the animist or pagan to God, the Scriptures indicate these essentials.

When Paul said there was no difference between the Jew and Greek because they were under the same Lord, we need to remember that this was a passage about salvation, about believing in Christ, about confessing Him whom Paul preached, about faith in His resurrection. Furthermore, the sameness was not of an existing condition, or of culture, but of a potential for salvation that required calling upon Him who could save—even our Lord only. Moreover, Paul goes on to ask how they can call on Him without having heard, and how can they hear without a preacher, and whence the preacher, unless one be sent? The passage hangs together very well (Ro 10:1-15) and brings together the Saviour and the Christian mission He commissioned.

The uniqueness of Christ as only Saviour, by His own personal claim (Jn 14:6), and also those who knew Him as man among them (Ac 4:12), is a basic presupposition of this article. I accept it on the word of Scripture and do not intend to discuss it anymore. An essay on "Possessing the Philosophy of Animism for Christ" would seem to require both the unique claims of Christ and the validity of the Christian mission. The Christian mission has been validated by numerous statements from our Lord: Mark 16:14-18, when

He found the eleven sitting at meat; Matthew 28:16-20, on the Galilean mountain; Luke 24:36-49, in Jerusalem after the incident of the fish and honeycomb; John 17:18, in the high-priestly prayer before His death; John 20:21, in the closed room after the resurrection; and Acts 1:8, on the day of His ascension. The common point in these passages is the Christian mission itself as a command from the Lord, but each would seem to be a different occasion and utterance, and each adds some dimension to the total mission. The rightness of winning animists for Christ is a presupposition of this essay.

We know that the New Testament church during its first quarter century grew among many groups—Jews, proselytes, Greeks and Romans. The linguistic evidence of this is found in the names of the Christians whom Paul greeted at Rome (Ro 16). However, for the purpose of this article, I desire to refer in particular to the *animists* who were won to Christ. I mean those who came out of animism into the church, and to whom a number of the things in Paul's letters were addressed. Consider for a moment the conversion of the magicians and sorcerers at Ephesus (Ac 19:18-20), and remember that it was to this kind of congregation that Paul wrote in terms of "standing against the wiles of the devil" and went on, "For we wrestle not against flesh and blood, but against principalities, against powers, against the rulers of the darkness of this world, against spiritual wickedness in high places" (Eph 6:11-12). This passage of Christian warfare with demonic dynamism has to be related to the narrative in the book of Acts.

Significant also is Paul's terminology to the foolish Galatians: "Who hath bewitched you?" (Gal 3:1). This introduces a passage on the Spirit and, after three chapters, leads up to a very neat contrast of the works of the flesh that are manifest, over against the fruit of the Spirit. This is the war in the soul, the power encounter, of the demonic and the Spirit. The significant thing about the catalog of manifest works of the flesh is that they describe perfectly the pagan religion which Galatian Christianity was encountering.

The word translated as "fornication" is *porneia,* prostitution, which was not only commonplace at the time but featured in many of the pagan cults. Another of the works of the flesh is "idolatry," which is itself the Greek word, *eidololatreia,* which according to Barclay, was an act of worship, not of the image itself, but of the deity localized in it. It was meant to visualize the god it represented.[1] Could there be anything more animistic than this?

The term variously translated in the different versions as "witchcraft," "sorcery" and "magic" (although these words represent quite different things) is *pharmakeia,* originally "the use of drugs," but which by New Testament times had degenerated into the use of medicines and charms in a "vicious and malignant" manner, which would make it sorcery. Apparently many deaths were attributed to this, judging by the sepulchral inscriptions, and regulations have been discovered which forbade the manipulation of sorcery to injure the crops of another person.

Barclay records a number of such usages—the melting of a wax image, the cursing prayer to the spirits of the underworld, the burial of bones, the use of love philters, astrological divination, the evil eye, etc.—for which he cites Greek and Roman authorities. He also shows the problem of Christians countering sorcery with magic, by wearing against their bodies, not heathen charms, but Christian texts and miniature copies of parts of the New Testament, "apparently manufactured for the purpose."[2] This has a strangely familiar ring to missionaries trying to break through animism in the pioneering period.

As with Ephesus and Galatia in Asia Minor, so with the Thessalonians on mainland Europe; they had been converted from idolatry (1 Th 1:9). However, Paul writes to them as having achieved the victory. The gospel came, not in word

only, but *in power,* in the Holy Ghost, and with much assurance (v. 5). With affection he points out how they manifested their new faith: they *received* the word (v. 6), they
turned from idols (v. 9), and they *sounded out* the word,
not only in their own locality of Macedonia, but as missionaries to Achaia (v. 8), and Paul can cite them as a model
(v. 7).

Let these cases suffice to show how the New Testament
church encountered animism from the very beginning. Her
problems and her victories, her obstructions and her growth
were remarkably similar to the experience of church planters
in the animist lands today. The importance of this discovery
to the Christian mission today is twofold: (1) We can
visualize the continuity of the Christian mission from His first
coming until He comes again, and see our labors in the same
momentum, with the same resources and moving to the same
goal. (2) Knowing that the early Christians faced the same
obstructions that we face, we may turn with confidence to
the Scriptures for direction. Whereas they had to depend on
maybe a single letter from the apostle, we have the advantage
of the collected books of a whole Bible. With such divine
provision we should take courage and push forward until He
comes again, for until then He promised to remain with us
in mission.

Therefore, having justified the Christian mission to the
animist, both by the command of Christ and by the precedent
of the early church, we now turn to an examination of the
philosophy of animism.

THE PHILOSOPHY OF ANIMISM

To what extent is there something inherent in the philosophy of animism which can be purified and won for Christ?
Or, is animism so entirely evil that it has to be completely
eradicated with conversion, signifying that a community has
to become foreign to become Christian?

Every cross-cultural evangelist, whatever his race or color, has to face this question. Granted, the evangelist is inevitably an agent of change, but of how much change, and what kind of change? If conversion has to bring people from darkness to light, from fear to joy, does becoming a "new man in Christ" mean denominationally and culturally becoming a foreigner?

In the last decade I have investigated the state of the church in more than a dozen different cultures, and often it is just this. Instead of a transfiguring joy, one often finds an aching void, a sense of something lost, and often a reaction against all foreigners in the land. Ethnopsychologists and anthropologists have spoken of this as "cultural distortion,"[3] as "despair due to deprivation,"[4] as "a loss of interest in life" leading to depopulation,[5] as *anomie*—cause of a category of suicide,[6] as *literal demoralization* or deinstitutionalization,[7] and as a "cultural void" of unmet social needs leading to nativistic resurgences,[8] which in theological terms could be called group *reversion* or *backsliding*. Anthropological research on social disequilibrium or malfunction has much to show to Christian missions with respect to the problem of reversion among converts due to cultural voids.

On the other hand, too generous an attitude toward animism has undoubtedly been responsible for a tragic syncretism, which is quite opposed to the teachings of the apostle Paul, for example, and this has cramped many a young church with myth and magic.[9] This unfortunate congregation discovers to its sorrow that it has merely exchanged one form of animism for another, and it is thus still enslaved. When a community is won for Christ as a group by multi-individual decision, this danger has to be met squarely with a consummation after incorporation into the fellowship. Or to put it in our own Western way, there must be effective follow-up after conversion. Subsequent manifestations of syncretism are more often the result of inadequate follow-up than of faulty conversion. (That is another subject, but I can document my affirmation.)

Above all, the evangelist must be warned against allowing his fear of syncretism to become such a bogeyman that he communicates a "pure" Christianity that is quite Western in approach, denominational in form, and foreign in its values. Every one of us is so ethnocentric in his missioning that he is in danger of transmitting an ethnocentric "gospel."

Now, the question I raise for discussion is: "Are we entitled to assume that a church universal, in which all "kindreds and peoples and tongues" must worship in multiethnic unity, will not draw something from each of its diverse components? My own personal experiences of multiethnic worship and social action, during the twenty years I spent on the mission field, greatly deepened my personal faith and religious understanding. My contacts with Fijian and Indian brothers in Christ, whose value systems were different from mine, rather than syncretizing my religion, drove me deeper and deeper into the Scriptures, and opened to me non-Western perspectives that greatly blessed my soul. I discovered that the Bible was more than a Western book. These young Christians had filtered scriptural truth to me through the filter of their ethos. They did not contaminate it; they isolated ingredients I did not know were there. To change the figure of speech, we were (after Tennyson) "ships that passed in the night and spoke to each other in passing," but something came from that contact which has entered my soul, and I have never been able to discover it again since my reentry into the West.

Perhaps in writing that, I have committed myself to a subjective rather than an objective role in finishing this article. In that case I shall go a step further. As a communicator of the gospel I believe that the process of communication must take place in the philosophical "orbit" of the animist, rather than in the Western "orbit" of scientific intellectualism. (Do not think that I am treating the animist as "prescientific." He is just as scientific as we are, but operates in a different scientific frame of reference.) This is why the growing edge of the church in the animist world is conservative and enthusiastic rather than liberal and rationalistic. One of my experienced advisees (by "experienced" I mean he had a decade of missionary field encounter behind him) analyzed three different Christian approaches to evangelism among Brazilian spiritists. The results were very clear. Those who were effective in winning spiritists for Christ were *operating on a common philosophical basis*. The spiritists regarded the liberal missionaries as nonbelievers, and therefore as being incapable of dialogue or encounter.

In this chapter I contend that the philosophical presuppositions of animism are such as permit our engagement in evangelistic dialogue in terms of scriptural values. The animist is open to Scripture. The Evangelical who takes the Bible at its face value has a common basis for discussion with the animist. This is not so with the demythologizer or the universalist.

Now, let me make quite clear something that I am certainly *not* saying here. I am not saying that animist *religion* as we meet it is anything but an unclean thing. The people among whom I have ministered have been saved from a terrible state of depravity—cannibalism, widow-strangling, patricide, infanticide, body-mutilation, human sacrifice, intertribal warfare, to name only a few of their religiously directed customs. (This is no missionary promotional write-up. I can document these and more from secular premissionary sources.) Only the grace of God could "save to the uttermost" like that. Yet, in spite of this, I believe that there are basic values and convictions in animist thought *that made possible their hearing of the gospel when it was preached to them, that permitted them to understand it, and to accept it.* This is the basic implication of Romans 10:13-15 which I have alread cited.

I have collected the testimonies of scores of the original converts from Fijian paganism in my documentary studies. It is clear that when they heard the gospel they recognized in it the solution to many of their problems and the answer to many of their felt needs. Despite the varied motivations of the early converts, the important thing is that they made a conscious acceptance of Christ, in a definite act of faith, and were prepared to demonstrate this new faith by publicly destroying their sacred heathen paraphernalia and "idols," by "bowing the knee" (their phrase for our "penitent form") before the congregation of those already Christian, and turning their heathen groves into gardening lands or building a Christian church there. In this respect Christianity was something entirely new, and it required considerable religious conviction for converts to take these steps. Despite his religious and social depravity, the animist was philosophically open to the gospel and capable of responding to it.

I have argued this on the basis of modern missionary history. Henri Maurier argues the same case on the basis of Romans 1 and 2:

> For pagans can in fact know God (1:19f) by virtue of a providential disposition: "God has made it plain" to them (1:19). An interior law "engraved on their hearts" (2:15) enables them to make judgements about good and evil (2: 14-16), to actually do the good (2:14) and to judge themselves deserving of blame or praise (2:15).[10]

The title of this chapter is "Possessing the Philosophy of Animism for Christ." I take that to mean that I am to demonstrate the animist's *capacity for the gospel,* and I am saying that in spite of the depravity of the pagan way of life, he has the natural capacity, under God, to see himself as a sinner in need of a Saviour, and to recognize that Saviour in Christ.

This is not just an intellectual problem for discussion. Over the whole period of modern missions—from the days of Hans Egede down to the present—many supporters of Christian missions, board directors and field missionaries have assumed that some kind of civilizing process is needed to prepare the way for a gospel of salvation. Trading stations, plantations, agricultural and educational programs have been set up to prepare the way for the gospel, not to mention colonialist and colonizing projects. These have been paternal in the extreme, foreign in values, unconsciously preaching a gospel of industry, sedentary rather than itinerant, and frequently neglectful of Scripture translation. This quite unbiblical approach to Christian mission has been a recurrent one, although its precise form varies with each generation. We see it today in such projects as the "mere technical-aid" type of mission. Christian mission, in the biblical sense of the *sending* and the *proclamation,* is a gospel of salvation, of seeking first the kingdom, and these other things being added afterward. The basic commission of our Lord cannot be changed by a mere semantic redefinition of the word *mission.* If Paul is right, that the animist is fully capable of knowing right from wrong, and the history of church-planting down through the centuries has been under God, the animist certainly has the capacity for hearing and accepting the gospel, and this renders us all the more responsible for our part in Christ's missionary program for our day.

Furthermore, there never has been a period in history like the postwar period we have experienced for large-scale religious change among the animist people of the world. The process goes on apace. The movement shows no fatigue or entropy as yet, but our days of opportunity are clearly numbered, and he is a daring missiologist who would advocate anything but a New Testament gospel mission in this period of history, the animist having, as he has, this capacity for the gospel.

THE ANIMIST'S CAPACITY FOR THE GOSPEL

Perhaps we have now reached the point where we must come to grips with some of the precise philosophical concepts of animism that demonstrate this capacity for the gospel. One is almost tempted to start with either the world view or the idea of God, but these are variables. Sometimes they offer a natural stepping-stone for the evangelist, but at other times they are serious obstructions (as, for example, in a matriarchal and matrilineal society with a female deity, and where the mother's brother performs what to us would be the father role). So I am forced to probe the philosophy of animism for evidences of what Maurier called "providential disposition," that which God had made plain. And because of the generalizing character of this chapter, I am looking for universals in animism. It seems to me there are at least four.

FIRST, THE SUPERNATURAL

The animist makes a clear-cut distinction between his own skill and technical know-how on the one hand, and the supernatural on the other. Although the two are found together, and there is no part of life beyond the influence of the supernatural, yet the two are never confused. When he plants his garden he knows how to go about it: how to recognize a suitable location, how to select his suckers, how to cultivate and irrigate, and he recognizes the time for harvest. To this point he knows his survival depends on his own knowledge and skill and diligence. But beyond this, the productivity of the soil, the rain and sun and fruiting of the crop, and many other factors are beyond his control. Whether he turns to magic or to religion in dealing with these forces beyond his control, he recognizes that there is a supernatural on whose goodwill he depends. It might be a friendly god whose aid he seeks, or an evil spirit who has to be bought off in some way. He feels the presence, though he does not understand. He merely accepts the notion that there is more in life than materialistic things and physical existence. The supernatural is there.

This is the starting point of his philosophy. Because he be-

lieves in the supernatural, he reaches out either with magic or
worship, "experimenting and coaxing and manipulating" or
"worshiping and praying and appealing." Somewhere out
there is "the unknown God," if only he can discover how to
know him. To speak of animists as materialistic is misleading.
True, they are concerned with obtaining material blessings,
but they are supernaturalists par excellence.

SECOND, THE DIFFERENCE BETWEEN RIGHT AND WRONG

The various types of behavior which the animist regards as
sins will differ from the particular sins we conceptualize in the
West because we operate in different social contexts, but we
both alike do regard certain things as offenses. In different
social contexts and value systems, one's responsibility to his
brother, for example, may work out differently. In one case
emphasis may fall more on the individual, in another on the
group. And there are sins against God or the gods. Social offenses are sins, in many animist societies, against the deified
ancestor, because he is responsible for social cohesion and
will punish the offender. This accounts for the mystifying am-
bivalent attitude of fear and affection to the ancestor. The
fortune of the tribe is his concern—its success in war, the
multiplication of population, the protection of tribal lands and
their fertility. To alienate these lands is a sin requiring
punishment of some kind. Thus the tribal deity, as judge and
preserver, is regarded with both fear and affection, and with
this goes the notion of right and wrong behavior—approval
of the former, and punishment of the latter. In a society without gods, this guiding and correcting role may be assigned to
spirits. There may be friendly and hostile spirits; these are the
variables in animist religion. The universal is the notion of
right and wrong action, the approval of the former and the
punishability of the latter. Having accepted the notion of the
supernatural, this second notion makes it possible for an
animist to see himself as a sinner in need of a Saviour.

THIRD, SALVATION

Although both the deity and the tribe are displeased with the offender, nevertheless the animist has always hope for some way of escape from judgment. This psychological compulsive in man has led to much of his experimentation in magic on one level, and in religion on another. Basically the animist is salvation-oriented. A complete list of atonements and sacrificial remedies for human offenses would fill hundreds of typed pages, if anyone could compile it. I think that I could list a hundred such occasions from Melanesia alone. The sacrificial descriptions and prescriptions of the Old Testament speak volumes to the animist world, and of course this is the biblical typology of the atoning work of Christ Himself. This is why the early translation of the letter to the Hebrews is so urgent in the many sacrificially oriented societies when they turn to Christ. It also explains why this letter is so much more frequently used in worship in such societies than in our own. Statistical counts from both Africa and Oceania have revealed this intensity.

We are here at the heart of the animist's capacity for the gospel. Let me cite a few brief examples of this salvation-orientation from my own field of special study, Oceania.

1. The pre-Christian Tahitians used a particular type of sacrifice after war. A new canoe with certain specific offerings—a model house, a basket of food and the effigy of a man—was taken through the reef and pushed off in the ocean current which carried it far into the Pacific. The offering symbolized the things destroyed in war—crafts, houses, gardens and humanity—destroyed because of intertribal war, which they recognized as wrong. As the priests sought forgiveness from the gods the sin-offering was symbolic of the taking away of the sin from the land.

2. The Ulawans of the Solomons, in the same way, annually drove a dog out to sea as a sacrifice to take away such sins

as brought sickness upon the people. The sicknesses of the year were identified with the dog, in the same way as the sins of the Hebrews were with the scapegoat sent out into the wilderness.

3. In a certain Fijian mountain village there used to be a large stone, called the Rock of Refuge. On this stone a manslayer could take refuge from the avenging chief and claim the protection of a tribal deity, all of which embodies precisely the same philosophy as the old Hebrew laws and procedures concerning the Cities of Refuge.

Such concepts (all quite pre-Christian) indicate that the animist recognizes the justice of penalty for sin, but nevertheless hopes somehow for a salvation escape from it. They also demonstrate his belief that such a salvation depends on an attitude of regret or confession of sin on his part, and an act of generosity from his deity. Such a philosophy surely suggests a mind capable of understanding the grace of God in Christ. The first requirement for salvation is that man should see himself as a sinner in need of a Saviour. The second is a readiness to reach out to receive that salvation. To people with this kind of religious philosophy, the gospel of the grace of God in Christ can indeed be *good news.*

FOURTH, RECONCILIATION BETWEEN MAN AND MAN ON A
BASIS OF RELIGIOUS EXPERIENCE

In one of the artificial islands off the coast of Malaita I talked with an old heathen priest at his tribal sacred place. I asked him the meaning of a sacrificial stone that stood before us which he called the Stone of Reconciliation. Two alienated members of the tribe, or the representatives of two alienated segments of the tribe, would make a sacrifice before this stone to the tribal deity, requesting forgiveness for disrupting the tribal cohesion, and registering their desire for reconciliation with each other. Such reconciliation mechanisms are not uncommon. I think they may almost be universal in animist societies—drinking the ceremonial beverage, eating salt together, smoking the pipe of peace, etc. Invariably a simple religious ritual links the ceremony with the tribal or family deity. People converted to Christ from such a background should have no difficulty with the Lord's injunction in the Sermon on the Mount (Mt 5:23-24), for both imply that human alienation is also a sin against God.

Thus I believe that, despite the inadequacy of the animist gods and spirits and their inability to save, that the basic philosophy of animism demonstrates a capacity for the Christian gospel, if it can be adequately presented to them. The basic notions of this philosophy—the notion of the supernatural, the notion of right and wrong with a just penalty for the latter, the notion of salvation, and the notion of reconciliation between man and man—are the principles on which the gospel hope stands.

SINCERITY OF FAITH—BUT FAITH IN WHAT?

However, to this point, we are only in the area of potential, of search, of hope. I stood at a heathen sacred place in the Solomons watching a sick man sweltering in the smoke of a sacrificial pig. He believed his god had sent the sickness to him because of his neglect of some sacred duty. The man was obviously sincere in his faith, for the sweat poured from his body in streams. Here was a petition of prayer, and an act of faith, far more agonizing than some of our shallow worship. Yet, in spite of his sincerity, the futility of it all hit me.

David Hill once had a similar experience as he watched a Chinese worshiper beating a gong frantically in his deep and urgent concern to penetrate somehow to his silent god. I have been told of a Japanese Buddha separated from his worshipers by a wire net. The people wrote their prayers on little pieces of paper and threw the pellets, hoping they would get through the netting and reach the image, but the scores of pellets adhering to the netting told the sad tale of failure.

Now, the first great difference between animism and the Christian faith is that, in point of fact, one really does not have to "get through" to Christ at all. The process operates in the opposite direction. Christ "gets through to man." "The Word became flesh and dwelt among us." This is not a philosophical concept at all. It is a historic event that is located in time and place: a story of a happening which can be told. The *idea* of incarnation is not unique, but the *historicity* of it most certainly is. To people who understand they cannot save themselves, who see themselves in need of a Saviour, the historic incarnation of God in Christ is wonderful news. The major hindrance to conversion here in the West is not the impotence of Christ, but the failure of man to admit he needs a Saviour outside himself. The sincerity and faith of the man trying to sweat himself to his god in the smoke of a pig sacrifice were worthy of a better Saviour than his religion could offer him. Demonstrating an awareness of his need for salvation from outside himself, this man was seeking a Saviour more than a teaching or a creed.

Millions of conversions have occurred in the last decade, many more of them animists than intellectualists. Effective mission is more "bringing men to Christ" than "teaching the Christian way," for the way cannot be taught to unbelievers; it has to be experienced as men tread it with Christ. Discipleship is a learning attitude toward a Master, not a state of achieved perfection. "Make disciples" (a single Greek word), Jesus commanded. To become a disciple, then, requires no more than an attitude of acceptance. Then, having become a follower, one has to grow in grace by obedience and learning from Him. The Christian way is not a legal code, or a "statement of faith," but a journeying with Christ. Christian ethics cannot be set down in a code book; they spring from a relationship between Master and disciple. There is no intellectual criterion for the Christian. Christ takes men as they are, and where they are, and transforms their lives.

THE CHRIST OF POWER

In the sense that a man becomes a new creature in Christ there is a commonality in all conversion experiences. In another sense, everyone is unique because each is a dynamic personal encounter with Christ and therefore intensely individual. In still another sense, multi-individual movements—either people. movements from animism or revivals in the West—reflect cultural features of the places where they occur. This is to be expected, for it demonstrates that something real is taking place in the core of the cultural system. It shows that Christ, who is really supracultural, is fulfilling again His incarnation, and breaking through into still another cultural pattern as Saviour and Lord. The cross-cultural evangelist must understand and expect this. (That is a subject which requires a whole essay for itself.) This raises the question of how the animist—the fetish-worshiper, for example, or totemist—conceptualizes the Saviour (and therefore salvation) and Lord (and therefore His authority). My experience and research have led me to see that usually conversion is *a power encounter* and Christ is a *Lord of power*.

The animist lives in a world filled with powers in a state of tension. Confronted with demons and the evil work of the sorcerer—often done through some evil spirit, he steers a perilous course among fears and demonic forces of all kinds. His gardening, his house-building, his personal relationships, his family encounters with sickness and the enemy tribe, and many other things involve him in a complex of powers and counterpowers. He finds himself a victim of one magical practitioner after another and spends his days making costly but futile sacrifices.

Then he hears the message of one who says, "All power is given unto me!" He discovers the evangelist has a Bible with a record of a life of amazing power, of a dramatic demonstration which speaks to his own situation. Here is a Lord

who sends forth His servants with a promise of "power . . .
over all . . . power" (Lk 10:19), the "power with authority"
(*exousia*) over all the powers (*dunamis*) of the enemy, and
this is the kind of Saviour he has been seeking. He gathers
together his charms and fetishes and religious paraphernalia,
which have always been too terrifying to handle (so that he
has had to carry them in baskets), and together with many
others like him who comprise a socially structured group, they
make a public bonfire, or throw them overboard into the sea.
The sacred, ornamented skulls, the *mana* repositories that
give them power in battle, are all now buried in a common
grave. The way of life for individual and group changes. The
demonic fears vanish; people dying of sorcery crisis recover
with amazing speed. I can document hundreds of cases of this
kind of thing from Oceania alone. In my anthropological
notebooks I also have records of interviews with nationals
from Mexico, Guatemala, and Navaholand to Taiwan and
Indonesia, and Ethiopia, so much so that I am persuaded
that the Christ of the animist-conversion experience is a Lord
of power.

The evangelist has no difficulty with this if he accepts the
Bible at its face value. The "demythologizing" intellectualist
has no spiritual resources for dealing with this situation, because the animist recognizes him as a disbeliever with no
gospel at all to offer. A temporary attitude of accommodation to animist belief for purposes of communication is also
recognized as phony. Furthermore, the evangelist may well
find himself personally involved in the struggle with demonic
evil; and unless he accepts the reality of this, he will not be
able to demonstrate the victory over Satan which he preaches.

Thus there is much in the philosophy of animism which is
in alignment with Scripture, and this should be possessed for
Christ. Animist religion, on the other hand, is sadly mis-
directed toward deities who cannot save, and many of its offensive elements are preversions of ideas which could be good

if redirected. The animist certainly needs Christ, for Christ alone can meet his needs. And this brings us back once again to Romans 10:14.

Notes

1. William Barclay, *Flesh and Spirit* (Nashville: Abingdon, 1962), p. 33.
2. Ibid., pp. 37-39.
3. A. F. C. Wallace, "Revitalization Movements," *American Anthropologist* 58 (1956): 269.
4. B. Barber, "Acculturation and Messianic Movements" (1941), p. 664.
5. W. H. R. Rivers, *The Depopulation of Melanesia* (Cambridge, England: U. Press, 1922), pp. 84-113.
6. E. Durkheim, *Suicide* (New York: Free Press, 1951; originally written in French in 1897), pp. 241-76.
7. R. K. Merton, "Social Structure and Anomie," *American Sociological Review* 3 (1938): 675.
8. Alan R. Tippett, *Solomon Islands Christianity* (London: Lutterworth, 1967).
9. See Tippett, *Verdict Theology in Missionary Theory* (Lincoln: Lincoln Christian College, 1969), pp. 25-33; and W. A. Visser't Hooft, *No Other Name* (Philadelphia: Westminster, 1963).
10. Henri Maurier, *The Other Covenant: A Theology of Paganism* (Glen Rock, N. J.: Newman, 1968), p. 27.

6

CHRISTIANITY AND TRADITIONAL RELIGIONS IN AFRICA

by
JOHN S. MBITI

THE TIME HAS COME when the church in Africa should look carefully at the relationship between Christianity and traditional religions. There is a growing interest in traditional religion and culture in many parts of Africa, and those who are showing this interest are in fact mainly Christians or people who have been exposed to Christianity. Schoolchildren, college and university students are all interested in rediscovering the area of African heritage which, as it turns out, is deeply religious. They are asking many questions which can no longer be ignored by the church. They are also, at the same time, seeking guidance about how to go about this rediscovery. There are individuals who even advocate setting up traditional religion in place of Christianity and Islam. Many others are deeply confused about the whole issue, and need both academic and pastoral guidance.

I wish that the church would hear the alarm and act with great urgency. Christianity has made a real claim on Africa, as evidenced by the fact that we have today almost 100 million Christians in our continent; and much of the educational

144

advance in the non-Muslim states of Africa is in fact through Christian presence. The question is: Has Africa made a real claim on Christianity? That is the crux of the matter. Christianity has christianized Africa, but Africa has not yet africanized Christianity. In the non-Muslim parts of Africa the momentum of evangelization has reached the point where almost every community and tribe has heard the gospel, even if the response varies widely. This momentum of the proclamation of the gospel is unlikely to be halted over the next thirty years. The church cannot sit back and rest, but evangelization has gained enough momentum to keep it moving with less energy than was necessary at the beginning of this century. Energy, effort, wisdom and grace should now be concentrated on africanizing Christianity in our continent; for until we do that, we may well have to face the risk of de-Christianization if not a near extinction of Christianity in Africa in the next century. The church in Africa has not been sufficiently prophetic to prepare itself for possible situations in the future. There are reasons for this, and we need not get into them here. We should, as Christian leaders, pastors and educators, smell the spirit of the times, take it seriously, and project our planning, efforts and preparation toward the future as the case might demand.

On the matter of deepening Christian presence in Africa, the voice of prophecy has been silent or, at most, feeble. If we cannot deepen Christianity at the point of African religiosity, then where else is it to find accommodation?

Christianity is a universal and cosmic faith. It was universalized on Calvary, and cosmicized on the first Easter Day. Our duty now is to localize this universality and cosmicity. Europe and America have Westernized it, the Orthodox Churches have Easternized it; here in Africa we must africanize it. It belongs to the very nature of Christianity to be

Reprinted from *International Review of Mission* 59 (Oct. 1970): 430-40. Used by permission of the author.

subject to localization; otherwise its universality and cosmicity become meaningless.

Evangelization is primarily an act of proclaiming Christianity's universality and cosmicity; africanization is an act of localization. Localization means translating the universality of the Christian faith into a language understood by the peoples of a given region. One cannot resist the temptation to quote the incident at Pentecost when those who had come from so many areas; Parthians and Medes, residents of Judea, Egypt, Asia, etc., "were amazed and wondered, saying, 'Are not all these who are speaking Galileans? And how is it that we hear, each of us in his own native language? . . . We hear them telling in our own tongues the mighty works of God' " (Ac 2:5-13, RSV). That was the beginning of the localization of Christianity—evangelism and localization went hand in hand. Are we to evangelize Africa only in the language of Western or Eastern Christianity? This has been done for too long, and few Africans can claim that they hear each in his own native language the mighty works of God. There lies the great challenge for the church in our continent.

SOME GUIDING PRINCIPLES

In discussing the relationship between Christianity and African traditional religions, it is necessary to work out some guiding principles. These principles should only be regarded as aids and not as an end in the discussion of the questions and problems arising out of the whole issue. The following formulations are put forward to serve as a basis for further discussion and reflection, and there are bound to be differences of opinion on some of them. But by opening up the discussion at least we are on the road toward reaching some degree of agreement or common approach.

AFRICAN PEOPLES ARE DEEPLY RELIGIOUS

That Africans are deeply religious is something that does

not require argumentation; there are many books to provide sufficient evidence about it. Christianity in Africa has, therefore, come to peoples who are profoundly religious in their own way. It must meet them on the religious frontier, for that is the language they know best. If Christianity gives them something less than that, or if Christianity removes from them this religiosity only to replace it with a religious vacuum or a halfhearted profession of religion, then it is landing them in trouble.

It must be stated clearly that to be deeply religious is not necessarily in itself taking a Christian position. African religiosity affects all areas of life, and people look at life and experience it through this religiosity. Therefore, the way they see Christianity is itself affected deeply by this traditional religiosity. In other words, by coming to Africa, Christianity lends itself to be judged by traditional religiosity, to find out whether or not it measures up to the religiosity which in effect it claims to have and intends to disseminate. It is an uncomfortable discovery for Christianity to realize that it is actually under judgment in this traditional African background. More so is the type of Christianity imported *in toto* from Europe and America.

AFRICAN TRADITIONAL RELIGIONS SHOULD BE REGARDED AS PREPARATION FOR THE CHRISTIAN GOSPEL

The old nonsense of looking at African background as devilish, and fit only to be swept away by Euro-American civilization, is or should be gone by now. We all know that Western civilization is not Christian, even though it does incorporate a lot of Christian influence in its long background and history. African religious background is not a rotten heap of superstitions, taboos and magic; it has a great deal of value in it. On this valuable heritage, Christianity should adapt itself and not be dependent exclusively on imported goods.

Here we face the difficult question of sorting out what is

valuable preparation for the gospel, and what is not. For that purpose, churches and theological institutions should make it a point to study this African background. Until we understand it well, in the totality of its cultures, languages and problems, we shall not be able to make a wise judgment on what is for Christianity and what is against it. For too long Western Christianity has condemned the African background and, in so doing, has not only thrown out valuable aids to the presence of Christianity in Africa, but also invited unnecessary resistance which, if not checked, could seriously undermine the future of Christianity in Africa.

What has been studied and formulated in African traditional religions would seem to fall into three areas. One area is that which clearly overlaps with Christianity and which, therefore, does not conflict with it. The second is that which clearly falls outside of Christian teaching and practice, and which is not for the cause of Christianity anywhere or at anytime. Third, there is the area of uncertainty which does not seriously injure the presence of Christianity or interfere with the profession of the faith. A diagram might illustrate this point as follows:

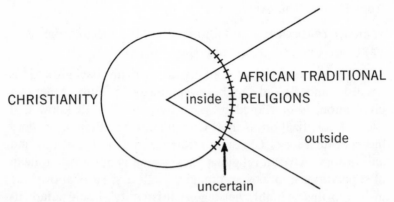

For this exercise of determining where to draw the line we should consider the four main expressions of religions, namely, beliefs, practices, personnel and religious objects.

Under *beliefs* we would have to consider the main beliefs or doctrines of both Christianity and African religions, and then compare what is said in both. For example, we would examine them under headings like God, Man, Creation, Sin, Redemption, Christ, Church, Hereafter, Spirits, etc.

The need actually forces us to study both Christianity and African religions carefully; otherwise we would be doing either or both of them some injustice.

Under *practice* we remind ourselves that African traditional religions are very concerned with celebrating life. Christianity also celebrates life, but perhaps in a different sense; and in addition, it meditates. Rituals, ceremonies and festivals deserve consideration here, so that we can sort out not only which Christian rituals, ceremonies and festivals should be celebrated, but also which ones in the African background should or could profitably be used in the type of Christianity we have in Africa. There is no reason why, for example, we should mark the harvest festival at the period when churches in England or America mark it. In fact, near the equator there are two harvests in the year and it may be wise to celebrate the harvest twice a year instead of once. But before the harvest there must come the planting festival, which in Europe and America is not observed, but which is meaningful in many African societies. Surely the church cannot celebrate the one and not the other as well.

In this section must also be raised questions that have to do with the whole area of the serving church—the service rendered by the church in the spiritual and social needs of the community. This is something which in a sense is foreign to the African traditional background as far as organized religious work is concerned. What social services we find in the traditional background are rendered primarily through kinship and neighborhood feelings. Can the church in Africa capture the spirit and utilize it? This is only one of the many questions of a practical nature which arise out of the encounter between Christianity and the African traditional background.

On the matter of *personnel* it would be necessary to study religious personages like the priests, medicine men and rainmakers, and themes like the Christian ministry and its structure, the laity, ordination, calling and training for the religious office, upkeep of religious personnel, etc.

In the area of *religious objects and places* there is plenty of work to keep us fully occupied. They include items such as shrines, altars, caves, mountains, groves, objects worn or otherwise carried by the individual, objects used at home and in the fields; to which should be added churches, crucifixes, crosses, Bibles, prayer books, hymnals, etc. Here too should be explored the whole area of art and symbolism, thus opening up the question of communication to which we return later.

Having sorted out, at least to some degree, what is to be considered as preparation for the gospel and what is not, the next question is a practical one. This is to ask ourselves how to make full use of the acceptable background, not only in the communication of the gospel but in the profession of the Christian faith in Africa.

AFRICAN TRADITIONAL RELIGIONS ARE LARGELY BUT NOT ENTIRELY COMPATIBLE WITH CHRISTIANITY

This principle can only be verified after a thorough examination of the situation along the lines indicated in the previous section. I mention it here primarily as a starting point rather than a conclusion. As such, it may turn out after much and careful study that, in fact, the opposite is the case. My own suspicion, if not conviction, is that Christianity and traditional religions are to a great extent compatible. If we seek after compatibility, the search will not be unrewarded; and the same search will help us see also where the line of incompatibility is to be drawn.

If we may return to our drawing in the previous section, we will see that in matters of belief there are clear areas of common ground like God, continuation of life after death, spiritual beings, the works of God, etc. On these both Christianity and traditional religions overlap to a large extent. On the other hand, magic, witchcraft, sorcery and divination which feature prominently in traditional religions, fall clearly outside the Christian orbit and are, therefore, incompatible with Christianity.

There are other issues which lie between and which need not be detrimental to the profession of the Christian faith for the individuals concerned. A clear example here is the matter of polygamy which the Bible neither condemns nor endorses. Christianity in Africa may have to put up with a certain amount of polygamy, instead of excluding so many professing Christians from the full fellowship of the Christian community. After all, war is a more satanic and devastating affair, and yet how long has Western Christianity not only kept quiet about war but actually participated in it and endorsed it? At this very moment there are professing Christians from the United States, fighting and killing Vietnamese people—with the blessings of their churches and chaplains. Who of those are excluded from Christian fellowship on the ground that that they have engaged in a war? Can we accept Western Christian endorsement of war which kills, and condemn polygamy (using Western Christian ethics) which, in fact, procreates? I don't wish to discuss polygamy, I only mention it here as a means of illustrating the difficulties and complexities of determining where to draw the line in some of the situations with which Christianity has to do in Africa.

Christianity and African traditional religiosity can find and establish common ground; but this has to be determined carefully, with the aid of academic understanding, the grace of God and the sympathies of the human heart.

CHRISTIANITY MAY BE SEEN AS A FULFILLMENT OF AFRICAN TRADITIONAL RELIGIONS

While Christianity and African traditional religions may at many points be compatible, when viewed in the light of the Christian faith something is lacking in traditional religiosity. I am thinking particularly of the message of the New Testament. We can find a great deal of interesting religious and cultural material in the Old Testament which parallels or matches the traditional background of African peoples. But when we turn to the New Testament, we find that African religiosity in all its richness is utterly silent and ignorant. Therefore, African religiosity must here assume the listening posture, be at the receiving end, whereas in the area of the Old Testament a certain amount of give-and-take or mutual enlightenment can be carried out.

I believe that this is one of the most exciting principles in the whole relationship between Christianity and traditional religions. It calls for a theological articulation of the fulfillment not only as an academic exercise, but to guide the church in its life, work and mission in Africa.

God spoke to Moses in the thorny bush of Sinai, and revealed Himself to Moses and hence to the children of Israel. Is God afraid of speaking to African peoples and revealing Himself to them through the thorny bushes of our continent— through our traditional religiosity? Howbeit, whatever means God used to speak to Moses and the children of Israel, they pointed to the fulfillment which came finally in and through Jesus Christ. The Lord God may have spoken Hebrew to the children of Israel; now He speaks the Christ-language. This is the language of the gospel; and the gospel comes to fulfill, not to destroy.

CHRISTIANITY IS TO JUDGE AND SAVE AFRICAN TRADITIONAL RELIGIONS

The task of fulfillment does not mean saying only yes; it

also says no. In order to preserve, it may be necessary to prune as well; and African traditional religions need a lot of pruning if their best values are to be preserved and taken up in Christianity. Christian fulfillment means, in effect, a universalizing act, and what cannot measure up to that height is not worth fulfilling. Only Christianity has the legal credentials to pass the right judgment on traditional religiosity; and unless Christianity does that in Africa, it will find itself wrapped up in a lot of religiosity not unlike the type that our Lord pronounced "dead" in Phariseeism and Judaism. Even religiosity can become dead, and not only dead but rotten. We must give Christianity the opportunity and freedom to remove deadness and rottenness from our traditional religiosity. If there were nothing to be judged and nothing to be saved in African traditional life, then there would be no need for Christianity in our continent. The individuals who cry out or write in the papers that we should have our traditional religions instead of Christianity (or Islam), simply do not realize the rottenness of their sincerity. They fear the knife which Christianity should bring with it as it deepens its roots in our continent.

AFRICAN TRADITIONAL RELIGIOSITY CAN BECOME AN
ENRICHMENT FOR CHRISTIAN PRESENCE IN AFRICA

The localization of Christianity cannot be carried out effectively without reference to traditional religiosity. This traditional background will assist, and even determine in some cases, the working out of methods of communicating the Christian message. It also affects a great deal the way in which Christianity should bring with it as it deepens its roots to ignore the fact that right now in Africa we have three worlds—the Old Testament world, that of the early church, and the world of today in which the church has to exist. All these must have a bearing on Christian presence in Africa, and it is my contention that the traditional world can bring rich insights into Christianity. This requires a lot of research and experimentation, but it seems to be a promising field.

The church should not fear to experiment and try out new things and new ways of being the church in the world. Examples can be drawn from many aspects of church life, such as worship, liturgy, church architecture, the meaning of neighborhood and kinship, the place of the departed Christians and the meaning of the communion of saints, evangelism, etc. For too long the church in Africa has been content to live and act as though it were still in America, and for just as long Christianity has largely remained on the surface. It is a grave mistake to perpetuate this one-way flow in which Christianity has all the time been flowing into the African world. Now the African world should be given an opportunity to flow into Christianity, if we are to be serious about africanizing Christianity. It will not do to listen only to what Rome, Canterbury or Athens tells us about how we ought to profess Christianity in our own house. If anything, these centers should also begin to look at and appreciate how we dress up the Christian way in our own style, which is dictated not from Rome but from the African soil. Romanism, Canterburyism and Athenism in Africa are on temporary visas; Christianity is on permanent terms as a *mwananchi** in Africa, and it must be enriched from within and not from outside. For too long we have sung borrowed hymns from Europe and America. Now we are beginning to realize that these imported hymns have nearly all become theologically extinct. The more we continue to sing them, the nearer we draw to extinguishing the freshness of the Christian faith in Africa. We must allow our rich heritage to make a contribution to Christianity. We who have been educated in Europe and America sometimes reach a point of despair for Christianity in those continents when we see what little impact it has on

* Swahili term meaning "citizen," which is much in use in East Africa at present.

the morals and life of people there; we almost despair when we recall that, in spite of Christianity in Germany, some thirty years ago six million Jews were massacred in the most abominable ways; we almost despair when we see that in spite of Christianity in America today, such a big nation is engaged in a senseless war in Vietnam, and Negroes are treated as second-class citizens; we almost despair when we see that the apartheid policy in southern Africa is backed up and given blessings by at least one brand of Christianity from Europe. What shall we do? Are we to inherit a largely bankrupt Christianity from the West, and cherish it in our bosoms without adding anything valuable to it? I believe that some enrichment can come to Christianity from our African background. We can add nothing to the gospel, for this is an eternal gift of God, but Christianity is always a beggar seeking food and drink, cover and shelter from the cultures and times it encounters in its never ending journeys and wanderings.

A SYMPATHETIC STUDY OF THE RELATIONSHIP BETWEEN CHRISTIANITY AND AFRICAN TRADITIONAL RELIGIONS MAY BE OF MUTUAL ACADEMIC BENEFIT TO BOTH

We have seen, or stated, that there is a great deal of similarity between the world of the Old Testament and African traditional background. The situation of the early church also has parallels with the situation of the church in today's Africa. These two areas of similarity (and sharp contrasts) can be of mutual academic enlightenment if sympathetically studied side by side. In particular, the world of the Old Testament might begin to shine in a new way if interpreted in the light of our knowledge of traditional African societies. The same applies when we look at the African world in the light of our New Testament understanding. Problems and experiences of the early church are, to a great extent, being duplicated in the church in Africa today; and by a careful study of both fields, academic light should be thrown on each of them. For

too long we have tried to solve problems in the church in
Africa by standards and criteria of modern-day churches in
America and Europe, with, probably, little success. Indeed,
a good number of the independent churches may have sprung
up as a result of this approach, though, obviously, we are all
aware of other factors in this movement for independency.
Let us not harass the church in Africa too much by expecting
it to be what the church is in Europe or America today.

CONCLUSION

We have enumerated these seven principles to open up a
serious discussion of our approach as Christians to African
traditional background, and particularly the religious field.
These principles are rough and unpolished in the sense that
more discussion and study are necessary before they can be
finally formulated. No doubt other guiding principles can be
added to them.

Christianity has spoken too long and too much; perhaps it
has listened too little. For too long it has passed judgment on
other cultures, other religions, other societies, while holding
the attitude that it is itself above criticism. The time may
have come now for Western Christianity to be more humble
in its approach to other religions and cultures if it is to be
effective here in Africa. Christianity has to approach this
traditional background with an open mind, with a readiness
to change it and be changed by it. In particular I would appeal to our brethren in and from Europe and America to allow us to make what in their judgment may be termed mistakes; allow us to make a mess of Christianity in our continent
just as, if one may put it mildly, you have made a mess of it in
Europe and America. When we speak or write on particular
issues about Christianity or other academic matters, we
should not be expected to use the vocabulary and approach
used in Europe and America. Please allow us to say certain
things our own way, whether we are wrong or not. We some-

times reach a point of despair when what we say or do is so severely criticized and condemned by people in or from Europe and America—often because we have not said it to their satisfaction or according to their wishes. Are we not allowed to become what we wish to become? The independent churches as a movement, may in fact be doing a great deal more to deepen Christianity in Africa than are the strictly historical churches which are too stiff to be shaped within the African situation. I have no doubt that the historical churches have a better theology, but the independent churches (speaking broadly) are more realistic and practical when it comes to taking the African situation seriously.

We are faced here primarily with the question of how best to communicate the gospel which, being an eternal message, does not change. But the means of containing and communicating it have to change. That is where experiments and mistakes come into the picture: experiments in that the church has to feel its way at every given place and period; mistakes in that Christianity as a human way of life is not free from error. The beauty of it all is that, in spite of the errors it makes, in spite of the criticisms which could rightly be leveled against it and against the church, Christianity is the vehicle of communicating the gospel, and the church is the living body of Christ. We should not use Christianity in such a way as to injure that body of Christ, whether the body is weak or strong, persecuted or peaceful, divided or united.

When Peter was called by God to go and take the gospel to Cornelius and his household, Peter objected that he had "never eaten anything that is common or unclean." To this, God told him that "what God has cleansed, you must not call common" (Ac 10:14-16, RSV). This happened three times, we are told. I wonder whether for too long (Western) Christianity in Africa has taken Peter's attitude toward the African background. My plea is that whether that background is common or clean, we should first of all understand it, experiment with it, and pray for God's careful guidance. I know that there are those who are ready to shout "Syncretism! Syncretism!" in order to dismiss this concern, but who of us is free from syncretism, pride, prejudice and sheer obstinacy? Are we not prepared to let the Holy Spirit guide us into all truth —the truth which, in this case, will no doubt show us where we are or that we could be wrong in our approach to the question of religion in Africa?

BOOKS

No books exist specifically on the matter of this article, but the following could act as a starting point for further reflection:

BAETA, C. G., ed. *Christianity in Tropical Africa.* Oxford/London: 1968.

DICKSON, K. A., and ELLINGWORTH, P., eds. *Biblical Revelation and African Beliefs.* London: 1969.

MBITI, J. S. *New Testament Eschatology in an African Background.* Oxford: 1971.

SAWYERR, H. *Creative Evangelism.* London: 1968.

TAYLOR, J. V. *The Primal Vision.* London: 1963.

WILLIAMSON, S. G. *Akan Religion and the Christian Faith.* Accra: 1965.

Also various studies on missiology and independent churches.

7

CHRISTIANITY AND CULTURE: BIBLICAL BEDROCK

by
LLOYD KWAST

The Problem

WHAT IS THE RELATIONSHIP of culture and Christianity? We ask the question not as Richard Niebuhr asks it in regard to Western culture, but as missionaries ask it when Christianity meets, mixes with, accepts and rejects aspects of other cultures.

Religion is the heart of each culture: the cement which holds it together, its authorized value system, its world view, and its mythical rational. As Christianity replaces religions (as it has throughout the Pacific islands and in many tribes in Africa), does it replace the culture? If Christianity replaces the heart of a culture, must it not radically transform all the rest? Even if old forms endure, will they not be filled with new meaning?

Is Christianity all of one piece? Or does it have a core and a periphery? If it does, what is the unchanging core and what is the cultural periphery which must be changed as Christianity passes from culture to culture?

What in culture is sacred and must not be changed? What

159

is utilitarian and must be changed to achieve a better life according to change of circumstances? Or is nothing in culture sacred? Is it all man-made and hence able to be changed by man?

These questions or others like them are crucial in missions today. Nationalism frequently finds its power in a sentimental defense of "national culture" even when Christian national leaders grant that Christianity is supreme and above all cultures.

These questions are particularly vexing because of the guilty conscience of Europeans in regard to the nations of Africasia. Having exploited them in the past, Europeans today lean over backward to avoid the charge of cultural imperialism. But the whole subject is really much bigger than European empires, for the basic questions were here long before there was a Europe. They troubled Peter and James and John back in Jerusalem in the year A.D. 50. They must be asked by Congolese missionaries evangelizing pagan Belgians in Belgium.

WHY DRAG IN THE BIBLE?

Obviously "to become a Christian" means to start living in the Christian way. It means becoming Christ's man. Equally obviously, it does not mean becoming a European or American. It has nothing to do with learning the English language or celebrating the Fourth of July.

But what does it mean to become Christ's man? And what is the Christian way of life? Today's missionaries and national Christian leaders are engaged in a crash program of defining the Christian way of life so that in Chile it is a thoroughly Chilean way, in Zambia a thoroughly Zambian way, and in India and Japan thoroughly Indian or Japanese. All this is easy to say, but difficult to do.

Becoming a Christian does not mean wearing Western clothes, singing Western hymns, or building Western-style buildings—agreed. But how about worshiping at 10:30 A.M. on Sunday, or having Christian women's associations, or Sunday schools, or using wine in the communion? Still further, are the principles in the following list *essentially* Christian? Must they therefore be adopted in every culture? Or are they dispensable, to be used or not as the Africasian denomination sees fit?

Episcopalian, Presbyterian or Congregational polity?

The Western custom of monogamy?

The democratic way of running a church through elected deacons and elders?

The renunciation of caste as an essential of becoming a Christian?

The wearing of hair long or short?

Quiet decorous behavior in public worship?

As the church advances from culture to culture, an enormous number of questions arise, many of which can be phrased the following way: Is such and such a custom in this culture acceptable as it is in the newly rising church? Can it be Christianized, or must it be rejected?

As Christian leaders answer this question, which arises in a thousand different forms, what is their authority? Are they to trust their own good judgment? Or the good judgment of the missionaries? Or of some anthropologist? Or of the nationals? Do they simply ask what does the Bible say? If so, on what grounds do they permit the eating of bacon? And on what grounds do they prohibit polygamy?

These questions are in reality very complex. Some missiologists are answering them from an unenlightened Western point of view. In effect they are saying, "Whatever we do in America (or England, or Norway) is the right answer. It is based on the Bible. Naturally it is God's will." This ethnocentric position is also the danger of missionaries from Africasian denominations and liberals from Europe. Missionaries sent by Korean denominations, let us say, are likely to assume that the form of Christianity which has developed in the Korean culture is mandatory for new congregations in Kalimantan or Calcutta. Liberals from Europe or America are likely to propagate as Christianity a particular world view and theological understanding which they have found appealing back in Pottsdam or London.

Other missionaries, much influenced by the relativism of influential schools of anthropology (which assert that cultures cannot be evaluated as either good or bad) and championing "vanishing cultures which are being ruthlessly trodden on by Western imperialists," are answering the questions from an uncritical point of view which assumes that the culture is always right. As people become Christian their cultures must not be disturbed. The missionary must not "stupidly meddle with things he does not understand." Whatever the nationals do is right. W. J. Hollenweger's article in the April, 1971, *International Review of Missions* beautifully voices this conviction.

Still other missionaries and missiologists are advocating cultural adaptations which in their limited experience seemed good to them. The subject is never discussed without wearisome reiteration of the error of promulgating Western tunes, Western church buildings, Western clothes, and Western ideas of punctuality. They never mention the difficulty which arises when Christianity adapted to Hinduism has to live peaceably with Christianity rigorously adapted to Islam.

All this is done without clearly setting forth the *authority* by which cultures, or better, the components of which cultures are composed, can be judged. By what standard are cultural components to be divided into those toward which Christianity can remain indifferent, those it welcomes, those it modifies and keeps, and those it must reject and replace with functional substitutes?

Often, the more aware that writers on this topic are of the problems and the importance of culture, the less biblical they become in their proposed solutions. The missionary seeking a truly Christian solution to the problems that culture presents must be willing to face the problems honestly and make the effort to see the issues clearly. And all attempts to provide answers must be made while standing firmly on biblical bedrock.

To do this the missionary needs a solid biblical hermeneutic—a sound system of interpreting and using the Bible—that speaks with authority to the questions of culture. Furthermore, he must be totally convinced that God has spoken a true, clear and fully understandable message in Holy Scripture for all men of all cultures for all time. This is absolutely necessary for any hermeneutic that would not cast him into a system of hopeless relativity of knowledge.

God has spoken. But what has He said? Is what He has said clearly comprehensible? Does it have meaning that is true for all time, for people everywhere? Is it equally true for people in every human culture? Can a hermeneutic be found that would render a true biblical interpretation applicable to all cultures? Is it possible to find a hermeneutic that can adequately bridge the gap between contemporary cultures and those of the biblical writers? Or can biblical truth at all bridge the language, culture and time gap?

Many today assert that diverse histories have made many societies on earth so dissimilar that cross-cultural communication with any degree of meaning is nearly impossible. They hold that the minds of men in totally diverse cultures are so different that what is evident to one must be unintelligible to the other. If some were to accept the Christian faith they would make of it something so entirely different that in the end it would not be the same religion.

Along this same line, the "New Hermeneutic" asserts that the mind and culture of the biblical writers cannot jump the historical gap to communicate anything meaningful to our time and culture. Modern man cannot understand the Bible without distorting the original meaning intended. Thus the Bible must be reinterpreted to have meaning and relevancy for our day, and every new day to which it speaks. Likewise, it asserts that every culture of man must come to its own understanding of what the Bible means to fit its unique cultural needs.

This writer rejects the view that the meaning of biblical truth is relative to time and culture. He firmly holds that the one, true and eternal God spoke through the writers of the Scriptures an unchanging truth for all men of all cultures for all times, and that the meaning of this truth can be clearly understood by those who sincerely seek it in the Spirit of Christ.

THE SIMILARITIES OF CULTURES

The Bible views the human situation as one. Its message is to all humanity; its appeal is to people in every culture and nation; its design is to communicate cross-culturally. From the first words in Genesis to the last in the Revelation, the Scriptures strongly assume that mankind is one and that all men share in a common origin and destiny. All men are of one race created by God. In Adam all men share in a common rebellion and fall into sin. And, regardless of culture or race, all men move toward an end destined by a sovereign, loving God. The Bible clearly presents only one way of salvation for all men, with no regard for historical period or ethnic origins.

The differences between men and their societies has long fascinated the students of culture and captured nearly all their interest and attention. But a more thorough look at the similarities among men and cultures can be impressive. All people on earth are physically similar; all are of one blood. Linguistic communications are strikingly similar, so that every human language, regardless of complexity, can be fully understood and completely mastered by one who does not naturally speak it. Though languages do express differing psychological or logical outlooks, yet they all express symbolically a common human reality. No dissimilarity between two languages can ever be so great that the barriers to precise meaning cannot be crossed from both sides.

The minds and thoughts of men everywhere are similar. Neill rightly observes that "the minds of men and women work in much the same way all the world over."[1] As intelligent creatures made in God's own image, all rational men seek after their Creator to find Him. In whatever culture he may be found, man is a creature who ponders the mysteries of life and universe, and he worships compulsively.

Until recently, most anthropologists have focused so much on cultural differences in human societies that they have almost entirely neglected the similarities. In recent years some anthropologists have given increasing attention to cross-cultural similarities or the "commonalities" among people of divergent cultures. Melville Herskovits, for example, acknowledges that "a degree of formal similarity exists even among the most diverse cultures." All cultures have language, religion, family, technology, morality, beauty, truth, good, evil.

Another anthropologist, Walter Goldschmidt, is not nearly so impressed by the dissimilarities of cultures as he is the similarities between human beings. He says, "People are more alike than cultures."[2]

He sees human universals in such things as the presence of dissatisfaction, selfishness, exploitativeness, conflict, tension, desire to escape, etc., and views culture as a necessary device "to preserve society against the essential self-interest of the human individual."[3] Goldschmidt essentially rejects the old emphasis on cultural relativism:

> . . . we must divest ourselves of the implications of cultural relativism. Certainly it was necessary for anthropology to go

through a relativistic phase in order to relieve social philosophers of the habit of evaluating cultures in terms of our
own culturally determined predilections. Yet by now we can
certainly appreciate the contextual value of infanticide without advocating it, or can see the merits and demerits of
polygamy without concern over our own convictions or
regulations. . . .

This means, among other things, that we anthropologists
must rid ourselves of the Rousseauean "good savage," must
cease to use ethnographic data either as an escape or as a
vehicle for expressing our personal social discontent, and
begin to look at primitive societies for what they can tell us,
not only about the possible but about the probable, and
about the consequences—to individuals and to societies—of
either.[4]

It is precisely because all men are similar that God can
and does address Himself in Scripture to all the nations (peoples) of the earth. God intended to communicate to the entire
creation in the "fullness of time." When the Roman Empire
provided some unity in the midst of cultural diversity, God
spoke through His Son. Perhaps the most remarkable development in recent history is the increasing oneness of mankind through modern communications, quick travel and
a growing world language. Could it be, as Neill suggests, that
a new human oneness is emerging out of many centuries of
cultural fragmentation as part of God's plan for all the nations, for the human race as a whole?

At the time at which the Gospel first appeared, the Roman
Empire had brought to a great part of the ancient world a
peace and a prosperity that had never been known before.
The Gospel could be preached in a language, Greek, that
was understood by educated men everywhere, from the
mountains of Afghanistan to Marseilles and western Spain.
Was this just chance? Or had God something to do with it?
Is it just chance that we live in a world which, for good or
ill, is unified as it has never been before? Or is the God who

revealed himself in Jesus Christ making it plain to us as Christians that he is interested in all the nations of the earth, and that this new unity is part of his plan for them all?

If we take the Bible seriously, we see that from the beginning God has been interested in all the nations of the world, in the human race as a whole.[5]

We can conclude that basic human similarities make cross-cultural communication not nearly so difficult as some would have us believe. The true, intended meaning of biblical revelation as delivered to an ancient Hebrew and Greek culture can be clearly and correctly understood by Spirit-directed men in every human culture today.

THE FOUNDATION, PURPOSE AND AIM OF CROSS-CULTURAL REVELATION

1. The foundation of God's true communication with men is that the biblical writers *were inspired to write what they did by the Spirit of God.* Thus the Bible is the revelation of a supracultural God, communicated to culture-bound people, through writers living at specific points of history and in particular cultural milieus. It is on divine authorship that the authority of the Bible rests as a *true revelation for all mankind throughout history.*

2. The *purpose* of biblical revelation is to make men of all cultures "wise unto salvation," and provide for God's children "doctrine, reproof, correction, instruction in righteousness, that the man of God may be completely equipped in all good works" (2 Ti 3:16-17, free trans).

3. The *aim* of biblical revelation is to effect *change.* The very design of God's truth is to change people, and communities of transformed people will quickly cause changed cultures. God's Word will not merely lead to correct understanding, but completely transform lives through right relationships to God. And right relationships to God will profoundly change all cultures in which it occurs.

HERMENEUTICAL PRINCIPLES

We are indebted to professors Dods, Ramm, and others for suggesting several hermeneutical principles essential in understanding the Bible in cross-cultural settings.

1. Only an individual who is indwelt by the Spirit of God can come to a correct understanding of God's truth in biblical revelation.

> In order to appreciate and use the Bible, the reader must himself have the same spirit which enabled its writers to understand their revelation of God and to record it. The Bible is a record, but it is not a dead record of dead persons and events, but a record inspired by the living Spirit who uses it to speak to men now. . . . It is the medium through which the living God now makes himself known. But to find in it the Spirit of God the reader must himself have that Spirit.[6]

2. The interpreter of God's Word must possess certain spiritual qualifications to correctly understand God's intended meaning: (1) He must be born of the Spirit of Christ. (2) He must sincerely want to know the truth of God's Word. (3) He must have a desire to be obedient to the truth he discovers from God's Word. (4) He must have a reverence for God and continue to exercise faith in Him. (5) He must have complete dependence on the Holy Spirit to guide and direct in his understanding of the Bible.[7]

3. The message of the Bible must be interpreted and understood as an accommodation of eternal, divine truth to the limitations of human language and thought. But this in no way limits the Bible in its ability to communicate fully and correctly to man. The Bible of necessity was written in several human languages in terms familiar to the cultural, geographical and historical setting of the people to whom it was written. God's communication of truth had to make contact with humanity at the points of language and culture, or else the

revelation would stand meaningless to those to whom it was addressed. In other words, the eternal truth of God was anthropomorphized in human language, in human thought forms, and in culturally relevant figures, objects and imageries *to convey precise meanings*. Because of human limitation God used human figures and imageries to convey exactly eternal, supracultural truth.

4. The clear and intended meaning of Scripture can be discovered by correctly understanding the meaning of the words and sentences of the Bible as they were ordinarily and literally used in the original biblical languages. Clear understanding of the Bible does not depend on fanciful, symbolistic or allegoristic interpretations.

5. However, Scripture uses numerous figures of speech, symbols, allegories, types and parables to present clear, true ideas of what God intended to communicate through the words of the sentences. These must be recognized.

6. The Holy Spirit, in using language (a particular language) and units of language (words and sentences), used an expression capable of meaningful thought communication for all men of all languages of all time in every place, since all men use language to think and conceptualize.

7. All truth that is *essential* in Scripture is clearly revealed and can be clearly understood by Spirit-filled individuals in every culture. The Bible emphasizes and often repeats essential truth to insure its clarity. "No really great or essential doctrine of the Bible is to be found in one passing reference or is to be founded upon slight Scriptural evidence."[8]

8. The Bible presents truth as *spiritual principles*. Usually the true, clear principle of truth in a Bible passage is an *unchanging one*, while the illustrations and applications of that truth might be *many*. "The Bible is a book of principles more than a catalogue of specific, minute directions."[9] If Bible teaching is seen as only specific it becomes culture-bound,

provincial and relative. We should constantly ask ourselves the question, What is the spiritual principle—the universal truth—behind the specific teaching? "The Bible emphasizes the inner spirit rather than its literal force that is to be our guide. . . . Commands in terms of one culture must be translated into our culture."[10] For example, biblical teaching on women in the church, cutting of hair and wearing of veils are purely cultural teaching, but yet hold spiritual principles for Christians of all cultures, that is, that women should avoid all appearance of immodesty, and be chaste and dignified in dress and behavior.

CONCLUDING OBSERVATIONS

It is wrong to view culture and language as a prison limiting the ability of God to communicate to men across cultures or distorting His revelation. Culture and language (the Hebrew and Greek cultures and languages in particular) should be viewed as a vehicle of universal thought and expression by which the truth of God is set free. In the same way the fullness of God was expressed and set free for human comprehension in the person of Jesus Christ (albeit in the limitations of the human body). Only in the weakness of human flesh could the truth of God's nature be freed for human understanding. In no way did Hebrew or Greek culture limit or distort the message God intended to give. God used these as ideal vehicles for communicating truth to people living in culture and history.

In revealing biblical truth, the Holy Spirit did not merely accommodate the message to reflect the narrow, provincial prejudice of Hebrew and Greek culture. The spiritual values of the Bible constantly surmount the values of the local culture. Consistently the prophets proclaimed spiritual values far more lofty than those of their culture-bound contemporaries. They consequently offended the cultural bias of their day and some of them were killed for it.

Jesus also surmounted the cultural bias of His day. Often His message and manner were offensive to Jewish cultural patterns, and He certainly did not reflect the cultural prejudice of His surroundings. His teachings, which clearly reflected an authority loftier than contemporary Jewish thought, often cut directly across accepted Jewish religious behavior. Likewise, the apostle Paul did not merely reflect his cultural environment, either Jewish or Greek, but presented bold, new spiritual concepts that quickly turned men of several cultures to the living Christ.

Notes

1. Stephen Neill, *Call to Mission* (Philadelphia: Fortress, 1970), p. 15.
2. Walter Goldschmidt, *Comparative Functionalism: An Essay in Anthropological Theory* (Berkeley: U. California, 1966), p. 134.
3. Ibid., p. 136.
4. Ibid., p. 137.
5. Neill, pp. 15-16.
6. Marcus Dods, *The Bible, Its Origin and Nature* (New York: Assoc. Press, 1912), p. 102.
7. Bernard Ramm, *Protestant Biblical Interpretation* (Natick, Mass.: Wilde, 1950), p. 8.
8. Ibid., p. 92.
9. Ibid., p. 116.
10. Ibid., pp. 116-18.

PART THREE
PRACTICAL ISSUES

8

QUALITY OR QUANTITY

by
RALPH D. WINTER

WHETHER MAKING SHOES or planting churches, one faces the constant problem of how much he should emphasize quality and how much he should emphasize quantity. People disagree about where to strike the balance. Billy Graham, for example, has been accused of being more interested in quantities of converts than in their quality. Over the years, therefore, he has added great emphasis to a follow-up program which relates converts to existing churches, gives them *Decision* magazine, the "Hour of Decision" broadcast, printed sermons, modern-speech versions of the Bible, even Bible dictionaries and other helps. All of this is the attempt to add quality to quantity.

Those who emphasize "church growth" are sometimes accused of being more interested in quantities of church members than in their quality. This is despite the fact that the very phrase *church growth* implies an additional dimension of emphasis beyond conversion, since it focuses not on how many raise their hands at an evangelistic service but on the *incorporation* of the new believer into *church* life. Other religions may consist of individuals worshiping at shrines, but the essence of Christianity goes beyond individual experience.

Thus, the very concept of *church* growth is an attempt to emphasize the quality of corporate life beyond the quantity of individual decisions.

Yet, of course, even the process of incorporation into a church can lack quality. This is why those who are known for their emphasis on church growth constantly talk about "postbaptismal" training, about "quality growth" and "organic growth" (Tippett's phrase referring to the development of structure within a Christian movement), and in dozens of other ways attempt to assess every conceivable aspect of the fullest, finest growth both in number of believers and in individual and corporate qualities of Christian life.

Quantity Versus Quality Is a False Issue

We are led into a booby trap, however, whenever we try to drive a theoretical distinction between *quantitative* and *qualitative*. Granted that Kodak's millions of inexpensive cameras do not have the quality of the fewer Leicas, Rolleiflexes, and Nikons that are made, but the inexpensive cameras must have at least enough quality to function properly. Furthermore, the "high quality" companies would be achieving nothing if they did not produce a certain *number* of their kind of camera. Thus, ultimately you cannot really choose between quality and quantity; there is room only for a difference in emphasis, and in different circumstances both emphases are needed.

Jesus certainly emphasized both. He talked to large crowds, and many of His hearers no doubt went away with only superficial understanding, sufficient merely to allow them to make only the very initial responses of repentance and faith. He also spent time in the "training of the twelve." Thus, He not only scattered the seed over a large area, but also returned to cultivate intensively the good ground that would effectively reproduce. Here is one emphasis of "harvest theology": even the high-*quality* soil is so labeled because of its ability to produce a *quantity* of fruit.

Paul also had both emphases. He talked to large, low-interest groups, and also spent time with his disciples—Timothy, Epaphroditus and Titus. He also wrote painstakingly to specific churches about specific problems, following their growth and development over a period of time. Yet Paul actually disclaimed the necessity of the same person working at every level. He was willing, in the case of the Corinthians, to have merely "planted" while Apollos "watered"; to have "preached" while someone else "baptized" (1 Co 1:17, 3:6). It is not strange then to note that in one sense John the Baptist performed one role, Jesus another, and Paul a third. Each sought *quality* in the particular ministry in which he was involved. John did not "follow up" everyone he baptized. Jesus did not go as far as Paul in organizing churches among the Gentiles. Thus it would be foolish to try to decide which of these three went for quantity and which for quality.

Every task, properly understood, has dimensions of both quality and quantity attached to it. We cannot choose between the two; we can only try to strike the right balance to meet the specific circumstances.

A similar warning is necessary in regard to a careless use of the two phrases, *quantitative growth* and *qualitative growth*. These must never be squared off against each other as if they were something entirely different. Why? Because *all quantities are measurements of certain qualities!* Whether we speak of a pint of ice cream, or even if we talk about the weight of ice cream per pint (a more complicated measurement), we are still talking about ice cream; and there is no ice cream that does not possess both weight and volume. If we speak of the number of church members, the average attendance, or, let us say, the number of people who both belong and regularly attend and have personal or family devotions, we are speaking of human beings who in some measure have been influenced by Christ. Whatever Christ does He does with *countable* people.

The crucial issue in missions in connection with quality
arises when it is assumed that either any numerical measurement of quality must be superficial, or that any important
quality cannot be measured. When you stop to think of it,
these common and erroneous assumptions fly in the face of
Jesus' insistence that "by their fruits you shall know them."
It may well be true that those who count things have not always counted the most important things, but the reality of the
impact of Christ on the world today is a phenomenon real
enough to be counted and measured in a host of different
ways. Our human judgment is not, of course, ultimate judgment. That is God's. But if we ever get to the place where we
are not quite sure whether the obedient following of Christ in
the power of His Spirit will make an *evident,* countable difference in a nation or community, we have most surely fallen
away from biblical faith.

Thus, highly important qualities do have quantitative,
measurable dimensions, and quantitative statements cannot
but refer to qualities of some kind, important or not. The
challenge is to make sure the qualities we measure are important. In fact, the people who set the quantitative in opposition to the qualitative are really trying to say that we are not
measuring the right things. They may be more interested in
how many people are engaged in public marches against civil
policies rather than *how many* people go to church. In both
cases, however, we are dealing with quantitative measurements of qualities, and we see that the issue of qualitative
versus quantitative is at best a superficial and misleading way
of talking. At worst it is an entirely false emphasis.

A recent letter from a church leader somewhat distantly
acquainted with the Institute of Church Growth is an excellent
example of what I have here suggested as an improper opposition of the two terms:

> Granted that qualitative aspects are not as measureable as
> quantitative, they are still as important, if not more so. . . .

> If [in your school] the same quality of scholarly re-
> search . . . as is given to the principles of numerical growth
> would be given simultaneously . . . to the concerns of quali-
> tative growth . . . a contribution could be made to the
> Christian mission that not only would enhance the validity
> of numerical growth but would make numerical growth
> principles much more widely accepted and practiced. . . .
>
> I am sure the curriculum of the School of World Mission
> must include offerings in the area of qualitative church
> growth, but the image given thus far to many, I fear, is one
> of such emphasis on numerical growth that qualitative
> growth must not be considered very important.

What I think this leader really is saying is: "You are measuring some qualities. I think there are other qualities that
should be measured as well." Perhaps he feels we are satisfied
with overall growth in church membership. Perhaps he does
not see that membership statistics properly interpreted are a
significant way of understanding qualities. His uneasiness
about statistical measurements is fairly common among some
Christian leaders. If such attitudes concerned only the grad-
uate School of Missions and School of World Mission at
Fuller Seminary, I would not mention it; but it is typical of a
widespread way of thinking among some church leaders and
missionaries which (unintentionally, I am sure) damages
Christ's cause by confusing the issue and underscoring how
easily people misunderstand the quantitative aspect of all
qualities. The error sets good Christians all across the world
against the very thing to which they are giving their lives,
namely, the propagation of the gospel.

QUANTITIES AS CLUES TO QUALITIES

The correct way to look at quantitative measurements is to
regard them—properly handled—as reliable indications of
qualities. Let me illustrate the point from the seminary where
I teach, the Fuller School of World Mission and Institute of

Church Growth. We certainly do teach national leaders and
career missionaries to calculate memberships accurately. But
these membership figures are not so much glorified as qualified, and statistics as such occupy only a tiny percentage of
our time.

We are almost always more interested in *changes* in church
membership—and in the hundreds of factors that may or may
not be related to such changes—and we recognize at least
six components of net increase in membership (conversion
in, reversion out, transfer in, transfer out, born in, die out),
so that simple *net* growth is rarely in itself considered defi-
nitive. We talk not only about *amounts* of growth but *rates*
of growth, and also *rates* relative to the growth of population
and subpopulation. We talk about the relative numerical *proportions* of at least five different kinds of important leaders
in a movement, the *ratio* of pastors to organized churches,
the relative expenditure of income on theological education,
and the costs of producing an ordained minister. These are
just a few of dozens of measurements of qualities other than,
and in addition to, gross membership. One of our recent
studies (on the Friends Church in Central America which
has been fathered by the California Friends) has over thirty
graphs and charts, only a few of which focus exclusively on
church membership.

In any case, most of our time is spent on the biblical, historical, theological and sociological realities of the world
Christian movement without any quantitative charts and
diagrams involved. A very major use of time results from our
concern that a new church should develop naturally within its
own linguistic and cultural forms. We are concerned that the
full meaning of the gospel of Christ might be transmitted, and
that individuals and groups—as many as possible—might be
incorporated into meaningful, growing, self-healing communities of faith that are durable and sound enough to witness
effectively on every level of their particular society, acting

as salt of the earth and light of the world. Anyone who has studied in our school or who has read a broad selection of our books and articles realizes that our use of numbers is a means to an end that is far more profound than membership figures. We continually deny that membership increase is a goal in itself. But I have described our procedures with the belief that they are typical of good procedures in all churches.

Nevertheless, while membership totals are not adequate as goals in themselves, in many situations in missions today they are a "necessary though not sufficient" evidence of faithfulness to God in evangelism. A medical doctor cannot be properly described as a man "preoccupied with body temperatures" just because he often (almost routinely) takes the temperature of his patients, and is not content when the temperature is not normal. He certainly is interested in body temperature, but only as a clue to something else. Body temperature is simply a "necessary though not sufficient" evidence of health or sickness.

Similarly in churches, 10 percent membership increase per year in a given church may not prove the *presence* there of all the fruits of the Holy Spirit, but on the other hand the absence of any growth, or a constant loss of membership, may often be a vital clue to the *absence* of certain fruits of the Holy Spirit. This is especially likely in many non-Western environments, where membership is mainly first-generation and a huge percentage of the population is yet to be won.

Can we not agree that if there are unreached winnable men anywhere, there must then not be complacent Christians anywhere? This is why it is important that if men and peoples are hungry and searching and responsive there are likely some *measurable clues* to this fact. Something must be wrong if 78 percent of the Japanese (in a government census) name Jesus Christ as the greatest religious leader in history, but less than 1 percent belong to any fellowship in which they will learn more about Christ. At the same time millions of Japanese are surging into Soka Gakkai.

Even churches that are apparently growing well may be better understood by means of quantitative clues to qualities. Figures A and B show two ways of looking at the growth of the Vietnamese section of the Evangelical Church of Vietnam. The top chart (fig. A) which shows the annual totals of members, seems to climb more steeply on the right than on the left. That is, the number of new members per year is about 900 during the recent decade (1960—1970), while it was only 600 between 1927 and 1931. However, be careful: it is natural for a larger church to win more people per year! The bottom chart (fig. B) shows the *rate* of growth—not the size of the church—by plotting the number of baptisms each year *per hundred members*. Comparing the same two periods, we find a staggering difference: In the earlier period there were well over sixty baptisms per hundred members per year, while during the latter period there were only five per year.

These facts are merely clues, of course, and are worth little unless they lead the ministers or missionaries to see the many factors behind the half century of experience of this Vietnamese Church. The leaders of this church must go on to learn more about the situation, using among other things the many clues these two charts give. But inattention to these quantitative clues could hide qualities that must not be hid!

Recently I was asked to study a church which I will not identify so that I may suggest some of my personal conclusions about it. My task as I went to this country was *not* to graph the growth of the church, but to see what could be done about the development of leadership and self-support. However, I discovered on arrival that this church had kept relatively good records and that the data on various aspects of growth were quite readily available. Somewhat routinely I jotted down the membership figures for the years 1936 to 1970. Figure C gives communicant membership totals in

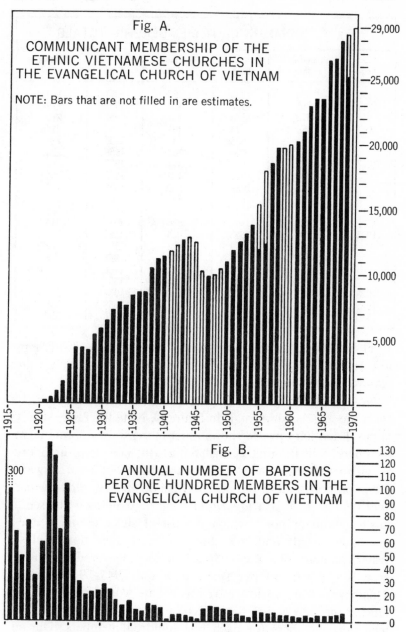

Fig. A.

COMMUNICANT MEMBERSHIP OF THE
ETHNIC VIETNAMESE CHURCHES IN
THE EVANGELICAL CHURCH OF VIETNAM

NOTE: Bars that are not filled in are estimates.

Fig. B.

ANNUAL NUMBER OF BAPTISMS
PER ONE HUNDRED MEMBERS IN THE
EVANGELICAL CHURCH OF VIETNAM

Fig. C. COMMUNICANT MEMBERSHIP TOTALS

Year	Member-ship	Year	Member-ship	Year	Member-ship
1910	355	1931	362	1951	1894
1911	362	1932	414	1952	1792
1912	378	1933	424	1953	2137
1913	364	1934	394	1954	2146
		1935	338	1955	2212
		1936	262	1956	2343
1917	362	1937	304	1957	2442
		1938	415	1958	2549
		1939	560	1959	2677
		1940	652	1960	2897
		1941	691	1961	3213
1922	280	1942	804	1962	3140
1923	256	1943	1023	1963	3079
		1944	1226	1964	3025
		1945	1440	1965	3145
		1946	1615	1966	3124
		1947	1768	1967	3509
1928	355	1948	1638	1968	3432
1929	400	1949	1657	1969	3457
1930	250	1950	1774	1970	3404

sheer numbers. Is anything immediately obvious? Perhaps not, for sheer numbers are rarely enough to give an accurate picture of the situation.

Now look at figure D which has been drawn accurately from the membership totals in figure C. Note the fairly steady climb. Each jog upward shows a net increase in communicant members. Still nothing earthshaking. But now look at figure E which plots the same data as the first, but each upward jog is proportional to the net increase *divided by the previous year's total*. This is a *logarithmic* chart. It helps us to see a most significant point which the list of sheer numbers does not show at all and the absolute chart does not disclose either, namely, that the 1936-47 period registered far faster growth (19 percent per year) than the 1947-1970 period. This 'sparked my curiosity. It was a clue worth investigating. During the first period there was an average increase of nineteen new members for each one hundred members. During

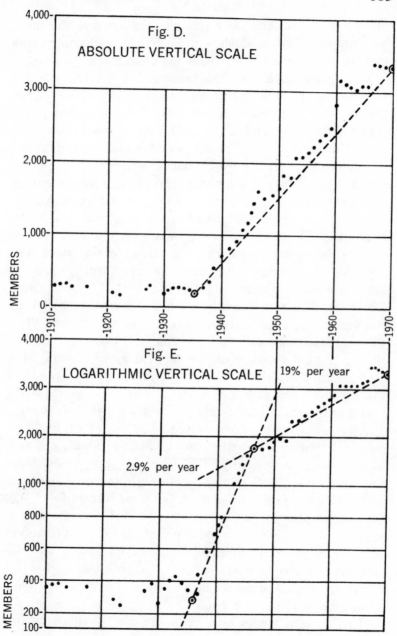

Fig. D.
ABSOLUTE VERTICAL SCALE

Fig. E.
LOGARITHMIC VERTICAL SCALE

19% per year

2.9% per year

the second period (almost a quarter of a century) this number dropped to three, which is no higher a rate of growth than that of the population in which the church was growing.

This quantitative clue led to other discoveries. I found that lay and national leadership predominated in the earlier period. Also there was a great deal of denominational self-consciousness surrounding the 200th anniversary celebration toward the end of the 1936-47 period, which challenged the church with concrete growth goals.

I discovered that in the earlier period there were far more active evangelistic efforts and a willingness to found congregations on a very humble base—in houses and shacks. An intermediate level of leadership was widely and effectively used in the earlier period but was phased out as more missionaries arrived and more nationals were sent abroad for university and seminary training. Also, by 1947, money from the United States had become essential for erecting buildings, training pastors, and paying highly trained pastors. When those funds could no longer increase each year, the church itself could not continue to increase. Each new congregation cost the church about a thousand dollars a year to run, and the mission board in North America, which was giving $70,-000 a year to this field, would not keep on giving more.

All of these observations—revealed by clues from membership and baptismal charts—are intimately bound up with both quantity and quality. The crisis the church now faces also partakes of both aspects: two-thirds (note: a *number*) of its budget comes from abroad, but these foreign funds will be reduced year by year to zero by 1980. Either the church stands still in membership and triples its giving, or it discovers how to triple its membership without increasing its paid ministry. I recommended the latter, but they had to describe the many ways (qualities) in which the church would have to change in order to expand.

This, briefly, shows how quantities and qualities are inseparable parts of the same reality. It is apparent that those who are alert to the quantitative measure of qualities are more likely to understand the situation than those who neglect the quantitative measures available. The same is true in medicine. Today doctors make more laboratory tests than ever because the enormous importance of quantitative measurements in the diagnosis of illness in the case of an individual human organism has been abundantly proved. Such measurements certainly have their parallels in the analysis of the living organism that is the church in all its various forms. The fact that we have sometimes made superficial or improper use of quantitative measures must not deter us from expanding and refining the quantitative measurements of the important qualities in the life and health of the Christian movement.

This matter is of crucial importance to the cause of Christ around the world in all six continents. As the churches grow in numbers and influence, in grace and power, in ability to serve and aid humanity, it is of the highest importance that Christian leaders learn how to measure qualities. Such measurement is helpful to the church, and we do a disservice to the cause if we belittle part of our task.

9

CRISIS OF IDENTITY FOR SOME MISSIONARY SOCIETES

by
DONALD McGAVRAN

A CRISIS OF IDENTITY occurs when people do not know who they are. Am I a sophisticated agnostic or a devout Christian? Am I a dutiful son, bound to the ways of my ancestors, or a modern who has rejected all parental authority and does whatever "feels good"? In times of rapid social change, confused individuals who are adjusting to radically new conditions and not sure of their function, are said to face a crisis of identity.

One of the crucial issues in missions tomorrow is that some missionary societies face identity crises. A few years ago every missionary society knew who it was and what its work was; it was an organization of devout Christians intent on carrying out the Great Commission. It existed to make Christ known in Asia, Africa and Latin America, and it had been commissioned to preach the gospel to every creature and was carrying out the commission. It was not the church. It was not the denomination. It was an agency of the denomination. It appealed to individual Christians and congregations, saying, "If you believe God commands every Christian to proclaim the gospel to the ends of the earth, then in obedience to God

188

either go as a missionary or help send others. Carry out your obedience through us."

No Longer Sure

But today, many missionary societies are no longer sure who they are or what their task is. Some of their leaders say one thing and some another. Several causes of their confusion are apparent:

1. With an enormous apparatus and an annual income of hundreds of thousands and, in some cases, millions of dollars, it looks to such missionary societies as if foreign missions might come to an end. Missionaries have been thrown out of China, North Korea, and parts of India. Younger churches are irked by missionaries. To be sure, nationals always say, "Send us missionaries of the right sort," but often they are not happy with missionaries and missionaries are not happy with them. Missionary societies wonder whether they can send missionaries to Asia, Africa and Latin America much longer. "Do we need another outlet for our resources?" they are asking.

2. Then, too, the word *mission* has been redefined. It used to mean "the proclamation of the good news to the non-Christian world," but now *mission* is held to be any activity of the church which God desires. Theologians say the mission is God's, not the church's, hence anything God wants done, anything God is doing, is part of His mission and therefore part of the mission of the church. This is a very wide mandate. The church-in-mission becomes the church-in-motion. American Christians sending their sons and daughters off to summer camp, winning their neighbors to Christ over a cup of coffee, or conducting a sit-in in favor of school integration are said to be "in mission."

As soon as this definition is accepted, the foreign missionary society is seen to be engaged in, not foreign missions (which may fold up) but God's mission everywhere, at home and abroad (which will never fold up). This new identity is pressed upon the missionary societies by some of their leaders.

3. The deviant theological positions, so well described by Dr. Beyerhaus in his significant chapter, require a very different kind of activity—I will not call it mission. They substitute humanization for mission. Once this theology and these goals are accepted by those in control of the society, a full-blown crisis of identity occurs. The old precious emotion-laden words are used—mission, evangelism, conversion, salvation—but with radically new meanings. The plane of missions has been hijacked. It looks like the old plane on its routine flight to Jerusalem, but it really is something new—a plane going to Havana.

4. Younger churches have helped create the confusion over the function of missionary societies. Some younger church leaders have resented their countries being the subjects of mission. It was time, they said, to end mission from the white churches of the West to the brown churches of Africasia. Mission must be defined in much broader and truer terms. Mission must be something which Africasia churches could do in sinful Eurica as well as what Eurican churches could do in sinful Africasia. *Mission must be mission in all six continents.* Helping older churches as well as helping younger churches is to be considered mission. From this new angle, *mission* ceases being gospel proclamation to non-Christians and becomes inter-church aid or good work done anywhere.

5. The missionary society becomes "The *Whole Church* in Mission." In the beginning, the missionary society knew very well that it was not the whole denomination and did not speak for it. It was a special agency. Often the denomination opposed it and accused it of siphoning off resources needed at home.

With the passage of the years, however, missionary societies became more and more powerful. Some became the most powerful organizations of their denominations. Each began to think of itself as *the* organization which spoke for the denomination in all matters concerning foreign mission.

6. Finally, the denominational society conducting missions in many lands became "a division of the denomination carrying on world mission." It now had a secure income—often in the millions, a competent staff whose task involved looking at ecclesiastical matters from a global point of view, and a new mandate arising out of the new concept of "the mission of God." It began asking questions like these: What is the mission of God for our great church? In the largest possible sense, what has God called us to do? What is the plan so comprehensive that it takes into account all activities which God wants done in this rapidly changing world? What should our whole church be doing in view of the hunger to come? What in view of the illiterate billions? What in view of racial tensions in North America? And revolutions in South America? Parochial North American concerns often outweighed those abroad, and empty stomachs seemed more terrible than empty souls.

THE DENOMINATIONAL MISSIONARY SOCIETY BECOMES THE CHURCH

In short, the denominational missionary society, which in the beginning had thought of itself solely as an agency for the proclamation of the gospel and the discipling of the nations, suddenly saw dangling within its reach a new identity: "The Church Carrying Out Its Worldwide Mission." Denominational societies have been particularly susceptible to this trend of thinking. They have the men and the resources. They have been getting rid of the connotation "foreign missions." They have been obtaining their funds not from "missionary" offerings, but from that portion of each congregation's income which is set apart for "outreach," a secular word covering everything any church might consider the mission of God. "The Church Carrying Out Mission"—this is the new identity of the missionary society which some leaders are strongly advocating.

WHERE HAS PROCLAMATION OF THE GOSPEL GONE?

In the confusion in identities just recounted, proclaiming the good news and "discipling the two billions who have yet to believe" have often been relegated to the background. In a few cases they have disappeared from view.

The church in the 1970s, like the church in every age, has many urgent and good things to do. As soon as the foreign missionary society assumes its new identity, it believes that its God-given duty is to do *all of these*. If William Carey were to stand before some modern denominational missionary societies, pleading for them to send evangelistic missionaries to faraway Bengal, they might in utter good faith reply, "The mission of God is far wider than the evangelization of those few million Bengalis. Urgent social and humanitarian needs at home and abroad must be met first, and then, if there is anything left, we shall consider your plea."

Christians, who supposed that missionary societies existed in order to preach the gospel and bring the nations to faith in Jesus Christ, suddenly find that their society has transformed itself into an agency of the mission of God, and is concerned with "many urgent duties." Preaching the gospel is—to it— only one small part of the whole. In some denominations if a Christian in some local church gives a hundred dollars to "our world mission," he can be certain that less than twenty dollars will get out of the United States, and less than two dollars will go into any kind of preaching of the gospel with intent to persuade men to become disciples of Christ.

As Pierce Beaver has pointed out, missions have become a vast system of inter-church aid and, he might had added, of general philanthropy. If Christians in the denominations wish to give to the conversion of the non-Christian world, they have to do one of two things:

1. Give designated gifts through their own church's mission society, spelling out exactly that they want this five dollars or that thousand to go "over and above the general budget to such and such a piece of church-planting evangelism."

2. Give through interdenominational or faith missions, dedicated to carrying out the Great Commission. The search for a new identity on the part of the denominational missionary societies has been paralleled by the growth of numerous interdenominational or faith missionary societies which have addressed themselves strictly to the preaching of the gospel and the multiplying of churches.

Denominational missionary societies, of course, since they have a hundred-year head start and have large affiliated Afericasian churches, are through them doing a respectable amount of church-planting. In fact, they can truly claim to be doing more church-planting than the missionary societies specifically dedicated to propagating the gospel. But the claim must be understood. They may *get* more church growth, but they are scarcely aiming at it. Indeed, many of their spokesmen go out of their way—as the Uppsala guidelines for mission in the seventies so clearly show—to define the program of mission in nonevangelistic terms. (See the minutes of the University Seminar on Mission quoted by Dr. Beyerhaus in chapter 2.) To some denominational missionary societies, in their new identity as "The Church Carrying Out Its Worldwide Mission," gospel proclamation and church growth are minor objectives.

INTERDENOMINATIONAL AND FAITH MISSIONS

Interdenominational and faith missionary societies also, which have demonstrated such an amazing growth during the past fifty years, while theoretically devoted to carrying out the Great Commission, often in practice have become as institutional and evangelistically ineffective as the denominational agencies. One typical conservative missionary society with a roster of about 150 missionaries engages most of them in orphanage, hospital, school, seminary, and other institutional tasks. The society talks as if its supreme goal were evangelism and church-planting, but the total membership of its affiliated congregations overseas is less than five thousand. Less than a third of its missionaries could be called evangelists in any sense and less than a tenth, church planters. Conservative missionary societies staunchly maintain that they have an overriding interest in evangelism, but they seem quite happy to carry it on in resistant populations and by methods which add few to the Lord. Dr. George Peters has been calling this fact to the attention of the missions world.

RETURN TO BIBLICAL MISSIONS?

I believe these confusions of identity among both old-line and new-line societies are temporary. In the rampaging flood in which we carry on Christian mission, so many changes have happened so fast, and so many adjustments are demanded, that most missionary societies which have deviated from their central goal have been *scarcely aware of it*. At least this is the way it seems to me in the 1970s.

It does not seem so to some of my friends. They maintain that the deviations of some denominational boards are permanent and due to theological latitudinarianism. "When you cease to hold that the Bible is God's infallible Word, belief on Jesus Christ is necessary for salvation, man is an immortal soul, and 'no man comes to the Father but by me'," they ask, "how can you carry on Great Commission mission? You will, naturally, continue philanthropic mission and humane assistance of your fellowmen on the physical plane. Even Gentiles do the same. But conversion mission will be forever beyond you."

When I listen to avant-garde spokesmen of some old-line denominations, the argument of these conservative friends of mine sounds convincing. But when I listen to other spokes-men of the old-line denominations, I discern rock-ribbed theological conviction. Furthermore, the unhappy fact that the conservative boards so frequently appear content to "carry on splendid mission work whether the gospel is, in fact, com-municated or not" must be held steadily in view as we decide whether the shift in identity is temporary or permanent.

The next ten years will be revealing. I hope old-line denom-inations will swing back to that which they had done faith-fully for so many years—carry on a vast program of church-planting together with a vast program of service. I hope they will begin again to meet men's need for life in Christ as well as men's need for loaves, fishes and social reconstruction. I do not infer that these should be assigned equal efforts. In-deed, the proportion between reconciling men to God and feeding them wheat bread or graduating them from the eighth grade is one which must be determined in each piece of the human mosaic at a particular point of time. The proportion needed in Harlem in 1970 is not that which was needed there in 1870.

I also hope that interdenominational and faith missions will resolutely bring their practice into line with their beliefs. With a theology like theirs, they ought to be greatly used of God to multiply churches.

LIBERATION OF MULTITUDES

The decades immediately before us are rich with promise that great populations will turn to Christian faith from ma-terialism, animism, and nominal membership in the ethnic religions and be liberated from old bonds. Dr. Barrett's pro-jection concerning Africa, originally published in the *Church Growth Bulletin* for May, 1969, and now widely copied in the religious and secular press, affirms that by the year 2000 there will be 357 million Christians in Africa. In Indonesia over 100,000 Muslims have turned to Christ in the last five years, and with them, 300,000 animists. In Taiwan, which had a Christian population of 30,000 in 1946, there are now 750,000 Christians. The church in Korea more than doubled between 1953 and 1963. In Latin America the enormous increase of evangelical churches shows no sign of leveling off. Great campaigns of evangelism—so well described by Dr. George Peters in chapter 10, and increasingly willing to measure themselves by the number of responsible Christians added to the church—are being seen on every hand. Even the absorption of some churchmen and some missions in the social, physical and intellectual improvement of mankind helps create a climate in which faith in Christ can multiply.

In these coming decades we shall see (1) whether the denominational societies (so often representing the interests of whole churches) *can* swing back unashamedly and enthusiastically to proclaiming Christ and multiplying His churches in receptive populations; and (2) whether the interdenominational and faith missions will go through that agonizing transformation of existing patterns of action so desperately needed. The goal of both should be to secure a proclamation of the gospel so biblical and so suited to each separate population that it is believed, men are baptized, and new churches multiply.

Denominational societies (in the face of their budget distributions and proclamations made by their most vocal leaders) can no longer assume that "of course we are concerned in church-planting." To be credible, they must demonstrate it. Interdenominational societies—in the face of miniscule growth of so many of their churches abroad and their unwitting drift to institutionalism—can no longer assume that it is sufficient for them to point to their own impeccable statements of theology. *They must find ways to evangelize effectively.*

In the meantime, the two billion who have yet to believe are living and dying without hearing of Jesus Christ. This cannot be God's will. He who sent Paul to the Gentiles, Judson to Burma, Patrick to the Irish, Morrison to China, Fraser to the Lisu, and Livingstone to Africa will—we believe—do two things: (1) raise up new agencies of evangelism which are sure of their identity as *missionary* societies; and (2) reform old agencies (both conservative and liberal) till they devote an adequate share of their resources to giving starving multitudes a chance to eat the bread of heaven and drink the water of life.

Possibly the word *missionary* will be so effectively captured by the whole-church organizations that it will cease to mean "those dedicated to the evangelization of the unbelieving world." If so, God's obedient servants, both old-line and new-line, will create organizations dedicated to the advancement of the gospel and give these another name. Under whatever name, the task will go on. Under whatever aegis, the discipling of the nations and the reconciling of men to God will continue. If the present denominations and interdenominational societies default, God can raise up true and evangelizing agencies and churches from the very stones.

But why talk of default? We all must fervently pray (1) that the old missionary societies so abundantly blessed with resources given by Christians for the evangelization of the world, will make sure that an honest proportion of their income, missionaries and national colleagues are devoted to conversion evangelism, to a "multiplication of cells of the redeemed" in every tongue and kindred, every tribe and nation; and (2) that the interdenominational and faith missions, remembering that they are *missionary* societies, will study their fields to find out where the Spirit of God is turning multitudes to responsiveness, and will renovate their methods and train their missionaries so effectively that the disease of slow growth which afflicts some of them may be cured and they may be the means under God of bringing population after population out of bondage into the promised land.

LIFE-GIVING MISSIONS

One of the crucial issues in tomorrow's missions is precisely this crisis of identity being experienced by missionary societies. The question is: Will they continue to see themselves as *missionary* societies? Will a chief and irreplaceable purpose of theirs be "so to present Jesus Christ in the power of the Holy Spirit that men shall come to put their trust in God through Him, to accept Him as their Saviour from the guilt and power of sin, to serve Him as Lord in the fellowship of the church, and to follow Him in the vocations of the common life"? This classic definition of evangelism—emphasizing the new life in Christ—originated in the Archbishop's Commission on Evangelism and after World War II was printed in the book, *Toward the Conversion of England*. Later it was slightly modified to the above form and adopted by the National Council of Churches of Christ in the United States of America and many other church and mission bodies. Charles Templeton, who had been Secretary for Evangelism of the NCCC, quotes it in his *Evangelism for Tomorrow*.[1] One must presume that till 1957 it was the definition of evangelism accepted by the National Council.

This kind of evangelism has been the way practically all missions, till about 1960, have understood their main task. Evangelism was their reason for being. Evangelism was what God sent them out to do. If missionaries went out as physicians or nurses, they understood that medicine was a way of presenting Jesus Christ which would help men to put their trust in God through Him. If they went out as educationists, they believed that through mission schools an influential segment of the community would come to accept Jesus Christ as its Saviour from the guilt and power of sin. If they went out as specialists of any kind, they hoped their specialties would help men serve Jesus Christ as Lord in the fellowship of His church.

Discipling has been "a chief and irreplaceable" purpose of Christian mission, and many missions have held that it has been "the supreme and controlling purpose." It has never, however, been the sole purpose, for it has always been accompanied by *multitudinous good works*. Missions and missionaries have always ministered to the whole man. William Carey brought into India various beneficial plants and trees. Mahogany was unknown in India; he introduced it. One of my prized possessions is a paperweight made from a mahogany tree he planted in Serampore. A missionary introduced vaccination to Thailand, and in many lands missionaries built the first girls' schools and leprosy homes. The first longings for land distribution, democratic government, and freedom from serfdom were generated in Christian hearts by the beneficent operation of the Holy Spirit. I need not labor the point. Like their Master, missionaries and missions have gone about doing good. Any scanning of mission budgets will reveal that varying proportions (but usually much more than half) have regularly gone to good works, nation-building activities, humanitarian labors, rural reconstruction, health services, educational institutions and the like. Evangelism, while it remained "a chief and irreplaceable purpose," has never been narrowly conceived.

Nor today is anyone calling on missionary societies to do evangelism and nothing else. The call, rather, is to make sure that, in the plethora of desirable good deeds, evangelism *is not crowded out. In every genuine missionary agency, evangelism should continue "a chief and irreplaceable part" of the total action.*

WHAT WILL YOU BE?

This crucial issue in tomorrow's missions comes before all branches of the church—Pentecostals and Roman Catholics,

large churches and small, Africasian and Eurican denominations, rich and poor, light-skinned and dark-skinned, denominational and interdenominational missions, older churches and younger churches, evangelistic missionaries and spe-
cialist missionaries—all must decide whether their missions
are to be *missionary* missions or humanitarian missions. "Are
we a missionary society or a general purpose society doing
many good deeds?" they all must ask.

To answer this crucial question intelligently, the society
should have before it the following data:

1. The statement of purpose in its constitution
2. An accurate record of the growth of the churches it has
   been planting
3. A twenty-year graph of the proportions of resources
   (men and money) going into church-planting evangelism, good works, administration and public relations
4. A reliable survey showing the general receptivity to the
   gospel of the population in which the society carries on
   work
5. An honest evaluation of the effectiveness of the systems
   of missionary training now used

The missionary society should answer the crucial question,
both by itself and in company with the younger church it is
assisting.

That church needs to face the issue just as frankly as the
missionary society. Does it demand that the missionary society furnish it rich services—or does it ask that the society
multiply churches among those who do not "know Him in the
power of His resurrection"? Is the younger church desirous
of partnership primarily because "younger churches should
be masters in their own countries"—or primarily in order
that there may be maximum reconciliation of men to God in
the church of Christ? This crucial issue of what mission essentially is will confront the younger churches in questions
such as the above.

Missionary societies of the younger churches also face this same crisis of identity. With the present climate of opinion, the political pressures which are being and will be brought on all openly evangelistic enterprises, and the active propaganda among Africasian churches carried on by some who redefine *mission* to mean *humanization,* it can no longer be assumed that the missionary societies of younger churches will "of course" engage in Asian or African evangelism. Missions of Africasian churches are tempted to think of mission, not in New Testament terms, but in terms of the heavy institutionalization so common in Eurican missions. Missionary societies formed by the devout in the churches of Asia, Africa and Latin America should make sure that their goal remains that men accept Christ as their Saviour from the guilt and power of sin. They should constantly review their *modus operandi* and budget distribution to make sure that, among the many good things which they do, the discipling of *ta ethne* is adequately emphasized.

In this crucial issue in missions tomorrow, the outcome devoutly to be desired is that increasingly all missionary societies, from all branches of the church of Jesus Christ, from all cultures and countries, keep steadily in mind that missionary societies, to earn the right to the name, must communicate faith in Jesus Christ. To be faithful stewards of God's grace, they must—in responsive populations—lead multitudes to serve Jesus as Lord in the fellowship of His church and to follow Him in the vocations of the common life.

Notes

1. Charles Templeton, *Evangelism for Tomorrow* (New York: Harper, 1957).

10

GREAT-CAMPAIGN EVANGELISM

by
GEORGE W. PETERS

THE NEW TESTAMENT abounds with illustrations of evangelism. I am not exaggerating if I state that the New Testament is basically a book about evangelism, for its content is the evangel—the gospel of God, the good news for man. The main characters of the New Testament—John the Baptist, Jesus of Nazareth, and the apostles Peter, John and Paul— are all evangelists, expounders and heralds of the evangel. The gospels and the book of Acts are the records of the activities and movements of the evangelists, and the epistles are the result of the follow-through and concerns and ministries of these evangelists. Evangelism is thus imbedded in the New Testament.

PRESUPPOSITIONS

This chapter concerns itself not with the message or messenger of evangelism, but with one specific method—great-campaign evangelism.

I presuppose that the message in evangelism is the gospel of God as recorded in the Bible unencumbered by cultural accretions and credal wrappings. It is Christ Jesus, our Lord in His humanity-deity mystery and His death-resurrection reality, His saviorhood and lordship in biblical fullness and biblical order. To the objective aspect of the salvation of God, the subjective aspect of repentance and faith must be properly related and proclaimed. Only repentance and faith relate man personally and savingly to the Christ who completed the work of salvation.

I presuppose that the messenger in evangelism knows himself personally related to Christ as Saviour, lives in humble submission to Him as Lord, and draws from the indwelling Christ his life, joy and strength. I assume that he knows himself indwelt by the Holy Spirit, possessed by Him and qualified by Him for his ministry. He is a man of God with the message of God for such a time as this and for the people to whom he goes to minister.

The message and the messenger can be biblically and dogmatically defined in detail and with precision, but this is not so with the method. There is only *one gospel* but many methods. The gospel is absolute, final, complete, perfect; *it is revelation given*. Not so the methods; they are conditioned by time, culture and psychology. Methods are relative. *They are people-related*. The Bible, therefore, does not lay down absolute patterns in methods.

Because of this, a method which may be very effective at one time, at one place, and among one people may be ineffective at another time, another place, and with another people. In fact, it may prove disadvantageous if not disastrous. Therefore, a method-bound movement cannot become an effective world movement. Neither can it last long; it will soon be relegated to the outdated and the outworn. We do not need renewal of the gospel, but we do need continuous renewal of methodology to communicate the age-old gospel in an intelligible, meaningful and purposeful manner.

Methodology must also be distinguished from abiding principles in evangelism. The gospel must be orally communicated, the gospel must be demonstrated in life and action, the gospel appeal must be made personal, it must be made intelligible, meaningful, attractive, persuasive and inviting. Man must be confronted; gospel communication must be preaching and speaking for a verdict. These are principles of gospel communication. They are qualities of communication and are biblically constant.

BIBLICAL FOUNDATION

Great-campaign evangelism does not lack New Testament support. Whether we term the ministry of John the Baptist *revivalism* or *evangelism* matters little. The fact is that he spoke to vast multitudes of people. We read of him as he preached in the wilderness of Judaea: "Then went out to him Jerusalem, and all Judaea and all the region round about Jordan, and were baptized of him in Jordan, confessing their sins" (Mt 3:5-6). Similarly Mark reports: "And there went out unto him all the land of Judaea and they of Jerusalem" (1:5). Luke says multitudes came to be baptized (3:7). John's great-campaign evangelism resulted in mass conversions and baptisms.

Though it cannot be asserted that great-campaign evangelism constituted a major method in the ministry of our Lord, it cannot be disputed that He proclaimed the kingdom of God to great multitudes.

Matthew is emphatic that great crowds (plural) from Galilee, Decapolis, Jerusalem, Judaea and beyond Jordan followed Him. And when He saw the crowds (plural) He went up into a mountain and taught (Mt 4:25; 5:1). It was in the presence of these crowds that Christ uttered the memorable words recorded in the Sermon on the Mount in Matthew 5—7.

It was to "many crowds" that His words in the unparalleled parables in Matthew 13 were addressed. The crowd of five thousand men (besides women and children, Mt 14:21), and again, the four thousand men whom Jesus fed, had been

His attendants at His great-campaign evangelism gatherings. Similarly, His message on the bread of life recorded in John 6 was spoken to a "great multitude" (v. 2).

We may well reason that these were typical incidents in the wonderful public ministry of our Lord. Christ accepted great-campaign evangelism as a practicable method for effective gospel communication.

Tracing the steps of Peter and Paul, we find that neither was apathetic to or critical of great-campaign evangelism. Though no one of the apostles is recorded to have majored in this method, neither did any shy away from it. In fact, Peter engaged in great-campaign evangelism on the day of Pentecost and sanctified the method for times to come.

Paul mastered it as one of his methods and addressed the multitudes with the gospel in Damascus, Jerusalem, Antioch, Iconium, Derbe, Thessalonica, Athens and Ephesus (Ac 9:22, 29; 13:44, 49; 14:4, 21; 17:4, 17, 22-32; 19:10, 20, 26). Such is the New Testament record.

DEDUCTIONS FROM NEW TESTAMENT RECORDS

From this brief survey of the New Testament records I deduce several principles:

1. Great-campaign evangelism finds biblical sanction and is well illustrated in the life of John the Baptist, Jesus our Lord, Peter and Paul.

2. Great-campaign evangelism in the Bible was effectively used in various cultures and among different people:

John the Baptist in Judaea

Jesus Christ in Galilee, Samaria, Decapolis

Philip in Samaria

Peter in Jerusalem, preaching to Jews and proselytes from among many different nations

Paul in Pisidia in Antioch among the Galatians (Europeans) and in Ephesus among a people strongly influenced by Hellenism and mysticism, and in Athens among the philosophers and intellectuals

3. Great-campaign evangelism was the methodological fountain which gave birth to the church of Jesus Christ, and it is a method which throughout the centuries has characterized dynamic churches which live close to and operate in the spirit of the fountain of Pentecost. Its neglect has always been a sure symptom of spiritual anemia, lost vision, lack of concern for and deep faith in the gospel of Jesus Christ. Neglect has almost always resulted in diminishing vitality, moralistic or institutional self-preservation, or legalistic paralysis.

4. Great-campaign evangelism was not the only method used in biblical times. In fact, it is doubtful whether it was a major method. History seems to indicate that personal, household and small-group evangelism were the prevalent methods, or at least soon became such. This may have been because of their general effectiveness, or their suitability to the lay movement which characterized early Christianity, or because of the severe persecutions of the times. However, great-campaign evangelism died only when the church became stale and static.

GREAT-CAMPAIGN EVANGELISM IN MODERN TIMES

Great-campaign evangelism was revived in the Christian church through John Wesley and George Whitfield. The latter transplanted it to America, where it soon became a part of the life of the church of Jesus Christ. While great-campaign evangelism has had its ebb and flow, modern history has witnessed at least four crests of it. One came under Wesley and Whitfield, another under Charles Finney, a third was experienced under the preaching of Dwight L. Moody, and the fourth has come in our times under the leadership of Dr. Billy Graham. Numerous other men have made significant contributions; we cannot begin to list them all, and only God knows the service the "average" evangelist has rendered to the cause of Jesus Christ.

In the countries around the world, none have made greater contributions to great-campaign evangelism than Billy Graham and his associates; the Foreign Mission Board of the Southern Baptist Convention, Richmond, Virginia; and the Foreign Missions Department of the General Council of the Assemblies of God, Springfield, Missouri. Evangelism-in-Depth and New Life for All are in other areas than great-campaign evangelism. Overseas Crusades, African Enterprise, Asian Evangelist's Commission, and the movement under the leadership of Bakht Singh of India must be mentioned as other instances of great-campaign evangelism in the fields around the world.

The Graham crusades have awakened interest and opened the eyes of Christians to the potential of great-campaign evangelism. This was particularly so in Europe, Asia and Latin America.

The Graham campaign in London in 1954 and his several crusades on the Continent in that same year became the turning point in the prospects of evangelism in the churches of Christendom. No less was the impact and response to his several visits to countries in Latin America and Asia.

The Southern Baptists are known for their "simultaneous evangelistic campaigns" in the United States of America. This pattern has been exported and practiced with good results. Joseph B. Underwood, Foreign Mission Board Consultant in Evangelism and Church Development, writes, in *The Commission*:

> For years the Board has sought to supplement and accelerate its regular missions program by cooperation in extraordinary evangelistic campaigns and by special projects in stewardship and religious education.
>
> What was perhaps the first simultaneous evangelistic campaign outside the United States was held in 1950 by thirty-seven Baptist churches of Recife, Brazil. The blessings were so numerous and far-reaching that Baptist church-

es there and elsewhere in the state of Pernambuco have continued such crusades annually with increasing effectiveness.[1]

Impressive Baptist programs in great-campaign evangelism were carried out in Japan in 1963, in Brazil in 1964-65, and the Crusade of the Americas in 1969.

The Assemblies of God have developed a program of great-campaign evangelism known at present as Good News Crusades. The program had its inception in 1958 as "Global Conquests," but due to imperial overtones, the name was later changed to Good News Crusades. It has a three-dimensional emphasis:

training of national leadership

providing literature for evangelism

conducting special evangelistic crusades

Good News Crusades are sponsored by the missionaries and national churches, with substantial subsidies in money and at times in personnel from the Foreign Missions Department in Springfield, Missouri. The program is thoroughgoing. Gospel saturation by visitation, literature distribution, and radio releases precedes the campaign. All efforts culminate in a great-evangelistic campaign.

A plan has been projected that, if successfully completed, will bring a great-evangelism campaign of the Assemblies of God to every major city of the world within this decade. From six to eight cities per year are being penetrated with the gospel message, with multitudes of people being contacted and large crowds confronted with the offer and claims of Christ.

In 1970, campaigns were conducted in the following cities: Salisbury, Rhodesia; Djakarta, Indonesia; Mexico City, Mexico; Bahia Blanca, Argentina; Kinshasa, Congo; Teheran, Iran; Noumea, New Caledonia.

Great-campaign evangelism has become "big business" in the kingdom of God. They are making their impact upon churches, missions and whole cities.

GENERAL OBSERVATIONS

GREAT-CAMPAIGN EVANGELISM IS A SYMPTOM OF A NEW
PULSATION IN THE CHURCH OF JESUS CHRIST

As the church rises to greater heights and man beholds clearer vistas, greater things for God are dared and undertaken. Our times are experiencing unprecedented revival in evangelism. The year 1966 will be marked in history as a year when the ebb was turned into a flow and a new tidal wave of evangelism began to be formed.

The numerous congresses and conferences on evangelism are bearing results as evangelism organizations and campaigns are increasing in number and effectiveness. Africa and Asia are rising up in evangelism, and great plans are in the making to reach entire nations with the gospel of Jesus Christ. A new pulsation is being felt. A new wave is forming. A new cloud is rising on the horizon. A breath of fresh air is being felt in many churches. Sad to say, till 1971 it has mostly bypassed the establishment.

The great campaigns are exerting their influence while at the same time they are being borne along by the tide of evangelism rising in many churches and individual hearts.

GREAT-CAMPAIGN EVANGELISM IS RIDING THE CREST OF A
PSYCHOLOGICAL AND SOCIOLOGICAL MOOD IN MANY
PARTS OF THE WORLD

It is evident that we are living in an age of anticipation. Excitement and expectation, mass production and mass movements are characterizing our days. Mass rallies, parades, processions, protest marches, workers' demonstrations and student meetings have become a world phenomenon.

A new freedom of inquiry, the availability of information via mass media, and the stimulation of hope and anticipation by emotional advertising are significant components in modern life everywhere. All these factors combine in creating a psychological and sociological "mass mood"—an "anticipation mentality"—a "movement temper" which the church cannot afford to ignore. Somehow great-campaign evangelism fits into this situation and, if properly timed, prepared and conducted, may successfully ride the crest of the waves to the benefit of many people. Certainly politicians and other propagandists are capitalizing on this mood.

GREAT-CAMPAIGN EVANGELISM IS CONTRIBUTING MANY BENEFITS TO THE CHURCH OF JESUS CHRIST AND THE CAUSE OF THE LORD

Dr. Joseph B. Underwood reviews some fifteen years of great crusades in an article entitled "Crusades and Missions." After giving impressive statistical data, he says:

> Spectacular evangelistic victories, however, constitute only one of many benefits resulting from these extraordinary campaigns. . . .
>
> Baptist bodies have been strengthened. These triumphs have liberated them from previous feelings of smallness and impotency in confronting tremendous obstacles and non-Christian majorities. . . .
>
> A growing sense of solidarity has developed among Baptists—an increasing oneness of soul and spirit. Individual hearts have been cleansed of personal rivalries, jealousies, and resentments. Dissensions have been eliminated as pastors and churches united in a cooperative endeavor to evangelize their own country and to extend the Gospel's influence to other areas. . . .
>
> A deepened sense of stewardship responsibility and practice has resulted. The value of cooperation has been vividly demonstrated as united efforts among Baptists made possible a tremendous impact on masses of people previously deaf to the Gospel. . . .
>
> Baptists have gained new recognition and respect by presenting convert artists, outstanding laymen and preachers, and by using newspapers, radio, and television to commu-

nicate the Gospel and to enunciate Baptist principles and distinctives. . . .

Lay persons have been utilized in large numbers and in diverse responsibilities.

Somewhat later he writes:

Experience over more than fifteen years in many countries has repeatedly underlined the value of large-scale evangelistic crusades as vital supplements to the regular program of missions. They can reinforce and advance the total world missions program, but must be prepared for and perpetuated by the regular, continuing work of churches, pastors, and missionaries.

The Rev. Melvin Hodges, Secretary for Latin America for the Foreign Missions Department of the Assemblies of God, speaks of great-campaign evangelism as one of the four most significant factors in the rapid multiplication of the churches of his denomination.

I spent one week at the headquarters of the Baptist Convention of Japan in Tokyo just one year after the great-campaign evangelism endeavor in that country. I talked freely to various secretaries and men of responsibilities in the offices, all of whom admitted that they had gone into the program with considerable hesitation. All stated, however, that their church had come out of it triumphant, encouraged, and emboldened to evangelize. Baptists had been liberated from a minority complex and feelings of smallness and inability. A negative defensive church had been transformed into a positive church. An ingrown church had been converted into one with face turned toward the world.

At a joint evaluation meeting, the executive secretary summarized his feelings by stating that he believed the Baptist churches in Japan had been pushed forward by at least ten years because of the campaign. To this several men added that they felt his evaluation was too conservative and that they would make it at least fifteen years.

The executive secretary felt that the greatest benefits were twofold. First, the crusades had taught the Baptist pastors the value of evangelistic preaching and the art of making an altar call. Second, it had taught the laymen the value and art of personal witnessing. The great campaign had brought a spirit of joyful witness to the churches.

Such evaluations cannot be dismissed lightly. These men know the cost of campaigns and the work involved, and they are anxious to achieve goals and effect positive results in church growth. They want transformed lives and transformed communities. Are such being achieved?

Before me are the annual reports of the past fifteen years of the two societies most prominent in the great-campaign evangelism. The Baptists report from thirty-two countries, and the Assemblies of God from eighty-two. The reports show that the Baptists have more than doubled in practically every field in the last decade, while the Assemblies of God have increased threefold in the past decade. These figures relate only to "members added to their congregations"; the number of "additional believers" is considerable.

Revitalization, reeducation, redirection and rededication have come to many churches. It is to this fact that Dr. Underwood speaks when he says, "Baptist bodies have been strengthened. These triumphs have liberated them from previous feelings of smallness and impotency in confronting tremendous obstacles and non-Christian majorities."

Arno W. Enns, Executive Secretary for Latin America of the Conservative Baptists, in his significant church-growth book, *Man, Milieu and Mission in Argentina,* points out that the Hicks campaign of 1954 was of immense significance for the evangelical community of Argentina. This was especially so for the Assemblies of God and the Christian and Missionary Alliance, the two chief supporters of the campaign. Of the latter body, he writes:

The graph (Figure No. 3) indicates that in 1949 the membership of the Alliance churches, after fifty-four years of missionary occupation, stood at only 513. By 1960 total membership was 1379, showing a net growth of 168 percent. This is respectable growth for this span of eleven years. The momentum generated through the new spirit released by the Hicks campaign was probably the predominant reason for the expansion.[2]

As a direct result of the campaign, the Alliance organized three new churches. However, the pattern of stagnation was not completely overcome, and a serious relapse soon overtook the new impetus.

This was not so with the Assemblies of God, where church growth has continued unabated to the present. Arno Enns describes the impact of the campaign upon this church body:

The largest church before the campaign had a seating capacity of only 150, and special halls had to be rented to accommodate the new converts. Five new churches were begun in the year 1955 alone. Enrollment in the Bible Institute, which had always stood at about twelve to fifteen students, in two years jumped to between forty and fifty. These young men were to be the future leaders of the continually growing movement. . . . An intangible but nonetheless solid result of the campaign was a new spirit of faith and spiritual optimism which pervaded the entire Evangelical community, even beyond the limit of the officially cooperating Churches. Humble and fearful Christians were made aware of their latent potential which could be released in saving power through the exercise of faith. Among the population in general, prestige and appreciation of the Evangelical Churches increased noticeably.[3]

Similar stories could be written about Mexico, El Salvador, Nigeria, Congo and several other countries. The Good News Crusades are giving to the churches that new impetus, direction and dynamism that send them on their path to further campaigns of liberation.

GREAT-CAMPAIGN EVANGELISM IS MAKING A RELIGIOUS
AND MORAL IMPACT UPON THE COMMUNITY

Evangelism campaigns must not be evaluated only in terms
of converts and benefits coming to the churches. We must
also think in terms of a general ministry to the world. There
is a mission the church of Jesus Christ (as the salt of the
earth and the light of the world) owes to the world, regardless of conversions and increase in church membership. Large-
scale evangelism campaigns provide an opportunity to become God's spokesman to the world in a unique way and to
make an impact for good which is difficult to measure.

In such campaigns the church can confront the world with
the reality and presence of God in history. Here the church
reinforces in the world an awareness of God and heightens
a sense of moral responsibility. It proclaims that God is not
only the Saviour, but also the Judge and Governor of history
and the universe. In great-campaign evangelism the church
not only announces the gospel; it shouts its prophetic message
to the world. This is a most significant and scriptural ministry. The prophets of old not only voiced precious promises to
the nations surrounding Israel; they also spoke a judging
prophetic word to them. They fearlessly uncovered the sins
of the nations, boldly speaking to them of their responsibilities in the light of ethical monotheism and common human
relationships. They courageously reminded them of their moral
responsibilities in terms of cultural developments for the
welfare of their people, and they emphatically pronounced the
judgments of God upon them unless they mended their ways.
They acted as God's men and announced God's commands
for the world.

Today the church is disgracefully failing in this ministry.
For the authoritative voice of the prophet, the church has
substituted weak "involvement" in the confusion, and its
wordless "presence" in all types of activities and me-too welfare programs. None of these does what a clear prophetic

voice can do while speaking in the name of the Lord and in the power of the Holy Spirit. Because the church has lost the fear of God, it has become ensnared in the fear of man. We desperately need a revival of the prophetic voice, and great-campaign evangelism provides the church a dramatic opportunity to become the spokesman of God to the world in re-direction, reconciliation and conversion.

KEYS TO EFFECTIVENESS

GREAT-CAMPAIGN EVANGELISM MUST BE CONDUCTED OVER EXTENDED PERIODS

That great-campaign evangelism must be conducted over extended periods has been well established by such campaigns as those of Richard Jeffrey in Panama City which went on for nine months and left a strong, organized church behind. The electrifying Hicks campaign in Buenos Aires, Argentina, last-ed for fifty-two days and transformed many Christian churches. The Jeffrey campaign in San Salvador continued for seven-teen weeks. The Bernhard Johnson campaign of 1969 in Greater Rio de Janeiro lasted two years. First the 250 church-es of the Assemblies of God in the Greater Rio de Janeiro area conducted local campaigns with Brazilian evangelists. Then all the churches combined in the great Maracan Stadium services led by Bernhard Johnson.

All these campaigns made indelible impressions upon the churches, added multitudes to the membership, and were in-strumental in founding scores of new churches, branch churches and preaching centers. Also, they called forth scores of new workers for the churches and numerous candidates for the training institutions.

The Baptist crusade in Japan continued for six weeks and in Brazil for more than a year.

The fantastic expansion of the Assemblies of God in Korea (rising from 1,500 members and 550 additional believers in 1955 to 2,443 members and 8,000 additional believers in

1965, and 18,000 members and 9,000 additional believers in 1970) is due, almost totally, to continuous evangelism campaigns in the impressive Evangelistic Center in the heart of Seoul, in the churches in and about Seoul, and in cities where no Assemblies of God churches previously existed. Several tents are in continuous use. In the Evangelistic Center, which seats some 2,500 persons, three evangelistic services are conducted every Sunday and several evenings each week. The center itself, with a membership of over 5,000, continually feeds converts and members to the several churches in the city, at the same time attracting and holding for the Assemblies of God those members who move into Seoul from other cities and rural areas.

Extended services have a sound psychological basis which makes communication possible in the true and deep sense. Since great-campaign evangelism attracts many who have no gospel background, no intelligent confrontation or decision can take place during a brief encounter, for it takes time to penetrate and permeate such minds. The presentation-penetration-permeation-confrontation process is logically sound and must be used if results are to be genuine and lasting, all of which means campaigns lasting weeks or even months.

Because we do not take time, many "professions" made in great campaigns are not conversions. Rather, they are expressions of need, guilt, desire, aspiration, or identification with the religion of the evangelist. They are not even intelligent inquiries; they are admissions that all is not well. Thus they are usually a "starting point" but not a profession of faith. Such a "starting point," however, is of tremendous significance for the counselor, whose task it is to help the individual make an intelligent decision for Christ. To fail here is to fail fatally.

Extended campaigns have additional advantages. They provide time for the new converts during their initial glow to become accustomed to attending services. This is very important, especially for people who have never or seldom attended church services. We cannot neglect the psychology and sociology of man in religious matters. He remains a creature of habit, and Christian habits of worship must be stamped in.

An extended campaign also affords an opportunity in training classes for baptism and church membership in order to establish new converts. The Assemblies of God have practiced this with good results in several of their crusades.

In Panama City they gathered the new converts an hour before the general service each evening in indoctrination classes. When the campaign came to a close, more than three hundred persons had been prepared, baptized and bound together into a fellowship. Related patterns have been practiced elsewhere with satisfying benefits.

GREAT-CAMPAIGN EVANGELISM MUST BE CAREFULLY AND PRAYERFULLY PREPARED FOR

Preparation may be the major, though not the only, key to effectiveness.

The Baptists prepared for several years before they began their nationwide campaigns in Japan in 1963. As early as 1957 the Rev. W. H. Jackson, Jr., an extraordinary man, shared his burden for such a campaign in Japan with a group of missionaries. In 1960 Mr. Jackson became pastor of an English-speaking Baptist church in Tokyo and, together with his church, he labored and prayed for a Japan-wide evangelistic crusade. When the Baptist General Convention in 1961 declined to accept the challenge, the Baptist Convention of Texas declared itself ready to underwrite the campaign, providing a budget of between $600,000 and $700,000. In addition, more than 600 American ministers and lay Christians paid their own expenses in 1963 to cross the ocean and assist in the campaign.

Approximately $200,000 went into publicity which was effectively handled by Detsu Advertising Company of Tokyo.

Literature, large billboards, the press, radio and television were utilized to draw the attention of the public to the coming great event.

The publicity was greatly enhanced during the time of the campaign by the appearance of many famous Christians from America such as Don Demeter of the Philadelphia Phillies and Bobby Richardson of the New York Yankees, who proved magnetic in baseball-loving Japan. They attracted the attention of the masses by radio, television, and extensive press coverage as they gave their testimony of their meaningful life since Jesus had become their personal Saviour and Lord.

The Cowboy Band from Texas was very popular, astonishing the crowds who for the first time saw cowboys with Bibles instead of pistols. The band participated in forty-one parades, fifteen evangelistic services, nineteen concerts, and twenty-eight other meetings.

The extensive publicity was equaled by fervent, widespread prayer which was offered that the unsaved and the Christians alike would look to God for a great harvest of souls.*

Southern Baptist Convention president Herschel Hobbs called on 32,000 Southern Baptist churches in the United States to conduct a special prayer meeting for the Asia crusade on Wednesday, March 27, 1963. The Japanese churches conducted early-morning prayer meetings for months in preparation for the thrust.

No less intensive but very much less expensive are the preparations by the Assemblies of God for their Good News Crusades. Their major method, besides much and fervent

---

* This extraordinary and expensive mode of evangelism was possible only because Japan has been a main mission field for the Southern Baptists, Mr. Jackson was a most able promoter, and the Japanese were very pro-American. If it startles readers, I would have them consider the hundreds of thousands of students who have attended plays put on by the Christian drama teams Biola College has sent to Asia. Enormous crowds also turn out for basketball games conducted by Overseas Crusades. A top-flight American team plays the champions of Djakarta, Manila, Hong Kong and other cities and, during half time and after the game, witnesses

prayer, is the distribution of specially designed gospel literature known as "Light for the Lost," which includes an invitation to the campaign. Such distribution is accompanied by door-to-door witnessing. In Panama City, 50,000 tracts and preparatory literature announced the coming of the campaign. In East Nigeria, 4 million pieces of literature were handed out in two years. In Santos, Brazil, 25,000 homes had been visited and 90,000 pieces of literature had been distributed prior to the campaign. In Niteroi, Brazil, 30,000 calls were made and 160,000 pieces of Light for the Lost literature were handed out before the crusade. In thousands of these homes the callers had also personally witnessed to their Saviour and Lord and prayed with the people.

Wherever possible, the local radio is utilized weeks and months in advance of the crusade, and newspaper space is widely used.

Perhaps the most thoroughgoing preparations for any great-campaign in evangelism were those carried out by the Billy Graham campaign in Tokyo in 1967. Too often "preparation" means organization, finances, and the spiritual vitality of the churches. None of these aspects can be neglected; however, *a social dimension* to great-campaign evangelism is often sadly neglected. Our Japanese brethren majored in social preparation, set a noble example, and carved a new pattern for others to follow.

Some 4 million homes were visited and gospel portions and other literature distributed. Each packet contained a stamped card on which anyone could express his desire for further information about Christianity. More than 40,000 cards were returned to the office, and more than 40,000 persons and families became the special objects in prayer. They were contacted several times before the campaign commenced,

to Christ and His power to save. Since the expenditure of a million dollars for an evangelistic campaign in one great American city is not exceptional, why should it be unwise to spend that much to touch an entire nation?

befriended by Christians, and introduced to the churches wherever possible and advisable. During the campaign they became guests of Christian families and churches and were encouraged to respond to altar calls. When some responded, Christian friends were there to accompany and encourage them.

A similar pattern was followed after the Graham campaign in order to assist the new converts in their Christian life and church affiliation. Thus, it is not surprising that more than 43 percent of all persons making professions could be found in the churches nine months after the meetings. The growth of churches in Japan is slow, and the membership of the churches affiliated with the Southern Baptists at the beginning of the campaign was about 16,000. Inspection of their steadily rising graph of growth four years later shows the campaign added at least a thousand to the church, causing marked upsurge in the line of growth in the year 1963-64. Growth continued steadily again in the years following. In 1968 the *World Christian Handbook* reported 18,279 full members.

GREAT-CAMPAIGN EVANGELISM MUST BE LAUNCHED BY
NATIONAL CHURCHES

Importations and impositions are not advisable in our day of deep and sensitive national feelings when cross-cultural, cross-racial, and cross-organizational tensions abound and strain Christian relationships to the limit. Very naturally also, churches will not cooperate enthusiastically unless the campaign is *theirs*.

The Brazil campaign (1964-68) was born in the heart of Dr. Ruben Lopez, pastor of the great Vila Mariana Baptist Church in Sao Paulo and president of the Brazilian Baptist Convention. Dr. Lopez enlisted a missionary, Dr. H. Earl Peacock, as crusade executive secretary. Drs. Lopez and Peacock, who gave themselves unsparingly to the cause and made the crusade a truly Brazilian endeavor, were successful in enlisting the 2,000 Baptist churches and 4,000 preaching points. A large percent of the finances was raised in Brazil, and most of the evangelists came from Brazilian churches. The Foreign Mission Board allocated between $300,000 and $400,000 for this campaign and sent some American evangelists to assist in special missions, such as the training of Brazilian workers for various ministries. As a whole, however, the campaign was conceived, planned, directed and manned by Brazilians.

The results are encouraging: 100,000 professions of faith; 43,552 baptisms; 300 new churches; 3,500 new preaching centers; and numerous dedications for special services. Above all, the campaign lifted the churches to a higher level and gave them a clearer vision. It convinced them of the possibilities and potential of aggressive evangelism.

Encouraged by the positive results, Dr. Ruben Lopez carried the challenge of evangelism to America. Appearing first before the Foreign Mission Board and later addressing in a letter the annual Baptist General Convention convening in Dallas, Texas, he became God's instrument in stimulating interest which eventually culminated in the "Crusade of the Americas" and now in the Baptist World Crusades. That which was begotten in Brazil is to spill over into the whole world.

GREAT-CAMPAIGN EVANGELISM MUST BE ORGANICALLY AND ORGANIZATIONALLY RELATED TO EXISTING LOCAL CHURCHES

True, in unchurched areas where the gospel is penetrating a new locale, evangelism has a right to stand by itself, to be carried on by a mission. Aside from such pioneer discipling, however, evangelism is basically and biblically a function of local churches. They are God's channels and instruments to evangelize their neighbors.

Because of the relationship between evangelism and local

churches, the Southern Baptists and the Assemblies of God have related great campaigns mainly to their own churches. To be sure, there have been exceptions. Tommy Hicks and Paul Finkenbinder, evangelists of the Assemblies of God, have conducted several large and successful campaigns on an inter-church basis.

"Going it alone" is not inspired by a spirit of separatism, but rather dictated by distinctive doctrines and working pro-grams. These two denominations feel strongly that great campaigns are more effective when done by one church. They see the following advantages in a one-church campaign:

1. It sets the evangelist at liberty to emphasize precious doctrines which, when speaking in interdenominational gatherings, he is bound not to preach. He can early begin a process of indoctrination of new believers for his own church.

2. It facilitates shepherding new converts. The denomina-tion feels more free and more responsible to follow up per-sons making professions of faith.

3. It facilitates the mobilization of the laity. In interde-nominational meetings, many laymen apparently hesitate to take a responsible part.

These denominations would not deny that interdenomina-tional campaigns can lead converts into local churches. Cer-tainly the interdenominational campaigns carried on by Graham in Tokyo, Hicks in Buenos Aires, and Finkenbinder in Lima were highly successful.

GREAT-CAMPAIGN EVANGELISM MUST MOBILIZE LOCAL
CHURCHES FOR AND IN THE CAMPAIGN

The principle of mobilization which has been much em-phasized in recent years is a sign of a return to biblical princi-ples in Christian ministries. It must be remembered that total mobilization is implied in the structure and function of the body in the priesthood of all believers, in the facts that all be-lievers have been baptized by the Holy Spirit, all are to be

His instruments, all are branches in the vine, all are to bear fruit, and finally, all are the church of Jesus Christ.

To the degree that a crusade succeeds in mobilizing the believers, the campaign will be of lasting value. Mobilization, though not the only factor, is tremendously significant.

CRUCIAL ISSUES IN GREAT-CAMPAIGN EVANGELISM

In the light of the above presentation, the reader may be surprised to hear of the concerns which creep over me as I study great-campaign evangelism around the world. I describe these not to discourage great campaigns but to alert us to certain built-in dangers. Whether these are averted or not is one of the crucial issues in missions tomorrow.

GREAT-CAMPAIGN EVANGELISM IS NOT THE ONLY METHOD

There are many good methods, some of them well illustrated in the Scriptures. Large-scale evangelistic crusades supplement the regular program of churches and missions. They can reinforce and advance the total program of world evangelization, but they are not substitutes for continuous evangelistic endeavors of local churches and for testimonies of believers in their regular relationships. There is simply no substitute for personal witnessing.

GREAT-CAMPAIGN EVANGELISM HAS LED FEW CHURCHES INTO LIFE RENEWAL AND WORK REVIVAL

Naturally the fact that great-campaign evangelism has led few churches into life renewal or work revival need not be the fault of the evangelistic team or campaign. However, the fact remains that most churches engage in campaign activities without becoming involved to the degree that the inner core of life is touched and transformed. Some, no doubt, are revitalized and renewed, but the majority remain untouched. Especially is this so in united, citywide campaigns.

GREAT-CAMPAIGN EVANGELISM QUICKLY BECOMES THE
"MENTALITY" AND LIFE PHILOSOPHY OF THE AVERAGE
CHURCH MEMBER

It is easy to condition a church to think of evangelism as "a special event" during the year. Evangelism thus becomes sporadic rather than spontaneous and continuous.

GREAT-CAMPAIGN EVANGELISM REACHES ONLY CERTAIN
STRATA OF SOCIETY

Only a certain strata of society is reached by this means of evangelism; others will not come no matter what is being done. A relatively small percentage come to any kind of "religious meetings," but the vast masses must be reached in other ways.

GREAT-CAMPAIGN EVANGELISM HAS NOT BEEN ABLE TO
RETAIN ITS GAINS

Such crusades in general are geared to bring people to the meetings, confront them with the offer and claims of Christ, and invite them to make a decision. Because crusades are not geared for aftercare, the loss of individuals who have stood before the altar and declared their sense of need and readiness is tragic. Some campaigns lose more than 90 percent— a grave shortcoming before God and man. Any campaign that does not retain at least 25 percent should deeply search its principles, method, motivation and message (Mt 13:3-9, 18-23). Retention from between 50 to 75 percent should constitute our goal. It should be possible, through tender and patient care, to assist multitudes who make decisions for Christ to overcome the "thorns," remove the "stones," and root themselves in the good soil, the source of life everlasting. Shepherding remains one of the major challenges of great-campaign evangelism, for putting the whole responsibility for loss on the churches is easy to do but not valid. The great campaign itself, with all its prestige, must learn how to get the sheep *into the fold.*

GREAT-CAMPAIGN EVANGELISM—THUS FAR—DISREGARDS
THE SOCIOCULTURAL MILIEU AND WEB OF RELATIONSHIP

There is no evidence that this type of evangelism has led to household, people, or community movements. Yet, it is these that have brought the vast majority of people into the kingdom of God and into the church of Jesus Christ.

The difficulty may not lie in the type of evangelism but rather in the fact that we Westerners tend to draw the individual into the church and away from his social relationships instead of using him as a door into the larger web of relationships. The individual would thus serve as a bridge to come with his kinsmen to the Lord. It must be remembered that people and community movements do not just happen but follow definite patterns of relationships, and such patterns can be built into evangelism.

The question arises: Is it possible for great-campaign evangelism to incorporate more and more sociological factors and thus serve even more dynamically? Why should it not be used by God to further people movements?

CONCLUSION

Great-campaign evangelism has solid biblical foundations and has been greatly used of God in the expansion of the church of Jesus Christ. Countless individuals have been brought into the kingdom of God by this method of evangelism. While it is not the only method, it is an important method and must not be permitted to become static. Honest evaluations and continuous study must accompany its course and assure its growth and development according to culture, time and people. Made more and more effective, it must continue a vital part of the program of the church of Jesus Christ to confront the world with the offer and claims of Jesus Christ our Lord and Saviour.

Notes

1. Joseph B. Underwood, article in *The Commission* (May 1965).
2. Arno W. Enns, *Man, Milieu and Mission in Argentina* (Grand Rapids: Eerdmans, 1971), p. 92.
3. Ibid., p. 79.

11

URBANIZATION AND MISSIONS

by
ROGER S. GREENWAY

"THE WORLD UPSURGE in urban populations is one of the most outstanding revolutions of the modern epoch."[1] As demographers, sociologists and economists everywhere are turning their attention to this phenomenon of urbanization, men concerned with missions must ask themselves what this means for the spread of the gospel. Missionary strategists cannot afford to ignore this worldwide movement to the cities.

Urbanization is one of the most important aspects of worldwide social change today. Changes are occurring with such unprecedented speed and with such far-reaching consequences that a constant reappraisal of missionary strategy is required. If the gears of missions are not shifted to keep up with social change, God-given opportunities for discipling the nations will be lost. This is unquestionably true with respect to the migration of the masses to the city. At the beginning of the twentieth century only about 13 percent of the world's population lived in the cities and 87 percent in rural areas. But by the end of the century the situation will be completely reversed. By then 87 percent of all people will reside in urban areas. Obviously the rural-orientated missionary patterns of past decades will be largely obsolete in the years ahead.

		Cities of 5,000 and over		Cities of 20,000 and over		Cities of 100,000 and over	
Year	World Popula-tion	City Popula-tion	Percent of World Population	City Popula-tion	Percent of World Population	City Popula-tion	Percent of World Population
1800	906	27.2	3.0	21.7	2.4	15.6	1.7
1850	1,171	74.9	6.4	50.4	4.3	27.5	2.3
1900	1,608	218.7	13.6	147.9	9.2	88.6	5.5
1950	2,400	716.7	29.8	502.2	20.9	313.7	13.1

Table 1
World's Urban Population Compared to World's Total
Population, 1800—1950 (Population figures given in millions.)

Source. United Nations, Economic and Social Council, Economic Commission for Latin America, Preliminary Study of the Demographic Situation in Latin America, E/CN. 12/604 (New York: United Nations, April 23, 1961), p. 31

THE WORLDWIDE PICTURE

ASIA

"The sheer rapidity of urban growth," says Paul Abrecht, "is one of the most astonishing and awesome aspects of the whole social change in Asia, Africa, and Latin America. It is both the cause and the effect of that change, and a measure of its depth."[2]

Asia's "teeming millions" are today, in increasing numbers, *urban* millions. Think for a moment of the great urban centers located in the Asian-Pacific area:

Karachi	3 million
Calcutta	5 million
Bangkok	2½ million
Saigon	1½ million
Puson	1½ million
Seoul	4 million
Tokyo	11 million
Osaka	3 million
Yokohama	2 million
Nagoya	2 million
Manila Gr.	3 million
Singapore	2 million
Sidney	2½ million
Djakarta	3 million

Metropolitan Tokyo is greater than half the population of Canada, and the first ten cities of India equal half the population of Britain. Our century began with only eleven cities with a population of over one million, but today there are more cities than that in Asia alone, which claim populations of more than a million.

A glance at any newspaper will tell you that the decisions which make the headlines regarding Asia and the Far East are made in their cities. The centers of political power, education, and mass media invariably are located in the cities. Christian leaders need to take these facts into account as they consider what strategy they should follow in world missions during the last third of this century. The decisive battles for the souls of men will be fought not in the jungles, or the mountains, but in the teeming cities.

AFRICA

The worldwide trend toward an urban culture, writes John Dilworth, is sweeping over the vast continent of Africa. "The city has become the focal point attracting hundreds of thousands of young people into its orbit, and its neon lights and technological wonders fascinate whole populations, even where the majority still live in the villages. The number of city dwellers [in Africa] increases literally daily."[3] Christian missions, however, tend to concentrate their efforts on the traditional rural population which has been thought to be more receptive to Christianity. There is something irrational about this, for the educational activities of Christian missions have been one of the major factors in the orientation of young people toward city life. Young people in Africa were first introduced to urban ways in the Christian schools, but when they reached the city they were left "high and dry" as far as the church is concerned. Missionaries have been slow to realize the challenge of African cities. This area of the world is a prime example of the rural orientation of Christian mission work.

Writing about urbanization in West Africa, Kenneth Little states that

> in the last twenty years the population of Nigeria has increased at an estimated rate of 1.5 per cent annually and with the control of epidemic diseases and improvement in maternity and child welfare, this trend should continue. However, so far as urbanization is concerned, the census figures leave no doubt that migration is the principal factor. Thus, no less than 58 per cent of the population of Lagos consisted in 1950 of people born elsewhere, while from figures provided in the Ghana census (1960) it may be estimated that only 25 per cent of the population of the city of Takoradi, about 40 per cent of the population of Sekondi, some 37 per cent of the population of Kumasi, and some 47 per cent of the population of Accra are of local origin. In 1948, over one-half the population of Takoradi and 36 per cent in the case of Accra had lived in those towns for less than five years. While in Ghana, as a whole, more than two-thirds of the urban inhabitants have been in the towns concerned for less than five years.[4]

Of significance for Christian evangelism is Little's comment that rural-urban migration creates a far-reaching network of social and other ties between the town and the hinterland. When people move from the farm to the city it does not necessarily mean a permanent separation between them and their kinfolk who have stayed behind. On the contrary, there is a constant coming and going of visiting relatives, traders, seasonal workers, and others, and this keeps the lines of communication open between the urban migrants and their rural kin. This means that new ideas and practices, including new religious beliefs acquired by the newcomers to the city, are transmitted to the countryside. In Africa, as everywhere else, towns and cities set the pace for society as a whole, and ideas and movements which have their base in the urban center quickly diffuse themselves over a much wider area.

LATIN AMERICA

Missionary leaders involved in Latin America should take careful note of what has been happening in that part of the world. "Latin America," writes Benjamin Higgins, "is more urbanized than the world as a whole. The proportion of the urban population was 39 per cent in 1950 and 46 per cent in 1960. During the 1950's the absolute increase in Latin America's urban population seems to have been about double the increase in the rural population."[5] In another recent study, the *Centro Lationamericano de Demagrafia* (CELADE) estimated that 51 percent of the population of Latin America is presently found in the urban areas, and that for 1975 an estimated 56.5 percent will be urban.

Another remarkable feature of the urban picture in Latin America is the fact that the urban population is often concentrated in one or two large cities, and the next towns in size are usually very much smaller. The large towns and cities, moreover, are growing faster than the small ones, with the result that the urban population structure in Latin America is "top-heavy" and tending to become more so every year. Most Latin countries are right now in the most dynamic and critical stage of the urbanization process. In one lifetime we are witnessing a colossal shift of population which will transform Latin America from a primarily rural to a primarily urban continent. What this means for Christian missions deserves most careful consideration.

OVERCOMING FRUSTRATION

By and large, Christian churches are not multiplying in the great cities of Asia, Africa and Latin America as they should be, or could be. Despite the volumes of literature being produced on the subject of urban ministry in the United

Crucial Issues in Missions Tomorrow

States of America, relatively little of it is useful as far as planting churches in non-Western cities is concerned. Studies are needed on how to evangelize urbanites so *that living churches eventuate and proliferate.* The literature on urban evangelism eminating from North America shows such overriding concern with urban social problems that it is not helpful in church-planting evangelism in Africasia. The impression is given that urban ministries everywhere can and should change urban structures. Social problems exist, to be sure, and American Christians—who are numerous and powerful in American cities—must face them squarely with all the resources at their disposal. But as we consider the Christian mission in the great urban centers of the Third World,—where evangelical Christians are very few—we should see that the task is first of all kerygmatic. Modern Ninevahs need to hear and obey the gospel, but first there must be some Christians!

An effective urban thrust, however, will require a large degree of openness and flexibility on the part of the evangelizing agency. The emerging urban expression of the church may startle some people. It may do away with some time-worn practices such as large, expensive buildings, somber organs and robed choirs. The emphasis may fall upon the neighborhood fellowship, informal Bible study, folk music and complete lack of clericalism. Jarring as some of the changes may be, they may more closely resemble the churches of Asia Minor in apostolic times than the sophisticated organizations we commonly call churches today. The crying need is for greater openness and sensitivity on the part of Third World churches as they seek to meet urban newcomers with their very pressing needs.

It is lamentable that precisely in this area the historic churches are especially weak. In his study of the African situation, John Dilworth reports that when new migrants "encountered loneliness and other difficulties in the city, they found little comfort in the orthodox Churches and turned for help to one or other of the Healing or 'spiritual' Churches. Here they find a more intimate sense of community, attention and special prayer and ceremonies are devoted to their individual problems!"[6] Dilworth is referring, of course, to the indigenous, Pentecostal-type of churches which account for the majority of urban Christian groups throughout the world. The Pentecostal forms of worship—with drumming, dancing and handclapping in Africa, and with guitars, wind instruments, and loud "Gloria al Señor" in Latin America—offer more release and relaxation to the troubled urban migrant than do the imported forms of worship of traditional denominations. Frustrated in their efforts to really reach the masses, many orthodox churches have settled for some form of social service through their established institutions and have left the multiplication of urban churches to the Pentecostals. The secretary for Latin America of one of the oldest and largest denominations said recently in Mexico City that except for the program which will be described later in this chapter, he did not know of a single church-planting enterprise being carried on by traditional denominations in Latin American cities. "Most churches," he said, "have written off the urban masses to the Pentecostals."

Credit should be given where credit is due, and in this case it goes to the Pentecostals who have indeed proven to be more responsive to the needs of new urbanites than have their older sister churches. The Pentecostalists have moved out among the receptive displaced masses with their simple message of the Christ who both saves and heals. They accept the slum dwellers where they are, with all their problems and frustrations, and provide them with a circle of religious fellowship where people count as individuals. Amid the whirlpool of urban life, the new urban immigrant discovers in the local Pentecostal church the face-to-face contact and sense of belonging which he can find nowhere else in the cold unfriendly city. The Pentecostal emphasis upon group prayer and divine healing touches some of his greatest personal needs. The unsophisticated sermons are rich in verbal symbols which convey the gospel to the unlettered far better than the high-toned rhetoric of the educated pulpit. Despite all their advantages, the traditional churches have not yet come close to matching the Pentecostals in their penetration of the urban masses.

The task of reaching the great cities for Christ need not, and should not, be left to the Pentecostals alone. "The clear implication," writes William L. Wonderley, "is that the church today has a responsibility, as never before in its history, to meet these culturally 'displaced persons' in their place of need and help them in their hour of transition to discover those values which alone can enable them to keep a sense of human dignity and to weather the storm of cultural change."[7] To do this, however, the traditional churches will have to move out of their middle-class shells and find out what the people on the fringes of urban society are really like. They will have to walk through the mud and the filth of their streets, climb their stairways, and sit in their homes. Amid the stench and the flies and the wailing children, they will learn what the needs and anxieties of these people are, and they will sense how the gospel can be made the most relevant thing in the world for their lives.

These things cannot be learned at a distance. Direct personal encounter with the realities of urban slums is required. Churches and missions with enough passion for souls to leap the cultural gap will discover a sea of humanity, weary and heavy laden, whom the Lord would have us call to His rest. If what God is doing in the world at large means anything to the church today, it should be clear that the phenomenon of urbanization is the work of God in preparing great multitudes of people for evangelization and the planting of tens of thousands of new churches.

MEXICO CITY EXPERIMENT

In January, 1968, an experiment began in the Mexico City area with teams of students from the *Seminario Juan Calvino* and, later, from the *Instituto Cristiano Mexicano*. Both schools are related to traditional Reformed and Presbyterian denominations, so we may consider this an experiment not only in urban evangelistic methodology but also in the adaptability of historic churches to the challenge of cellular multiplication in a Third World urban situation.[8] Mexico City is representative of the many great cities of the Third World that have experienced rapid urbanization in the last few decades. The 1970 census shows a total of over eight million in the metropolitan area, with an annual growth of over half a million. The sprawling slum communities which surround the city give ample testimony to both the rate of urbanization and the incapability of the present city to absorb such an influx of rural-urban migrants.[9] As we began our urban evangelistic efforts, natural instinct caused us to avoid the slums. We tended toward the paved streets and the better neighborhoods. It was not until later, after we had discovered the amazingly high degree of receptivity in the *colonias* (colonies) of the newer migrants, that we began to direct our major efforts in their direction.

The theory which we set out to test was this: that the simple method of house-to-house visiting by trained and highly motivated young people would be the key to establishing neighborhood churches which would form meaningful fellowships of Christian witness and service.[10] Our method would consist of intensive visiting in selected areas of the city where, as far as we knew, no Protestant church was established. We would sell Bibles and New Testaments from house to house, give a verbal testimony to the gospel wherever we could, and we would seek out families that would allow us to begin Bible classes in their homes. We hoped that in this way we would be able to establish *iglesias hogareñas* (churches which meet in houses) in each neighborhood.[11]

Before going on to tell about the results of this experiment in Mexico City, something should be said about the missionary ideology which lay at the heart of our effort. This ideology, quite frankly, has shaped every stage of our urban program. Both the goals and the methods have been determined by it. We have taught it to our students and we have continually used it to test each phase of the program. Simply stated, it is this: that the organized local church is the God-ordained institution for the corporate worship, witness, and fellowship of Christians. The church is as important to Christians and to Christianity today as it obviously was to Paul in the first century. In order to make a Christian impact on society as a whole, you first of all need born-again Christian people who are obedient to the Word of God. They in turn should be organized into churches, not just big, central churches serving people from all parts of the city, but local, neighborhood churches where parents and children together can meet with their neighbors for instruction, fellowship and worship.[12] With this ideology behind us, we set out to experiment in church-planting in the sprawling megapolis that is Mexico City.

"Nothing succeeds like success," they say, and it would be easy to write only about the areas of the city where we have been successful in planting healthy growing churches. But to limit our report would be misleading. Our churches-in-houses approach has been hounded by the inavailability of houses with adequate space. Our teams have spent days and weeks in neighborhoods where we seemed to get nowhere. We have managed to organize some promising groups only to see them evaporate before our eyes. Sometimes we have come home so tired and discouraged that we wondered if we were following the right procedure at all. The truth is that we have failed in almost as many places as we have succeed-

ed.[13] Certain neighborhoods proved to be virtually in-
penetrable; others showed only moderate receptivity. Some
left us thinking that only a divine visitation could break
down their resistance to the gospel.

In this connection, we want to single out the great apartment complexes as an area which to us posed almost insur-
mountable difficulties. In many of the apartment buildings
tenancy regulations forbid the holding of religious services,
which makes occupants reluctant to allow any kind of gathering, especially if there will be singing that can be heard in
the next apartment. Visiting is not easy either, for there are
guards at the entrances and "peep holes" in the doors. Moreover, the desire for anonymity seems to make many apart-
ment-house residents particularly resistant to any personal
contact. We have visited every home in four of Mexico City's
largest apartment complexes, and we managed to hold meetings for some weeks in two of them. But in neither case were
we able to organize a permanent congregation.

Great apartment buildings, now a worldwide phenomenon,
are characteristic marks of urbanization. In Mexico City our
strategy has largely failed to reach either the wealthier homes
or the apartment dwellers, so it is our feeling that these two
segments of society require a very specialized approach. With
the erection of every new *condominio* and apartment complex, the need for such a strategy grows more urgent.

Success in church-planting came for us in Mexico City in
the neighborhoods composed of ground-level, upper-lower
and lower-middle-class homes. Considering the time and effort involved, these are the areas which show the greatest results. In the Colonia Pedregal Carrasco, for example, after
only three weeks of Sunday morning house-to-house visiting,
we had Bible classes started in three different homes.[14] That
was in March, 1969. The first formal service was conducted
on April 17, and within six months the group had built a
humble chapel on a piece of land provided by one of the

members, was contributing regularly toward the erection of a larger chapel, and was taking on the characteristics of a responsible, self-perpetuating church.

In varying degrees but with basic similarities, we have experienced results like these in a dozen different parts of Mexico City. This has led us to believe that the densely populated fringe *colonias* are the most receptive to the gospel. A large percentage of these people, though not all of them, to be sure, are new immigrants to the city. In the newfound freedom and independence of the urban environment they can decide for themselves whether they wish to continue to follow the traditional religion or whether they will give the new way at least a hearing. In these neighborhoods the man or the lady of the house comes to the door when the evangelist knocks. You meet the whole family in their home situation.[15] Face-to-face contact with both parents and children soon establishes the visitor as one who is known and is trusted, and as one who is interested in the family and its needs. House-to-house visiting, concern for the family as a unit, clear testimony to the gospel, Bible instruction in the home: that has been our formula, and *it has worked*.

CASE HISTORY OF A NEW CITY CHURCH

On Sunday afternoon, March 13, 1968, five students sat huddled around a map of Mexico City in our living room. It was decided to make our next target the Colonia A. Lopez Mateos, a heavily populated area of the city just east of the airport. It was originally settled by squatters, but through the patronage of the wife of the late president of Mexico, after whom the *colonia* was later named, the squatters had been given some assurance that they could retain the land.[16] A government school was under construction. After prayer and a hymn we loaded the station wagon with Bibles and tracts and headed for the *colonia*. We covered every home in the area, working in teams of two. My nine-year-old daughter was my companion. To relieve the shock of a towering *gringo* appearing at the door, I have found that taking along a son or daughter is quite effective. The sight of the child and father together removes the suspicion and hostility toward foreigners which one naturally can expect to find. The only wrinkle on this particular afternoon was a troublesome drunk who followed us for several hours.

My notebook shows the following entry for that day:

> Door-to-door visiting in the Col. A. Lopez Mateos. Excellent response. Three homes invited us to hold services. We will begin in the home of a "sometime" Presbyterian woman next Wednesday night.

The reference to the "sometime" Presbyterian points up an important factor to be found not only in this *colonia* but in almost all our new city churches. Roughly two-thirds of the members were Christians before we contacted them. Half of these were members of Protestant churches either in some other part of the city or in their village before moving to the city. The other half is composed of persons converted through some form of mass evangelism (Bible distribution, radio, correspondence courses, tracts) but who had never joined a church. The final third is made up of new Christians won to the Lord through the personal work of the students and the services they conduct in the homes. However, we prefer to hold services, not in the homes of these very new people, for that can be risky, but rather in the home of a family that already has made some form of Christian commitment.

An interesting sidelight on the beginning of the work in the Col. A. Lopez Mateos is the fact that when we began we knew just one person living there. He was a retired Presbyterian pastor. We had hoped that he might open his home for services and for this reason we visited him first. However, while on the one hand he greeted us warmly, he rebuffed our suggestion of evangelizing the *colonia* and beginning services.

"It can't be done," he told us. "These people are too hard; they will never accept the gospel." As we went down the street, selling Bibles to his very own neighbors, the elderly pastor stood in his doorway watching us. He was a classic example of "limited expectations."

For four months we held services on Wednesday nights in the home of the Presbyterian woman. She was very poor, having been abandoned by her husband, and neither she nor her young son had been to church for several years. We equipped their two-room house with four benches for the services, and they were always dusted and in order when we arrived. Before the service began each Wednesday night we generally spent an hour visiting in the neighborhood. In addition, student teams continued to work the area on Sundays, inviting people to the Wednesday night services. My notebook shows that at one time, in the month of May, when the attendance had dropped sharply the previous week, we revisited the entire *colonia* with a team of ten students, searching for new families. It was on that particular occasion that two new families were contacted who eventually became the leading families in the church.

Records show that the attendance wavered between fifteen and twenty during the first few months. The entry in my notebook for April 24 states: "Growth continues but the rains are now hindering attendance. The unpaved streets are all mud." All mud they were indeed. On several occasions my station wagon was buried in mud down to the axles and the students had to literally lift the vehicle out of the ruts. During this period we began the services rather late in the evening because the men in the area had to take two or three different buses in order to get home from work. They arrived home late, and therefore, in order to get the men as well as the wives and children, we began the services late and continued until 9:30 or even later. We usually showed a Bible filmstrip at the close of the service and that kept the children both awake and quiet until the end.

The main part of the services consisted in learning and singing new hymns and choruses, Bible teaching and preaching, and prayers for the sick and for those with special problems. No rigid order of worship was followed, though quite naturally a certain routine was gradually fixed. Opportunity was always given for questions to be asked, and if anyone had something special to say, he was free to stand up and address the group. Offerings were taken right from the start, and it was always explained that we would keep this money on behalf of the group until they themselves could erect a chapel building. Records of the weekly offerings and attendance were carefully maintained in both the mission and the school office.

A faithful nucleus began to appear by the month of May, and by the middle of June we felt that it was time to turn this young church over to a Mexican pastor. On June 26, we introduced Mr. and Mrs. Santos Galan to the group and explained that while we would still visit them from time to time, Mr. Galan would now be in charge of the affairs of the congregation. From that day on Mr. Galan, who is employed by the World Home Bible League in Mexico City, became the volunteer pastor-evangelist of the church. At about the same time the services were changed to Sunday and the members began looking for larger facilities.

By the beginning of 1969, the Colonia A. Lopez Mateos Church was renting a large room for their services. In the month of May a "steering committee" was elected from among the members. Mr. Galan prepared a large sketch of the church building they hoped to erect and this was hung on the wall near the entrance for everyone to see. While, on the one hand, the strength of the congregation was evidenced by the large proportion of complete families and men in attendance, there were also some internal problems involving members who had formerly been Pentecostals. Severe attacks were made by the Jehovah's Witnesses, who hoped to take away some of the new Christians. The Seventh Day Adventists also tried to get something started but were largely unsuccessful. Two adult members, however, did leave the church and joined the Pentecostals.

Baptisms of whole families together has been the general rule. Upon occasion, baptism has been immediately preceded by a marriage ceremony since some couples had not been legally married before. The men are almost all employed in factories or in construction, or work in small businesses. The women are all housewives, though one operates a small store in the front part of her house. The biggest gap is in the teenage group. But since nearly all the members are parents with small children, this problem will probably disappear in a few years.

Sunday school is now held at 11:00 each Sunday, followed at 12:00 by a worship service. Almost all the members attend both. The average attendance stands between seventy and eighty, and some remodeling had to be done recently to facilitate the increasing attendance. Thursday night services continue to be held for the main purpose of attracting new families who normally would not interrupt their Sunday outings or visits to relatives by coming to church.

Two major steps have been taken very recently. First, the Colonia A. Lopez Mateos Church has obtained a loan of $3,-200.00 from our board of missions to buy the property which they are now renting and begin the construction of a church building. Second, they themselves have begun a mission in an adjoining *colonia*. It so happened that a family of the church moved to this new area and, finding no evangelical church there, immediately invited Mr. Galan to begin services in their home. There is every reason to believe that before long this very young church will have a daughter in the Colonia Arenal, and both Mr. Galan and a team of our students are working hard toward that end.

If the Colonia A. Lopez Mateos in Mexico City can be considered a kind of urban laboratory, and our evangelistic efforts there can be regarded as a laboratory test of planned action resulting in church-planting, then we may have something here that is significant not only for Mexico but for urban centers throughout Africasia. It has been shown how urban masses can be effectively evangelized in their own neighborhoods and how new churches can be established among them. What is more, it has been demonstrated that Christians from traditional denominations, if they are willing to adapt, can do the job.

Here lies an important point. As Henry D. Jones has pointed out, this is not the task of the missionary alone. *It is primarily the task of the church in each nation.*[17] Churches and seminaries throughout Asia, Africa and Latin America need to be aroused to confront an urbanized people with the claims of Christ in a meaningful way. The rapidity of worldwide urbanization demands a reorientation of missionary strategy in which church workers, both foreign and national, catch the vision and share the responsibility.

Notes

1. United Nations Economic and Social Council, *Preliminary Study of the Demographic Situation in Latin America* E/CN. 12/604, (Apr. 23, 1961), p. 30.
2. Paul Abrecht, *The Churches and Rapid Social Change* (New York: Doubleday, 1961), p. 149.
3. John Dilworth, "The Growing City," *African Ecclesiastical Review* 10, no. 4, (Oct. 1968), p. 321.
4. Kenneth Little, *West African Urbanization: A Study of Voluntary Associations in Social Change* (London: Cambridge U., 1965), pp. 19-20.
5. Benjamin Higgins, "The City and Economic Development" in *The Urban Explosion in Latin America,* ed. Glenn H. Beyer (Ithaca, N. Y.: Cornell U., 1967), p. 118.
6. Dilworth, p. 328.
7. William L. Wonderly, "Urbanization: The Challenge of Latin America in Transition," *Practical Anthropology* 7, no. 5 (Sept.—Oct., 1960).
8. The Seminario Juan Calvino and the Instituto Cristiano Mexicano are related to the Board of Foreign Missions of the Christian Reformed Church and the Iglesia Presbiteriana Independiente of Mexico.
9. It has been observed that the slums of Mexico City are not, in fact, as wretched as those of Caracas, Lima, or Sao Paulo. For vivid accounts of the life of the urban masses, see Oscar Lewis' books, *Five Families*

(New York, Basic Books, 1959) and *Children of Sanchez* (New York: Random House, 1961). The setting of these books is in Mexico City, but they apply throughout Latin America and into other continents as well.

10. For a most stimulating booklet on the use of students in evangelism, see A. Clark Scanlon's *Church Growth Through Theological Education,* published in Guatemala in 1962.

11. By "churches" we mean congregations of baptized believers who meet regularly in a given place for worship, and who both corporately and individually seek to proclaim the full message of the gospel to their community. This, we believe, is the New Testament understanding of the local church.

12. This preference for neighborhood churches as over against central churches whose membership is drawn from many different parts of the city presupposes the social and economic situation of most city dwellers outside the more advanced countries such as the United States of America. In areas of the world where comparatively few people have cars and where bus travel is difficult and uncertain, the need for neighborhood churches close at hand is all the more important.

13. "Failed" here is used relatively. The fact must not be forgotten that even in the areas where we were unable to establish a church, many people were brought into contact with the gospel and eventually may become members of a Christian church.

14. See *Church Growth Bulletin* 6, no. 3 (Jan. 1970), for a fuller description of this project.

15. The main problem, as I see it, with the so-called "Industrial Evangelism" approach is that it generally fails to involve the whole family as a unit in Christian worship and fellowship. When asked: "What about the wives and children?" a well-known advocate of industrial evangelism in Great Britain is quoted as saying: "We leave them to the churches." Very well. Churches are what we aim to establish. We want the whole families, both fathers, mothers, and children, for both practical and theological reasons.

16. The development of this *colonias* appears to have followed to the letter what Richard M. Morse calls the "Spanish municipal tradition." Commenting on the historical parallels between the growth of modern urban slums and early Spanish traditions, Morse says: "It is not far-fetched to say that the Spanish municipal tradition is vigorously perpetuated in today's squatter invasions, which may recapitulate all the ingredients of a town-founding by a conquistador's band: careful staging and role allocation; solicitation of patronage from a powerful political figure; legitimation of the claim by planting of lags and strategic publicity; meticulous distribution of building lots; common resistance to low-echelon police; discrimination against later settlers; formation of a committee of *vecinos;* mutual-aid arrangements; a gridiron layout with provision for plaza and common facilities; erection of community chapel, school and council house; priority for legalization of land titles; efforts to create a channel for claims and grievances to the highest political authority, even the president or his wife" (Richard M. Morse, "Recent Research on Latin American Urbanization: A Selective Survey with commentary," *Latin American Research Review* 1, no. 1 (Fall, 1965), p. 61.

17. Quoted by W. Stanley Rycroft and Myrtle M. Clemmer, in *A Study of Urbanization in Latin America* (New York: Commission on Ecumenical Mission and Relations, the United Presbyterian Church in the U.S.A., 1963), p. 135.

12

GUIDELINES FOR URBAN CHURCH-PLANTING

by
EDWARD F. MURPHY

SINCE DR. GREENWAY, in his splendid chapter on "Urbanization and Mission," has described so adequately the worldwide spread of urbanization, my task is to emphasize the tremendous evangelistic opportunities and to suggest guidelines for urban discipling. My work for the last dozen years has been evangelism in the great cities of Argentina and Colombia. Out of scores of evangelistic campaigns and thousands of evangelistic conversations I present aspects of the task which are of vital importance to all ministers, missionaries, and lay Christians who seek to obey the Great Commission in the cities of our time.

SOCIAL CONSEQUENCES OF URBANIZATION

William L. Wonderley, in a review of that shocking book, *Five Families* by Oscar Lewis, says:

> . . . urbanization presents almost unbelievable problems of adjustment for millions in Latin America who have left their Indian, peasant, or small-town backgrounds because of land shortage or in search of a more modern way of life, only to find themselves alone and near the bottom of the socio-economic scale in the big, unfriendly cities.[1]

Urban migrants become culturally displaced persons. Coming mostly from close-knit face-to-face societies, the impersonal atmosphere of the big city produces a terrible loneliness. There is a breakdown of the social ties that formerly gave life its meaning, for families break up and friendships that have endured for generations are severed. Having once been part of a homogeneous unit, and now finding himself a nobody, one out of an agglomeration of unrelated individuals, the new urban dweller loses his sense of security.

Furthermore, his value system takes a terrible shaking. Family, home, neighbors, the church and other loyalties were once highly regarded. In the city, with its money economy and ruthless materialistic philosophy of life, these allegiances are gradually eroded and his entire value system undergoes a transformation. Stripped of his former moral stimulation and higher value system, the urban migrant finds that his life is little more than a battle for existence and a constant struggle to hold down a job. He vainly tries to find a decent place to live and to earn enough money to feed his growing family.

During the first ten or fifteen years of the life of the urban migrant the common social consequences of rapid urbanization are devastating. Yet, they often produce a receptivity to the gospel that would not exist under normal circumstances. The authors of *Latin American Church Growth* affirm that

> the current wide-spread migration to the city, with concomitant changes in labor and wage patterns, is more likely to render people responsive to the Gospel than to make them resistant. The areas of urban expansion throughout Latin America are uniquely open to the evangelical message.[2]

THE IMPORTANCE OF PLANTING NEW TESTAMENT CHURCHES IN CITIES

The present wave of urbanization (just a foretaste of what is to come) provides a church-growth potential never seen since, perhaps, the days of the early church. At whatever cost, we must restructure our missionary strategy to step into this open door of opportunity. Allocation of both personnel and funds must be made in the light of the opportunity for church-planting that world urbanization presents to world missions. Both theological and sociological factors support this conviction.

THEOLOGICAL FACTORS MAKING GROWING CITIES PRIME FIELDS FOR CHURCH-PLANTING EVANGELISM

The mission of the church is "to give every person in the world an opportunity to say 'yes' to Jesus Christ."[3] Obviously we must seek persons where they are. In the past, men lived largely in the rural areas and in the small face-to-face communities, the towns and villages scattered across the world. All this is now rapidly changing with the move to the cities.

In Latin America as a whole, "The projected growth rates for urban population between 1960 and 1975 are three times those for rural populations. For the South American countries these rates are 67 and 22 percent respectively; for Mexico and Central America, 85 and 26 percent."[4]

The world in general presents other examples of the rush to the city. Tokyo's population was eleven million in 1966. By the end of this century, it will contain over thirty million people.[5] By that time perhaps half of the world's population will be living in huge apartment complexes.[6] *The church must evangelize the cities to be theologically sound.*

A second theological factor has to do with responsiveness. We are told in the Scriptures that, while the whole world is to be evangelized, we are to give priority to "the fields white unto harvest" (Mt 9:35-38; Jn 4:1-42). That is, *the strategic people are the responsive people.*

Generally speaking, recent migrants who live in the working-class suburbs of the great urban centers are responsive to the gospel.

The acculturation which characterizes . . . urbanization provides good opportunity for church growth based on personal conversion. The old structured nature of family life gives way to a more open stance toward life, which in turn necessitates new values of discipline, education, family relationships and social contacts. . . . The introduction of these new elements is altering the old fabric of Latin American life. . . . The fast-growing indigenous churches with their urban base and lay orientation have particular appeal to the new urban dweller. In them he finds opportunity to belong to a group whose activism fits his new-found sense of personal power. The positive evangelical message helps answer his questions concerning the new society in which he finds himself. . . . As urbanization increases, so the opportunities for evangelical growth also increase. As the evangelical churches multiply themselves in the opportunities presented by social change stemming from urbanization, they can influence the direction that the urban masses will follow. *Only as they multiply themselves, however, will they have any such influence.*[7]

This, written of Latin America, is true of many cities in all six continents.

Sociological Factors Making Cities Significant for Evangelization and Church-Planting

The influence of the rapidly growing cities over the life of the undeveloped nations is an important sociological factor. Large cities are the centers of government, transportation, education, industry, communication, religion and, in short, of all the essential areas of life. Though this is seen in most nations, it is much more in evidence in the underdeveloped, emerging nations. An amazingly high percentage of the population lives in or near the state or national capital. This makes urban evangelism more potent than rural evangelism, for the whole life of the nation can be influenced by multiplying churches in major cities.

The transiency of responsiveness is another factor. As we have already seen, the newer city dwellers are in a state of tremendous social flux. McGavran says that the migrating city dwellers have been jolted out of old adjustments and set social, political, economic and religious patterns and are searching for better, truer and more satisfying ways of life. This *searching,* the first step in any journey that finally leads to God, is evidence that the Holy Spirit is at work.

Yet the period of responsiveness is usually very limited. "Specific cases of urban church growth in Mexico City, Bogota and Belo Horizante indicate that it takes a rural migrant a decade or two to adjust to the new urban situation. During such a period of adjustment, he is responsive; we must act quickly if we are to act effectively."[8]

The rapid growth of heterodox sects in the growing urban centers, sometimes excelling that of all the evangelical churches combined, is a third factor. In most of these urban centers, spiritism, Jehovah's Witnesses, and Mormonism are rapidly multiplying. For example, during the past few years in the city of Cali, Colombia, the Mormons have gained more adherents than those gained by all evangelical churches in the city combined. Christians must "act quickly if they are to act effectively."

GUIDELINES FOR URBAN CHURCH-PLANTING

Having considered the cities—the setting in which evangelization takes place—we now propose certain principles to govern and direct the evangelism done. These will be presented under three headings: theological, sociological, and methodological.

THEOLOGICAL GUIDELINES

A theology of harvest. Much urban evangelism is intended to be little more than seed-sowing. This will not do. God has sent us to reap a spiritual harvest. It is not enough to distri-

bute literature, use radio and TV to proclaim the gospel, and
organize evangelistic crusades, visitation evangelism, and
open-air preaching. Such efforts must be seen as only the
first step in the evangelism cycle. New Testament evangelism
brings men to Christ and *incorporates* them in New Testament churches. Anything less is sub-Christian. Churches and
missions must *intend* church growth.

A theology of discipleship. The Great Commission speaks
of making disciples, not just converts (Mt 28:19-20 in the
original Greek). A disciple is one who believes in the doctrine of his teacher and follows him. The idea of following
Christ is implicit in the word *disciple*. Professions of faith,
therefore, that do not produce followers of Christ do not
represent the New Testament concept of evangelization.
Those who "accept Christ" but do not follow Him are not
true Christians. Much of our evangelization so overempha-
sizes "the saving work of Christ" and so ignores His lordship
that we continually produce non-Christian Christians. Thus
the "spontaneous multiplication of the Church"[9] dies with
the falling away of the first converts.

A theology of the church. The purpose of the incarnation
was at least twofold: Jesus came "to seek and save that which
was lost" (Lk 19:10). He also came to "build [His] Church"
(Mt 16:18). The two are completely interrelated. When men
are saved, they must immediately become church-related.
This means they must become members of local churches
which, as Louis King has said, are societies "in which man
is perfected [and] God is glorified."[10]

The church glorifies God. As a true theist, this is my deepest desire: that God should be glorified. The church perfects
man. As a true humanist, this is my deepest desire: that man
should be perfected. Therefore to extend the church to the
ends of the earth is the most important task and the highest
privilege that God has given to Christians.

Church-planting, therefore, must have priority over other

forms of Christian service, and is must be the rule by which we evaluate every aspect of mission. A valid theology of the church demands multiplying churches in cities.

A theology of indigenous churches. Much is being written about indigenous churches. Most missions strive to make their churches self-supporting, self-governing and self-propagating, for it is felt that in this way they will be true indigenous churches.

It is important to bear in mind, however, that a local church can practice these three "selfs" and still be far from truly indigenous. Such churches are "indigenized" but not indigenous, since they have been structured according to Western, traditional Protestant patterns, not local, native patterns. They are still foreign, even if they are guided by national pastors.

What is required is a theology which, while cleaving to the Bible, takes culture seriously. The worship patterns, self-image of the church, its hymnology, and its concepts of its structure and leadership must all be *harmonious with the culture of the people who are being discipled.* These practices must be formed by Scripture in light of local culture. Therefore church planters must, from the very beginning, allow the emerging church to take its own form and shape, express its theology and life in its own way, in concepts meaningful to the local believers. It is essential, of course, that all of this be in accordance with scriptural truth.

A theology of responsiveness. As we evangelize the great urban centers, experimentation and investigation will enable us to discover which sectors are responsive to the gospel and which are resistant. The theological truth must be grasped that the responsive must be favored in church-planting evangelism. Those who want to be liberated have a higher priority than those who resist their liberators.

So important was a theology of responsiveness to our Lord that He told His disciples that they should let responsiveness

determine the "where" of their church-planting mission.
Where people persistently rejected their message, the disciples
were to "shake the dust off their feet" in judgment against
them and pass on to more responsive peoples (Mt 10:14;
Mk 6:11; Lk 9:5). That the early church understood what
Jesus meant by these words is evident by Paul's action described in Acts 13:43-52 and 18:1-6.

SOCIOLOGICAL GUIDELINES

The personality of each city or urban center. We must
know the city we are attempting to evangelize, for every
city has its own personality. Los Angeles is different from
Indianapolis; Buenos Aires is even more different from
Quito, and Tokyo still more from Mexico City. There is no
substitute for careful investigation before we attempt church-
planting in any urban center. We must become thoroughly
familiar with the major sociological, anthropological and
church-growth studies available which deal with the urban
center in question.

The cultural mosaic of the urban center. In *Church Growth
and Christian Mission,* McGavran compares the general population of a city to a great mosaic. He says, "Each piece of the
mosaic is a society, a homogeneous unit. It has its own way of
life, its own standards, degree of education, self-image and
places of residence."[11]

All of these factors, and many more, affect the responsiveness of each subculture or part of the mosaic. Its degree of
responsiveness, in turn, should guide us in our church-multiplying mission. Let me illustrate by citing the case of Cali,
Colombia, where I spent many years in missionary service.

Cali is booming. Its population has doubled during the
past ten years to almost one million people. It is one of the
fastest-growing cities in the Western world, yet Cali is not
one but at least eight different cities.[12]

The first Cali is the inner city. It is, almost 100 percent, a business area. Very few people live there.

The second Cali is composed of the semibusiness residential barrios, completely surrounding the inner core of the city on the north, south and east. It is a stagnant area. Here is found the market, surrounded by a vast red-light district and barrios of the middle-lower class.

The third Cali is found directly west of the inner city and separated from it by the Cali River. Running both north and south and nestled between the river and the foothills of the western range of the Andes Mountains are found the largest middle-and-higher class residential barrios.

The fourth part of our mosaic is lovely Santa Terresita and adjoining barrios. Composing one of the newest residential sectors of Cali and built on the lower foothills of the Andes Mountains, it is filled with hundreds of higher-middle to higher-higher class families.

The fifth Cali spreads south of Santa Terresita for miles. It is made up of dozens of middle-middle class to higher-middle class barrios. We will call it San Fernando, the name of its principal barrio.

Our sixth Cali is located south of Santa Terresita and west of San Fernando, also occupying the foothills of the western range of the Andes. Rising to quite a height, it is visible for miles throughout the valley. These hills are covered with several lower-class barrios where some 50,000 people dwell. The barrios were formed by invasions of homeless families who simply moved in and took over the land. We will call this piece of the mosaic Siloe after its most prominent barrio. Siloe is a world in itself and is unlike any other sector of the city. It is important to observe that some residents of Siloe have moved up the social ladder and could be considered lower-middle class.

The seventh Cali comprises the middle-middle-class areas

north and east of San Fernando. We will call it Alameda after its most prominent market area.

The eighth Cali is the largest in the area, the most populated, and the most strategic for church-planting. It is composed of the dozens of working-class barrios, which are rapidly expanding, being fed by continuous migrations from all over Colombia. The city is completely surrounded by these barrios which are multiplying so rapidly it is impossible to provide them with sanitary facilities, water, and power.

What does all this have to do with church-planting in Cali? Much, for churches grow in society, among men, not in vacuum tubes. If we desire to plant indigenous churches in Cali which can continue to grow and multiply, where should we plant them? By seeing Cali not as one, but as eight, we can begin probing to find which is the most responsive and shows the greatest promise for rapid church multiplication.

Many missions engaged in church-planting in Cali, though sincere, have been largely ignorant of the mosaic of the city or have chosen to ignore its significance. Some have tried to plant churches in the inner city, where few people live. Others have tried to raise up churches in the stagnant semibusiness-residential areas surrounding the inner city. It has been difficult going, and these congregations show little growth. Others have deliberately chosen the middle-class barrios and find their churches growing very slowly. It is important to observe that the fastest-growing churches in Cali and those which multiply themselves are in the working-class barrios.

If a church or mission desires to plant more rapidly multiplying churches in Cali, where should they evangelize in light of these observations? The answer is clear. It should concentrate on the eighth Cali. Dozens of small-house churches, churches meeting in rented buildings or under thatched roofs, can and should be established all over this eighth Cali. It is a great city.

What a difference it would make in the direction of the

social revolution now sweeping the lands of the younger churches if the great masses of migrating lower-class peoples moving to the cities would find vigorous evangelical churches established in the areas where they are going to take up residence. This could be the greatest single factor in the spiritual transformation, moral regeneration and social uplift of these masses.

The strength of living relationships in growing urban centers. Christians from the Western world are strongly individualistic. We act independently from our friends, and even from our families. This is not true, however, in the lands of the younger churches where family and friendship ties are very strong, and people like group action and group decision. This fact can become either our friend or foe in the spread of the gospel. If we seek individuals, calling them to come out of their groups, it will be our foe. If we attempt to win to Christ whole families or geographical, occupational or friendship groups, it will become our greatest ally.[13]

The local church can become the ideal functional substitute for the group-belongingness lost after migration from the rural or face-to-face communities. Dr. Eugene Nida has written,

> These people need to experience a kind of fellowship which is even more satisfying than what they have known in the community as a whole. If people can be taught the meaning of the new fellowship in Jesus Christ and what the new community of saints can and should mean, they can be brought into a type of fellowship which will be not only satisfying, but creative. . . . The Protestant Church has a very special ministry [in the urban environment], for it can help to create effective, mutually beneficial social groups in the midst of the impersonal environment, and thus meet people's basic needs for fellowship.[14]

For this to occur, it is necessary that the convert move into a church in the company of a group of his fellows. Thus he will not have to suffer a second social dislocation coming soon after the social upheaval incurred in his migration to the urban area.

METHODOLOGICAL GUIDELINES: WHO PLANTS CHURCHES?

Church multiplying can be a mission venture. Missionaries can still be effective church planters in the lands of the younger churches. The myth that the day of the missionary church planter has now passed is substantiated neither by the facts nor by Scripture.

In most of the lands of the younger churches there remain vast areas with few evangelical churches. In their great urban centers, huge sections are either without any local church at all or are served by one or two small struggling churches. Missionaries with an apostolic gift can move into these unevangelized areas and raise up indigenous New Testament churches. Two things must always be kept in mind, however. (1) If national denominations already exist in the area, their support and blessing must be sought. Simply to move in, ignoring the churches already laboring there, is religious imperialism. (2) All converts must immediately be organized into indigenous local churches. These new churches must be brought into a living relationship with the other evangelical churches found in the area, for to hold them aloof from the rest of Christ's body is a violation of Scripture, a sin against God, and evidence of spiritual pride and sectarianism.

Church multiplying can be a younger church venture. As soon as a church is planted, it must in turn plant more. This is what is meant by "the spontaneous expansion of the church"—God's blueprint for world evangelization.

The chain of continuous church-planting too often breaks after the first few are established. A paternalistic relationship is formed between them and their spiritual fathers, and these churches become sealed off from their community. They continue dependent upon the mission, missionaries, or national pastors who become substitutes for the missionary.

Many churches complain that they do not have the necessary financial resources nor the highly trained leaders necessary for further church expansion. This is unscriptural. A new church, experiencing the power of the Holy Spirit and motivated along New Testament lines, can multiply cells of believers without dependence on missionaries or ordained ministers. The early churches did not depend on foreign missions for financial aid before planting more churches. Neither did the apostles import ordained men from Jerusalem or Antioch to pastor the hundreds of new churches being planted all over the Roman Empire. Pastors were found within the churches themselves. Local men gifted by the Holy Spirit, were given on-the-job training by the apostles and other leaders, and thrust out to work.

One of the most thrilling experiences of such church establishment is now in progress in El Salvador, Central America, under the guidance of the Assemblies of God. In 1953 the Assemblies had 3,940 baptized church members in that country. After a period of waiting on God, the Holy Spirit sent a refreshing revival. Bible institute students, pastors and laymen began evangelizing and planting churches everywhere—in homes, in the ranchos of humble believers, and in rented halls. By 1966 the baptized membership had increased to 13,000. Sunday school attendance went up from 3,356 to 30,-000. Even so, in 1966 only 1 percent of the population of El Salvador was attending one of the Sunday schools of the Assemblies of God.[15] Tremendous potential for growth remained.

The organized churches multiplied from 78 in 1954 to 313 in 1968. Their annex churches, called "whitened harvest fields," increased from 200 to over 1,000.[16]

This remarkable growth has been basically the work of laymen and Bible institute students, not highly trained nationals or missionaries. With very little formal education these men, gifted by the Holy Spirit, and trained on the job by their leaders, who themselves had little academic preparation, have become instruments in God's hand to carry forward a notable church multiplication. This is one of God's blueprints for world evangelization.

Church multiplication can be a joint venture of a younger church and a foreign mission. The younger church can provide gifted church planters, while the mission gives some financial backing. It is helpful if church planters are on the same social and educational level as the people among whom they labor. The Christian and Missionary Alliance followed this procedure in a high-potential area of Colombia. The result was one of the finest examples of spontaneous church multiplication seen in Colombia during the past few years.[17]

The reverse plan also produces good results. The younger church provides guidance and financial assistance while the mission provides a church-planting missionary. The Central Presbyterian Church of Cali, Colombia, in cooperation with the Cumberland Presbyterian Mission follow this procedure in a working-class barrio. The church rented an old home in Barrio Popular and the mission sent in a church-planting missionary released from all other responsibilities. He was specifically commissioned to *raise up a church in Barrio Popular*. St. Mark's Presbyterian Church is the result. It continues now under a national pastor trained by this fine missionary, and is continually multiplying itself in Cali.

METHODOLOGICAL GUIDELINES: HOW ARE CHURCHES PLANTED?

Now to the "how" of urban church-planting. Four basic methods are bringing good results: evangelistic crusades, visitation evangelism, the extension program of existing churches, and planting by students of Bible institutes and seminaries.

Prolonged evangelistic and Bible-teaching crusades. These

have proven effective ways of establishing growing churches in a short period of time in the urban complexes of the Third World. Two important factors must be kept in mind: (1) The purpose of the crusade is not mass evangelism. *It is to found New Testament churches—churches which will reproduce themselves—in a short period of time.* (2) The strategy involved is that of continuous, vigorous evangelizing and systematically instructing new converts until a local church is born.

Dr. Melvin Hodges, Latin American Field Director for the Assemblies of God, says this was the main method that led to the remarkable multiplication of churches in El Salvador, already referred to. He cites the growth of the churches in the capital, San Salvador, as an example. In 1956 there was only one church in the city, with a membership of less than one hundred. That year an open-air evangelistic campaign was held.

> Crowds of approximately 3,000 attended nightly. At the end of two and a half months, 250 new converts had been instructed and were ready for baptism. Six weeks later, an additional 125 converts were baptized. Instead of trying to hold all these people in one congregation . . . the city [was divided] into twelve sections. A call was made for workers to take charge of new meeting places. Some . . . were Bible school students, others were men who had had outstation experience. . . . Each was assigned to a section. . . . At the end of one year there were 12 new churches in the city and a combined total of approximately 1200 in Sunday school. Yet, the story does not stop there. For these churches have continued to grow and extend their influence in establishing new churches. In 1964, eight years later, there were 27 Assemblies of God churches, with 200 outstations [branch churches] in the city and surrounding areas. In the city alone, combined Sunday school attendance was fluctuating between 7,000 and 9,500.[18]

The same procedure was followed by the Four Square Gospel in a remarkable church-planting movement in Guayaquil, Equador. Wayne C. Weld in his book *An Equadorian Impasse* comments,

> At the close of the six-week campaign a baptismal service was held with 30,000 in attendance. Fifteen hundred were baptized in a river in Guayaquil. *The instruction for these baptismal candidates was given during the campaign.* It was discovered that by 9:00 p.m., when the evangelist was already well into his message, people were still coming. Therefore the main message was set back, and [first] an associate gave a message of instruction on the Christian life. . . . Those who attended every night received more pre-baptismal instruction than many candidates ever do. The pattern successful in Guayaquil was followed for planting churches in other areas.[19]

Shorter evangelistic and Bible-teaching crusades. When there already are a few believers living and meeting in the area to be evangelized, a shorter crusade can be very effective. The strategy is to concentrate on winning those persons with whom the believers enjoy a living relationship. This rather than the gathering of unrelated individuals is the effective method.

The author has had considerable experience in this type of church-founding in Colombia. A case in point would be the request in 1965 that Overseas Crusades help a Mennonite Brethren missionary and a group of eleven believers begin a church in Barrio Villa Colombia in Cali. In just a few nights of evangelistic emphasis, there were over one hundred professions of faith. These people were immediately given studies in the Christian life. I was present when most of them gave their first public testimony of their new faith. Ninety-five percent were either relatives or friends of the original eleven believers. Within a few months most of these new converts were baptized and a vigorous church was formed. This church continues to evangelize and grow in this working-class barrio.

Church-planting through extension programs of existing churches. In most cities responsive to the gospel, some churches have already been planted. True, many are sealed off and introverted. Others, however, need only a little stimulus to launch an effective church-planting program in the surrounding barrios.

Once again, the remarkable church-planting ministry of the Assemblies of God in El Salvador has lessons to teach us. As we have noted, the organized churches multiplied from 78 to 313 between 1957 and 1967, and their branch churches grew from 200 to over 1,000 during the same period of time. Their strategy has been to make each church responsible to bring to birth a daughter congregation. Laymen, gifted by the Holy Spirit and trained by the pastors of the sending churches are the church planters. Hodges writes,

> Churches have so consistently followed the pattern of establishing other churches through their work, that in some areas the mother churches find themselves completely surrounded by daughters. For example, in the area within a thirty-mile radius of Santa Ana, there are at least 100 established churches. This is partly the work of Bible school students, but mostly it is a development of local church outreach.[20]

Visitation evangelism church-planting. At least two different approaches to visitation evangelism are leading to successful church-planting in urban centers:

1. *Visitation without living contacts.* This is usually exploratory, to find which areas show the greatest potential for church-planting. First, an area is mapped out for house-to-house visitation. Second, believers going two by two offer Christian literature to each home. Third, being alert to anyone who shows interest in the gospel, they find homes willing to open for a weekly Bible study. These then become evangelistic cells or even house churches.

Ernie Poulson describes the success his students are having

in Singapore with this type of evangelism and church-planting.
For a couple of years they have regarded each high-rise apartment house with its 1,000 residents as a parish—a small
town—and have tried to plant a congregation in each. Their
best "apartment house church" has eighty members, most of
them new Christians, and contributes about $1,000 Singapore
($330 U.S.) per month for the Lord's work. He writes,

> More than half a dozen such churches have emerged as
> a result of intense door-to-door evangelization within multi-
> story apartment buildings. In some instances, services have
> been held in the flat of a believer. At least three worship-
> ping groups are housed in a ground-floor shop. During the
> week [the church] is used as a kindergarten, the fees of
> which pay the rent. Other congregations have been helped in
> the initial stages by an older sponsoring church or by a
> group of concerned individuals.[21]

2. *Visitation of living relationships.* The gospel flows best
over living bridges, the channels of family and friendship.
Visitation evangelism directed to relatives and close friends
of Christians can produce exciting results.

One large evangelical church in Buenos Aires had an interesting experience along this line. A dynamic, soul-winning
pastor encouraged his members to visit every apartment
in the large apartment complexes in the nearby barrios.
Thousands of pieces of literature were distributed and
hundreds of visits were made, but there was almost no fruit.
The pastor then tried a different approach. Knowing that one
of his most faithful church members lived in one of those
apartment complexes, he encouraged her to win her friends to
Christ. Over a short period of time this lady won forty-five of
her neighbors to the Saviour. Her friendship with these people was the bridge over which the gospel moved. The relatives
and close friends of the forty-five new Christians should prove
even more responsive.

In the city of Armenia, Colombia, a woman living in a

small apartment complex was converted during one of the first nights of a crusade. She invited a few of her neighbors in nearby apartments to attend the meetings the following night. They also were converted. By the end of the crusade all twenty-two persons living in her apartment area came into a living relationship with Jesus Christ. Once again, friendship ties formed the bridge over which the gospel moved.

Bible institute and seminary church-planting programs. Bible institutes and seminaries have been established in many large urban centers, and their students represent one of the greatest resources for church-planting. Furthermore, such on-the-job training is the best way of discovering which students have received the spiritual gifts necessary for leading ongoing churches. If for this reason alone, Bible institutes and seminaries should engage their students in systematic church-planting in their own and nearby cities.

Roger Greenway's chapter in this book tells of just such church-multiplying by seminary students and missionaries in Mexico City. The instance is particularly significant because it is done by the staid orthodox Christian Reformed of Grand Rapids, Michigan. To those inclined to believe that city evangelism can only be done by new and ardent branches of the church universal, I say, "Look at the Christian Reformed in Mexico City."

Melvin Hodges states that the same thing is happening in El Salvador. The mission has established

> an aggressive Bible school program which trains both doctrinally and in evangelistic methods, such as literature distribution and outstation work. Many students are actively engaged in church planting. . . . Because students play such an important part in establishing churches, the school has now been moved to the capitol, San Salvador, to provide this new sphere to activity.[22]

CONCLUSION

The growing cities in the lands of the younger churches are among the most strategic and important mission fields in the world. In the new emphasis given to urban church-planting, we must not merely "reach" the cities, not merely sow seed there, but *must multiply congregations and cells of Christians on a magnificent scale.* Both nationals and missionaries should be trained in the complex and exciting task of establishing churches which will continuously reproduce others. It is of the greatest importance to recognize that *the strategic people are the responsive people.* Since the most responsive seem to be the working classes, the barrios where they live should be recognized as the fields of highest priority. May God usher in a day of church-multiplying in the great cities of the world.

Notes

1. William Wonderley, "Urbanization, the Challenge of Latin America in Transition," *Practical Anthropology* (Sept.—Oct. 1960).
2. W. R. Read, V. M. Monterroso, and H. A. Johnson, *Latin American Church Growth* (Grand Rapids: Eerdmans, 1969), p. 280.
3. Edward Dayton and John A. Klebe, "PERT, Newest Tool for Mission," *World Vision* (Oct. 1966), p. 10.
4. Read et al., p. 243. Quoting Frank Bonilla, "The Urban Worker" in *Continuity and Change in Latin America* (Stanford, Calif.: Stanford U., 1964), pp. 186-205.
5. Akiri Hatori, discourse given at the World Congress on Evangelism, (Berlin, 1966). From notes taken by the author.
6. Ibid.
7. Read et al., pp. 241-43.
8. Read et al., p. 274.
9. Roland Allen, *The Spontaneous Expansion of the Church* (Grand Rapids: Eerdmans, 1964).
10. Louis L. King, *The Church's Worldwide Mission,* Wheaton Congress, ed. Harold Lindsell (Waco, Tex.: Word, 1966), p. 18.
11. Donald McGavran, ed. *Church Growth and Christian Mission* (New York: Harper & Row, 1965), p. 71.
12. Various statistical reports published in Colombia.
13. Eugene Nida "Culture and Church Growth" in *Church Growth and Christian Mission,* pp. 94-96.
14. Eugene Nida, "The Relationship of Social Structure to the Problems of Evangelism in Latin America," *Practical Anthropology* (Mar.—Apr. 1958).
15. Melvin Hodges, "Spiritual Dynamics in El Salvador," *Evangelical Missions Quarterly* (Winter, 1966), pp. 80-83.
16. Edward F. Murphy, *Preliminary Essentials for Producing Growing Churches in Latin America* (Bogota, Columbia: Latin American Congress on Evangelism, 1969), pp. 20 ff.

17. Murphy, "How a Dead Church Came to Life," *Evangelical Missions Quarterly* (Fall, 1969), pp. 41 ff.
18. Hodges, pp. 80-83.
19. Wayne C. Weld, *An Equadorian Impasse* (Chicago: Evangelical Covenant Church of America, 1968), pp. 61-63.
20. Hodges, pp. 80-83.
21. E. N. Poulson, "Every Thirteen-Story Building a Parish," *Church Growth Bulletin* (Jan. 1970), pp. 45-46.
22. Hodges, pp. 80-83.

EPILOGUE

by
DONALD McGAVRAN

THE CRUCIAL ISSUES in tomorrow's missions—both those described in this book and others—are being resolved by the risen and reigning King. He who declared that the gospel "will be preached throughout the whole world as a testimony to all nations" guides His church that His Word may be fulfilled. He, who under circumstances of great solemnity gave the command to disciple the nations, will continue to give His disciples power to carry out the command.

The Christian approaches mission problems and issues, confident that they will not be solved by giving up world evangelization as a dream of Western imperialism, discovering that missions are no longer necessary, or redefining missions to mean brotherly behavior toward all men. He approaches them believing that they will be solved in such a way as to make more certain that *ta ethne* will be brought to faith in and obedience to Jesus Christ. This is the very purpose for which the gospel has been disclosed (Ro 16:26), the very reason why the Word became flesh, and the Father sent His only begotten Son.

We trust this book has been read seeing these issues as studies in tactics. In tomorrow's missions the end remains the same, but the means chosen to achieve that end change. Take one continent, Africa, for example. The goal is the evangelization of Africa. In the nineteenth century the best means

266

available seemed to be bands of missionaries from Europe and America. In the end of the twentieth century to reach the same goal other means must be added, including total mobilization for evangelism and the training of leaders of African independent churches in the use of the Bible.

Agreed then that missions are being carried on by the risen and reigning Lord, toward the unchanging end taught in the Bible, the church gives its attention wholeheartedly toward so adjusting to current conditions that the end is more effectively achieved, more men come to know Jesus Christ as Lord and Saviour, and more churches carry on God's program of justice, peace, evangelism and worship. But the church must not hope "to bring in the kingdom of God." Until Christ's return, when He sets up the kingdom, all the brotherhood, peace, mercy and righteousness which Christ's servants, living under His Word, are able to achieve will be partial. Yet their labors, especially the proclamation of the gospel to all men, bring that end time closer. Christians work at these crucial issues, seeking to resolve them that the water of life may flow freely to every hamlet and high-rise apartment in the world.

This book is written for all Christians—Eurican and Afericasian alike. The crucial issues of today face every church. The dangers are no more threatening to North than to South American churches, to Asians than to Africans, to Europeans than to Japanese. The opportunities and exciting challenges of missions beckon to Afericasians as much as to Euricans. True missiology must not be adulterated with advice to ex-imperialists or recently emancipated. The great obstacles to missions do not lie in conditions peculiar to any one kind of men, but rather in the humanity, sinfulness and skepticism common to all men. The great open doors stand before all followers of the way.

Christ's mission and His missions go on. Each newly discipled segment of society, as well as the ones discipled centuries ago—ramifying throughout the vast complex mosaic which is mankind—disciples both individuals and ethnic units. Newly converted Muslims from Indonesia send gospel witness to West Pakistan. An infant denomination in Mexico sends fourteen missionaries to Spanish-speaking lands south of it. A Christian scientist from Kerala in India wins pagan Americans to Christ in California. Swedish Baptists from Minnesota are used to spark a revival in the highlands of Ethiopia. A Lutheran layman from the fiords of Norway gives himself to mastering the Borano culture and discipling those nomads. Basketball players from Texas put on demonstration games in that part of Indonesia where multitudes are turning to Christ and bear witness at the half time and after the game to the saving power of Christ. A brilliant scholar gives his life to central Nigeria in the training of a Bible-knowing ministry. There is no end to the list. The risen and reigning King Himself directs His people in a million different situations to spread the light and multiply units of God's peace and righteousness (churches) throughout the world.

In reality, there is only this one crucial issue in missions tomorrow: Will the King find willing and loyal subjects, eager to carry out His commands, alert to the changing scene? Will the King find good stewards of the grace of God? Will He be able to say to you—and to me—"Well done, good and faithful servant. Enter into the joy of your Lord"?

INDEX

Abrecht, P., 228
Accommodation, 142, 145, 168, 170
Acculturation, 248
Afghanistan, 166
Africa, 21, 28, 61, 63, 66, 80-81, 98, 115, 145, 146, 151, 154, 156-59, 195, 197, 201, 228-29, 231, 266-67
African
  Christianity, 145, 154-55
  heritage, 144, 147-48
  religions, 149-53
  traditional, 147, 149
African Enterprise, 207
Allen, R., 85, 95
Animism, 77, 126, 127, 129, 195
  different from Christianity, 140
  philosophy of, 129-34, 135, 139, 142
  universals in, 135-39
  world of, 132
Animists
  capacity for gospel, 133-39
  conversion of, 92, 125, 127, 129
  and supernatural, 135-36
Anomie, 130
Anthropologist(s), 6, 114, 165
Anthropology, 25, 26, 62, 78, 84, 99, 142, 152
Argentina, 27, 208, 215, 245
Asia, 189, 201, 207, 228, 231
Assemblies of God, 207, 208, 212, 213, 215-18, 222, 257, 259, 261
  Foreign Missions Department of, 207, 208, 211

Barney, L., 103
Barrett, D., 28, 195
Bavinck, J. H., 78
Beaver, R. P., 112, 192
Bengal, 192
Beyerhaus, P., 13, 25, 54, 190, 193
Biola College, 218
Blake, E. C., 36
Bloch, E., 72, 75
Brazil, 65, 82, 132, 219-21
Bright, J., 46, 49, 51
Brotherhood, 11-12, 20, 21
Burma, 197

Cali, Colombia, 252-54, 258, 260
Campus Crusade, 19
Carey, W., 192, 199
Change
  agent of, 130
  culture, 79, 130, 167, 188, 227, 234

individual and group, 142
  religious, 99, 134, 167, 180
  structures of society, 64, 71
Chile, 160
China, 189, 197
Christian and Missionary Alliance, 25, 212-13, 258
Christianity
  Africanizing, 145-46, 154
  core of, 159
  enrichment of, from Africasia, 131, 155
Church
  definition of, 23, 47, 104, 109, 118-19, 189, 250-52
  growth, 17-18, 20, 27, 57, 63, 99-100, 129, 175-76, 193, 247, 250
  local, 221-22, 236, 252, 261
  mission of, 10, 33, 45, 49, 57, 111
  planting, 64, 78-79, 129, 193-96, 200, 237, 247-51, 256-58, 261-63
  role of, 58-61
  sending, 11, 15
  social concern of, 58-61, 115, 149, 232
  task of, 10, 36, 61-67, 118, 234, 243
  universal, 131, 145
  urban, 249-51, 258
  witness of, 43, 49, 211
  younger, 65, 71, 115-16, 189-90, 200, 256, 258
Church Growth Bulletin, 64, 65, 195
Colombia, 27, 245, 252, 258, 262
Commission on World Mission and Evangelism, 36-38, 64
Communism, 19, 21, 106
Congo, 208, 213
Conservative Baptists, 212
Consolidate, 20
Conversion, 6, 23, 77, 80, 85, 93, 105, 114, 127, 129-30, 141-42, 180, 190, 193-94, 197, 214
Cross-cultural, 141, 167
Cultural accretions, 202
Culture
  change, 130, 162, 167
  relativism, 165-66
  similarity of, 164-67
Cumberland Presbyterian Mission, 258

Demons, 43, 51, 59, 75, 127, 141-42